Academic Writing Demystified

Navigating the world of academic writing and publishing can be overwhelming. This book provides the antidote. Written by a team of authors who are at different stages of their careers, this book provides hands-on advice and strategies to turn academic writing from a daunting experience to a joyful journey. It gives a complete overview of the publishing process, from how to write an academic paper, chapter, or book to areas that are often overlooked, such as indexing a book, working with images and copyright, dealing with advertising and disseminating the book, ethical issues, open access, predatory publishing, and much more. The chapters are short and clearly labeled, with questions for reflection and discussion at the end of chapters, making them a handy reference for readers to dip in and out of. Demystifying aspects of academic writing, academic writers will come away with the confidence and knowledge to "publish and thrive."

SALVATORE ATTARDO is Professor of Linguistics at East Texas A&M University. He has published over 100 articles and 15 books.

HILAL ERGÜL is Assistant Professor of Applied Linguistics and TESOL and the Coordinator of TESOL Programs at the University of Northern Iowa. She's currently working on a book on oral corrective feedback for teachers.

ELISA GIRONZETTI is Associate Professor of Spanish Applied Linguistics at the University of Maryland. Her recent publications include *The Multimodal Performance of Conversational Humor* (2022).

HEATHER JERÓNIMO is Associate Professor of Spanish at the University of Northern Iowa. Her recent publications include *Performing Parenthood* (2024).

Academic Writing Demystified: Publish and Thrive

Salvatore Attardo
East Texas A & M University

Hilal Ergül
University of Northern Iowa

Elisa Gironzetti
University of Maryland

Heather Jerónimo
University of Northern Iowa

CAMBRIDGE
UNIVERSITY PRESS

Shaftesbury Road, Cambridge CB2 8EA, United Kingdom

One Liberty Plaza, 20th Floor, New York, NY 10006, USA

477 Williamstown Road, Port Melbourne, VIC 3207, Australia

314–321, 3rd Floor, Plot 3, Splendor Forum, Jasola District Centre, New Delhi – 110025, India

103 Penang Road, #05–06/07, Visioncrest Commercial, Singapore 238467

Cambridge University Press is part of Cambridge University Press & Assessment, a department of the University of Cambridge.

We share the University's mission to contribute to society through the pursuit of education, learning and research at the highest international levels of excellence.

www.cambridge.org
Information on this title: www.cambridge.org/9781009418836

DOI: 10.1017/9781009418805

© Salvatore Attardo, Hilal Ergül, Elisa Gironzetti, and Heather Jerónimo 2026

This publication is in copyright. Subject to statutory exception and to the provisions of relevant collective licensing agreements, no reproduction of any part may take place without the written permission of Cambridge University Press & Assessment.

When citing this work, please include a reference to the DOI 10.1017/9781009418805

First published 2026

Cover credit: 'Escaping a Maze with a Ladder' – Getty Images

A catalogue record for this publication is available from the British Library

A Cataloging-in-Publication data record for this book is available from the Library of Congress

ISBN 978-1-009-41883-6 Hardback
ISBN 978-1-009-41879-9 Paperback

Cambridge University Press & Assessment has no responsibility for the persistence or accuracy of URLs for external or third-party internet websites referred to in this publication and does not guarantee that any content on such websites is, or will remain, accurate or appropriate.

For EU product safety concerns, contact us at Calle de José Abascal, 56, 1°, 28003 Madrid, Spain, or email eugpsr@cambridge.org

Contents

List of Figures	*page* x
Preface	xiii
Acknowledgments	xvi

Part I The Fundamentals — 1

1 The Philosophy behind This Book — 3
 1.1 Finding What Works for You — 4
 1.2 Demystifying Writing — 4
 1.3 Finding Joy — 5
 1.4 Writing Regularly — 7
 1.5 Celebrating Your Accomplishments — 8

2 Mental Well-Being — 10
 2.1 Being in the Right Place — 11
 2.2 Writing Hurdles and How to Leap Them — 12
  2.2.1 Writer's Block — 12
  2.2.2 Procrastination — 14
  2.2.3 Impostor Syndrome (IS) — 15

3 Getting Started — 20
 3.1 Building Momentum — 21
 3.2 Tracking Your Progress — 23
 3.3 Defending Your Writing Time — 24

4 Finding a Writing Group That Works for You — 28
 4.1 Types of Writing Groups — 28
 4.2 Reasons to Join a Writing Group — 30
 4.3 Considerations for Choosing a Writing Group — 32

Part II The Mechanics — 37

5 Ethical Considerations — 39
 5.1 Resources on Ethics — 41
 5.2 Avoiding Plagiarism and Self-Plagiarism — 42

	5.2.1	Plagiarism	42
	5.2.2	Self-Plagiarism	44
5.3	Avoiding Conflict of Interest		45
5.4	Authorship Issues		46

6 Outline 48
- 6.1 Example Outline — 50
- 6.2 Reverse Outlines — 53

7 Abstracts and Keywords 56
- 7.1 Writing an Abstract — 56
  - 7.1.1 Writing an Abstract for a Conference — 58
  - 7.1.2 Things You Should Not Put in an Abstract — 58
  - 7.1.3 Formatting — 59
- 7.2 Keywords — 59
- 7.3 Using AI — 61

8 Introductions and Conclusions 62
- 8.1 Introduction Structure — 62
  - 8.1.1 Attention Getters — 64
- 8.2 Conclusion Structure — 67
  - 8.2.1 Conclusion Strategies — 68

9 Literature Review 72
- 9.1 How to Write a Literature Review — 72
- 9.2 Synthesizing Information from Various Sources — 77

10 Data Visualization 80
- 10.1 Data Visualization with a Purpose — 80
- 10.2 The Right Visualization for the Right Purpose — 81
- 10.3 Some Tips to Avoid Common Mistakes — 85

11 Reproduction of Images and Copyright Issues 88
- 11.1 Basic Concepts of Copyright Law — 88
  - 11.1.1 Copyright — 88
  - 11.1.2 Fair Use — 89
- 11.2 Reproducing Copyrighted Products — 90
  - 11.2.1 Text — 90
  - 11.2.2 Images — 90
  - 11.2.3 Other Products — 91
- 11.3 Getting ahead of the Copyright Problem — 92

12 Creating an Index 95
- 12.1 Indexing Techniques — 95
- 12.2 Indexing Decisions — 98

13 Dealing with Reviewers' Comments (Including the Dreaded Reviewer #2) 102
- 13.1 The Emotional Aspect of Rejection — 103
- 13.2 Whether or Not to Make Revisions — 104

13.3	Working with the Actionable Parts of Reviewer Comments	106
13.4	A Thematic Approach to Your Response to Reviewer Comments	108
13.5	Staying within the Word Limit While Revising	110

Part III The Genres   113

14 Writing for Different Audiences   115

14.1	Publishing Your Dissertation	115
14.2	Turning Class Papers into Publications	116
14.3	Turning Conference Papers into Publications	118

15 Choosing the Right Outlet   121

15.1	Journal Rankings	121
15.2	Tiers and Expectations	122
15.3	Predatory Publishing	123
	15.3.1 Avoiding Predatory Publishers	125

16 From Dissertation to Publication   128

16.1	Reasons to Publish Your Dissertation	128
16.2	Turning Your Dissertation into Several Papers	130
16.3	Turning Your Dissertation into a Book	133

17 Book or Media Reviews   136

17.1	Book Reviews in Academic Journals	136
17.2	Media Reviews in Academic Journals	140
17.3	Alternative Types of Reviews	141

18 Journal Articles   144

18.1	Types of Journal Articles	145
	18.1.1 Research Articles	145
	18.1.2 Review Articles	146
18.2	Submitting Your Article	147

19 Chapters in Edited Volumes   151

19.1	When to Contribute to an Edited Volume	152
19.2	Invitation to Contribute to an Edited Volume	153
19.3	Types of Edited Volumes	154
	19.3.1 Handbooks	154
	19.3.2 Research Volumes	155
	19.3.3 Conference Proceedings	156

20 Writing and Submitting Book Proposals   158

20.1	Parts of a Book Proposal	159
	20.1.1 Title and Summary	159
	20.1.2 Outline and Chapter Summary	162
	20.1.3 Market and Readership	164
	20.1.4 Timeline and Reviewers	165
20.2	Submitting Your Proposal	167

viii   Contents

21	Edited Volumes	169
	21.1 Coeditors	170
	21.2 Proposal	171
	21.3 Authors	174
22	Grant Proposals	178
	22.1 Finding the Right Funding Program	178
	22.2 Crafting the Narrative	179
	22.3 The Work Plan and Timeline	182
	22.4 The Budget	184
	22.5 Additional Items	184
23	Nontraditional Academic Writing	187
	23.1 Types of Nontraditional Academic Writing	188
	23.1.1 Blogging	188
	23.1.2 Podcasts	189
	23.1.3 Social Media	190
	23.1.4 Video Pieces	192
	23.1.5 Interviews	193
	23.2 Advantages of Nontraditional Academic Writing	194

Part IV   The Community   197

24	Having an Online Presence	199
	24.1 ORCID, Scopus ID, and Researcher ID	199
	24.2 Google Scholar	201
	24.3 Curating a Professional Website	202
25	Self-Marketing	205
	25.1 Academic Conferences	205
	25.2 Panels, Round Tables, and Symposia	207
	25.3 Book Launches and Talks	208
	25.4 Getting Your Book Reviewed	210
26	Professional Networking	213
	26.1 Navigating the Department	213
	26.2 Organizations You Can Join	214
	26.3 Conferences	215
	26.4 The Elevator Pitch	217
27	Mentorship	219
	27.1 Formal and Informal	219
	27.2 Choosing a Mentor	220
	27.3 Guidelines and Expectations	222
	27.4 Becoming a Mentor	223
28	Writing with Others	225
	28.1 Collaborative Writing Tools	225
	28.2 Strategies for Collaborative Academic Writing	226
	28.3 Collaborating with Students	228

29	Open Access Science		231
	29.1 What Is Open Access?		231
	29.2 Gold, Diamond, and Preprint Open Access		232
	29.3 Green OA		233
	29.4 Standards of Quality		234
	29.5 Preregistration and In-Principle Acceptance		235
	29.6 Transparency		236
30	Serving as a Reviewer		238
	30.1 Getting Started		238
	30.2 Do's and Don'ts		239
	30.3 How to Deal with the Perception That You Are Doing Free Labor		240
	30.4 How Much to Review		241
	30.5 When and How to Say "No" to Review Requests		243
	30.6 Reviewing Books and Grant Applications		243
31	People in the Publishing World		246
	31.1 Journal Editors		246
	31.2 Acquisitions Editors		248
	31.3 Series Editors		249
	31.4 Agents		249
	31.5 How to Reach Out		250

Appendices: The Occluded Genres	253
Appendix A: Say-no Punch Card	254
Appendix B: Sample Submission Emails for a Book Proposal	256
Appendix C: Follow-up Email after Submitting a Book Proposal or Journal Article	258
Appendix D: Email to Inquire about a Possible Book Talk	259
Appendix E: Sample Panel Invitation Email	260
Appendix F: Sample Email to Potential Reviewers of Your Book	261
Appendix G: Sample Email to a Review Editor	262
Appendix H: Sample Cover Letter for Article Submission	263
Appendix I: Sample Initial Emails to Authors for an Edited Volume	265
References	268
Index	275

Figures

6.1	Initial part of a sample outline	page 51
6.2	Remaining parts of a sample outline	52
7.1	Sample annotated abstract	57
8.1	Parts of an introduction	63
8.2	Sample annotated introduction	65
8.3	Parts of a conclusion section	67
8.4	Sample annotated conclusion	69
9.1	Sample secondary source notes with annotations	76
10.1	Sample box plot (left) and histogram (right) showing suspiciously tall graduate students (outliers)	83
10.2	From left to right, sample waffle chart, isotype chart, and donut pie emphasizing a single piece of information (percentage or count)	83
10.3	Sample single line chart (left) and comparative line chart (right) showing percentage change over time	84
10.4	Sample Mekko chart (left) comparing variables within a data set and tornado chart (right) comparing two sets of data across different variables	84
10.5	Sample scatterplot (left) and bubble chart (right) showing the positive relationship between number of siblings and GPA	85
13.1	Sample disagreement response to a reviewer comment	105
13.2	Sample response to reviewer comments with a preface	107
13.3	Thematically arranged responses to reviewer comments	109
13.4	Partial disagreement response to a reviewer comment	110
13.5	Response to a reviewer comment about expansion of content	111
17.1	Descriptive comments in book reviews	140
17.2	Examples to clarify criticism in book reviews	140
17.3	Suggestions for improvement in book reviews	140
17.4	Examples to frame criticism within context in book reviews	140
19.1	Portion of an invitation email to contribute to an edited volume	154
20.1	Original and modified book title	160
20.2	Abstract that tells without showing	160

20.3	Abstract that shows and tells	161
20.4	Sample book outline and chapter sections	162
20.5	Word count allocation for chapters and sections	163
20.6	Discussing competing books	165
20.7	Sample book-writing timeline	166
21.1	Sample timeline for an edited volume	171
21.2	Sample chapter description for a handbook	173
21.3	Sample internal organization of chapters for a handbook	173
21.4	Sample tracking document for edited volumes	176
22.1	Breakdown of the first paragraph of a grant narrative	180
22.2	Sample Gantt chart	183
31.1	Sample submission email to a journal with annotations	251

Preface

This book came from a joke that Sal, one of the book's authors, misunderstood. Seriously. Several years ago, Sal started a writing group for his doctoral students. The intention was to keep students accountable for their writing; they would show up each week and report how many words they wrote. The department chair inquired if the group was going to be called "Doom and Gloom" or something equally fitting. Sal instead quipped he'd called it "the Joyous Writing Group," because there is, of course, nothing more joyous for a doctoral student shrouded in constant stress, self-doubt, and crippling anxiety than to report tangible results to their supervisor week after week. Naturally, some of the students fled the scene as soon as they could, but many eventually finished the dissertation and graduated, and those of us who already got their PhDs and are now less shrouded in constant stress, self-doubt, and crippling anxiety (the other authors of this book) caught wind of the group and started coming to the weekly Zoom meetings. All joking aside, Sal did promise a zero-judgment environment for our weekly reports and has lived up to it. We sometimes admit to producing zero words with our heads hung low, while at other times we report thousands of words with absolute pride in our eyes. We congratulate each other, encourage each other, and console each other. At the time of writing this book, we still show up every single week to keep ourselves accountable. After reporting our word counts for the week, we ask each other any professionalization questions we have. I've emailed my dean for funding and haven't heard back; how long should I wait before reminding them? This journal has been sitting on my submission for a while; when is it OK to write to the handling editor, and what should I say? My publisher wants advertising materials; what on earth are those? And so on and so forth. One day, we wondered out loud what other people did when they had similar questions. Who do they turn to when they have such specific questions that everyone is supposed to "just know" but there's no one telling them? Someone said we should turn our conversations into a book and we had fun with the idea. We were completely joking. Then the next day, Sal sent us the first draft of our table of contents, and the rest is history.

Our working title was *The Book of Joyous Writing* until more sedate views prevailed, and we came up with a title that is even more fitting. Going by the motto of "publish or perish" is quite depressing; no one enjoys operating under pending doom. We like to think that this book will help you change the narrative, so you can "publish and thrive" instead.

In this book, we aim to do for you exactly what we have been doing for each other: help demystify very prominent aspects of academic life that no one tells you about (and some that are talked about elsewhere, but giving you our take, backed by research and our own extensive experiences) and answer the professionalization questions you wish you could ask someone.

As you read the book, you'll also find questions for reflection and discussion, as well as questions for your mentor at the end of every chapter. We hope that these questions will allow you to revisit each chapter several times, as you will get something different out of the chapters based on who you're discussing these ideas with and whatever career stage you're in. To make this book even more useful and practical, you will find that in most chapters, we included Action Items to give you concrete ways to start putting our suggestions and resources into action.

Throughout the book, where relevant, we provide you with real-life examples, including samples of things that we wrote ourselves, such as responses to reviewer comments or article outlines. To protect the identities of the writers, we have fictionalized anything written by others, such as emails, book proposals, and reviewer comments. So if you find yourself wondering where the examples came from as you read through the book, they are from real people but have been modified in a way that maintains their essence. Any examples that are directly discussed within a chapter appear in-text. We also added a list of appendices with additional examples of what are known as the occluded genres (after Swales, 1996), the kind of writing that usually is never seen publicly. This is where we provide templates that you can adapt to your own needs.

We would like to point out that you will see some overlaps among chapters, which is inevitable considering the nature of the contents. Writing a chapter for an edited volume, for instance, is mentioned in several chapters. It has its own chapter, but it has to be talked about in edited volumes (from the editor's perspective), and it is also relevant when talking about writing for different audiences. Likewise, we have a chapter on writing outlines, but this topic is also relevant in a variety of ways in other chapters. When we mention these items elsewhere, we make sure to direct you to the chapters dedicated to these topics.

We believe that there is no one-size-fits-all solution that works for everyone when it comes to academic writing. In fact, our approach is exactly the opposite. You need to find what works for you. If stringent organization is your recipe for success, organize away. If creative chaos rocks your boat, be creative. Our role is to provide you with ways to make your work more effective, as well as easier and more pleasant. You can reap the benefits of our collective couple of lifetimes of experience in academe.

You may wonder, perhaps with an undertone of fear, whether the advent of Large Language Model (LLM) driven Artificial Intelligence (AI) systems will not make the whole idea of writing research papers, books, and other scholarship obsolete, and hence this book unnecessary. Given the unbelievable amount of hype surrounding anything AI-related, you'd be justified in your concern. However, LLMs can do plenty of things, except be original. And, guess what? Original is the name of the game in research. We are a long way away from AI replacing humans in researching and creative endeavors. Sure, AI may help (and we point out a few ways in which it can in the book), but AI will not come up with research programs any time soon.

Finally, we'd like to point out that this book can be read linearly, from cover to cover, but also lends itself to being used as a handbook, where you can look up information when you need it. Need to write a book proposal? Go to Chapter 20. Puzzled by open access journals? Go to Chapter 29. Another reading strategy is to use the book as a sort of "book club" reading. You may want to use a given chapter as a "conversation starter" for mentoring faculty and graduate students or as an assignment in an academic writing class. As you use this book individually, with book clubs, in the classes you teach, or in conversations with others, we would love to hear from you about topics we didn't discuss or those upon which we could expand. If you have a different perspective or further examples on the topics we wrote about, let us know, as well. Feel free to reach out to us at publishandthrive@gmail.com.

Acknowledgments

We would like to acknowledge each other's contributions to this project and note that the author order for this book is alphabetical. We would also like to acknowledge all the editors, reviewers, students, colleagues, and others in the academic profession whose expertise and examples have helped shape our journeys with academic writing. Sal would like to acknowledge the help and support of Lucy Pickering. Hilal would like to acknowledge the support of her friends and family. Elisa would like to thank Alberto for his constant support and patience, as well as Javier and Manel for their guidance and friendship. Heather would like to thank Josh Gregory for his constant support.

Part I

The Fundamentals

1 The Philosophy behind This Book

If you are someone who gets to produce academic writing as part of your job (and we're assuming you are, since you opened this book ... thanks and welcome, by the way), you are part of an important community of researchers and thinkers. In a way, you're living out the dreams of all those little kids who wanted to be writers when they grew up. Academic life can present a lot of challenges to overcome before you can feel good about your professional writing, but we're here to tell you that you can (and should) be confident in your writing. You've surely experienced a long journey to get where you are in your academic career, and we want to help you embrace your awesomeness and offer you some strategies to feel empowered and enthusiastic about your writing.

With this book, we see our job as demystifying the process of academic writing, to help you approach this important aspect of your career from a perspective of confidence and even joy. We talk about the things you may even be embarrassed to ask about; shouldn't someone in your shoes know all this already? Well, no. And this is where we come in. We have asked the questions and searched out the answers, and we would like to share them with you. By clarifying those aspects of academic writing that seem frustratingly mysterious, we hope to help you move your relationship with academic writing away from a "publish or perish" attitude, one that has been used to describe academic writing in the following ways: demanding, challenging, difficult, exasperating, inaccessible, bad, mediocre, formal, high expectations, disenchanting, esoteric babble, tortuous, a bummer, and some might even say the worst form of writing ever invented. And these aren't our words; they are from the Corpus of Contemporary American English (COCA). While the list could go on indefinitely, our goal is that by the end of this book, you'll be able to create a new, more positive list of adjectives to describe your academic writing process (bonus points for adjectives with more than four syllables) that reflects your newfound sense of self-assurance and the perspective that you can publish and thrive.

So what can our philosophy do for you? By eliminating (some of) the anxiety of writing and simplifying the process, our philosophy can make you feel more confident about the process. That's what we call "demystifying" writing. Academic writing becomes effective when you know what you need to accomplish and how to get there. When the process is clearly outlined for you and there is little mystery left to the steps you need to take, you can reduce any daunting task to bite-sized pieces that don't seem so scary.

This book, in sum, aims to help you shift your mental narrative about academic writing to a more joyous perspective by demystifying the processes involved. Now, this doesn't mean that every time you sit down at your computer to write, you'll feel like you've been magically transported to a sunny field full of flowers where you can twirl around to your heart's content. This isn't a tampon commercial, after all. Instead, success comes from the certainty of having a plan to follow or someone or something to turn to (like this book) to help you keep going forward at any stage of the writing process. By maintaining consistency and following the principles and guidelines described in the book, you can feel confident about the writing process and become a more efficient writer.

1.1 Finding What Works for You

There is no "one-size-fits-all" approach to writing, and comparing yourself to other writers is the quickest way to undermine your confidence and diminish your joy. Dr. So-and-So may have published twelve articles this year, but you don't know how many years of work went into those publications or how many rejections they received before finding a home for their scholarship. You need to focus on your own writing agenda and find what works for you – and stick to it.

The first part is relatively easy, the second much harder. We'll help you with both. Sal likes to write in his office, with some classic Frank Zappa or Pink Floyd playing, usually after 10:00 pm and sometimes until late, often for a couple of hours. Hilal likes to meet with other people to write. Having to meet someone on Zoom or face to face is what ensures that she doesn't do anything else at that time. Heather blocks out two to four hours each week for writing, adding that time to her calendar as an appointment that cannot be scheduled over. Elisa writes best when she is home alone, early in the morning, with the help of many, many cups of espresso. She tries to block out a couple of mornings every week to make sure she has the quiet she needs to write.

1.2 Demystifying Writing

There is still a Romantic idea of the writer sitting in their garret, directly inspired by the muse, writing alone, preferably with a quill on loose foolscap paper, until they drop from exhaustion, only to have their manuscript snatched from their hand the next day by a publisher who rushes it to print to the applause of the masses. The only part of this picture that rings true for most of us is the exhaustion.

The big problem with this Romantic stereotype of the writer is this idea that writing is some sort of mystical communion with an unknowable entity (call it the muse, the spirit, the subconscious, whatever). Inspiration is great – when it happens – *but you cannot wait for inspiration to strike*. A large part of writing is a conscious, deliberate process that can be controlled and done "on command." Take a moment to come to terms with that fact, and let us elaborate. Suppose you have the idea of testing a hypothesis. That's the creative moment. What follows (operationalizing the hypothesis, gathering data, analyzing them, compiling the results, and interpreting them) is simply the application of a method and can be described explicitly. In fact, even having the original idea can be planned to some extent: engaging in extended reading in a field is bound to trigger some idea (e.g., spotting a gap in the literature). So, you may not be able to plan having an insight, but you can put yourself in the position of being more susceptible to it. You will most likely find that the writing you produce on "uninspired" days is every bit as good as what you create on those days when you're really vibing with the muse. Taking ownership of the writing process, rather than waiting for inspiration, is a joyous act, because it eliminates panic and creates space for confidence. When you're in the practice of writing regularly, you know that those off days won't matter in the grand scheme of things, because you're consistently moving toward your goals.

So, a significant part of our writing philosophy is aimed at demystifying the writing experience and turning it into a process that you can control and harness. For example, by breaking down a complex (and daunting) task, such as writing a book, into smaller tasks (put together an outline, write an introduction, complete a paragraph, craft a topic sentence for a paragraph, etc.), we can create an easily digestible list of tasks, so simple that we expect anyone would be able to perform them.

1.3 Finding Joy

Just like a runner, as you continue to train as an academic writer, you might find your "writer's high." Let us elaborate: You probably have heard of the runner's high. As you run, your body starts to produce endorphins, which are essentially a natural morphine. Sal has never experienced runner's high. When he tried running, he experienced runner-I-want-to-die and sensibly stopped and went to eat a donut. Remember that each writer is different; some people experience joy, and some don't, but everyone can write. In this section, we offer some potential sources of joy that may or may not work for you.

Remembering your "why": When you're under pressure to publish for a promotion or annual review, it can be hard to see the positive side of academic writing. You most likely got into this field, though, because you are passionate about your area of research and you wanted to make an impact on the field, your peers, and your students. Maybe your research is going to provide representation for first-generation scholars or another underrepresented group in academia, or maybe your investigation of firefly mating habits will create sparks of change at the next conference you attend. Either way, you're where you are because you have something to say, and there are people who want to hear it.

Before the publish-or-perish mentality weighed you down with anxieties, we're willing to bet that you were pretty fascinated with the subject of your academic writing. It's good to be realistic and understand how your writing productivity will affect your ability to keep or get a job, but anxiety related to writing productivity can snuff out your spark of curiosity related to your research topic. Establishing a writing plan for consistency helps to minimize anxiety so that you can thrive as an academic writer. By shifting the narrative in your head from what you don't have time to do, don't know how to do, or don't like about academic writing to a focus on that thing that you know you do well, you will enjoy the experience of writing more.

Sense of achievement: It's not "achievement" in the sense of writing hundreds or thousands of words or finishing a manuscript (though they are most welcome when they happen!). Hilal finds joy in the sense of achievement she feels every time she manages to clear out a block of time in her schedule and sits down, officially, to write. It *is* an achievement; she made time for her writing, saw it through, and now with the uninterrupted time she has ahead of her, she is going to make *some* progress.

Curiosity: Heather finds joy in those moments when a new research project has her feeling like a detective about to uncover juicy secrets. There is nothing like the rush of finding a novel that deals with exactly the themes she is hoping to analyze, especially when it's by a relatively unknown author. In addition to learning and sharing that knowledge with others, Heather is especially excited when she is able to elevate marginalized voices from underrepresented demographics through her research.

Flow: You may experience flow, "a state in which people are so involved in an activity that nothing else seems to matter; the experience is so enjoyable that people will continue to do it even at great cost, for the sheer sake of doing it" (Csikszentmihalyi, 1990, p. 20). This sometimes happens to Elisa. The whole house could be burning down and people could be screaming and running around her, but she would not even notice because she is in the zone. Flow feels like an unbreakable bubble, created by Elisa's engagement in the task (disclaimer: she only experiences flow when she is writing, not completing some other task like unloading the dishwasher). When she's in the zone, Elisa can work on the same task for very long stretches of time, ignoring other arguably more important needs such as eating or drinking water.

Path to discovery: Much like you don't really know something until you teach it to someone else, you don't really know what you know until you write it down. We write to find out what we think. Writing as a path to discovery can be energizing and, frankly, exciting.

External validation: Who doesn't like being told that they did a great job? Producing research that is both meticulously investigated and beautifully written can be thrilling. When others commend your writing or cite you in papers or at conferences, this can give you a confidence boost to encourage you to keep writing.

Control: At least until you reach the editing stage, you have 100 percent control over your writing. Nothing is on the page until you put it there; nothing is changed unless you change it, which you may find soothing.

Creativity: Many of us get to decide what we are working on and writing about, and most of the time we come up with our hypotheses and arguments. Even if someone else assigned you a topic to research or write about, you still have control over the writing process, who gets quoted, what sources you use, and all other creative choices.

Action item!

Have a look at the potential sources of joy we listed above. Are any of these reflective of your own experience? Is anything missing? Write down your own example of how one or more of these bring you joy when writing or add a new writing-related item that brings you joy.

1.4 Writing Regularly

The most effective way to write is to write regularly in order to build momentum (Chapter 3). Write *something*; be it the acknowledgments, entering items in your bibliography, copying citations from your references, or just taking notes while you read some of the literature. It doesn't matter. The day before writing this paragraph, Sal wrote a whopping 290 words (two paragraphs, to be precise) of his eye tracking book. It isn't much, but he is now 290 words closer to being done than he was the day before.

Find what works for you in terms of writing frequency and time, and stick with it. Perhaps writing on the weekends is more reasonable, or writing an hour in the morning before the kids wake up, or two hours at night after your lovely wife goes to bed (Sal's strategy), or writing in your office in time slots you've pre-scheduled into your calendar (what Heather likes to do). The details don't matter, but it's important to establish a routine that involves repeating writing sessions which will become a habit. Habits are momentum; they are self-sustaining, and they can be comforting. When your routine gets disrupted (and it surely will), you will just get back into it when the disruption has passed. Once you have a consistent plan for writing, you will see the benefits of maintaining that routine, which should make you less willing to give up the time you have earmarked for that purpose.

1.5 Celebrating Your Accomplishments

Writing can be a very lonely activity. When you write, you most likely sit alone in front of a computer or a piece of paper. An important part of our philosophy is the sharing of experiences, struggles, epiphanies, questions, answers, hunches, and moments of triumph when a paper gets accepted or a good review comes in. Your writing group (Chapter 4) should be a place to share with people and find community and shared experience.

We recommend you start tracking your progress. It is very rewarding to look back on your week and to see how many hundreds (or thousands?) of words you produced in a week. It quantifies your efforts, shows you how far you have come, and makes the hard work you've put in even more worth it. If you don't have a number you are satisfied with, just remember that it's that many more words than what you would otherwise have, so it's still worth celebrating.

In our writing group, we applaud each other's weekly reports. They may be small or in the thousands of words, but they are always better than nothing and worth celebrating. It feels good to say, "I did it! I wrote 500 words this week, and I am now that much closer to my goal." When you can share your wins (word count, paper acceptances, positive reviews of your book) with a community of academic writers, everyone participates in your celebration and benefits from a sense of momentum. What if you didn't write at all this week or feel like you don't have anything to celebrate at the moment? No worries, get back on the saddle and write next week. It happens to everyone. Even great athletes lose a set or miss a shot from time to time. They just move on to the next point.

If you don't have a writing group yet, you can consciously remind yourself to take the time to acknowledge your hard work. Elisa knows by now that she is not really good at celebrating her accomplishments, so she now keeps a Post-it note on her computer that says, "Take a few minutes to celebrate after each accomplishment." It does help. Finally, remember that it gets easier. Writing is like any complex activity where practice will improve your performance. You'll get better and better. Even impostor syndrome diminishes over time (see Chapter 2).

1.5 Celebrating Your Accomplishments

As you read the chapters in this book and apply them to your academic writing, we hope that the tools, techniques, and strategies we discuss will help you to gain confidence in your ability to grow as a writer little by little, day by day. By having a plan for your writing and forging ahead without waiting for that elusive strike of inspiration, you will realize that academic writing is attainable, even in the busiest of schedules. While academic writing may not be a non-stop laugh fest, demystifying the process and feeling confident in how to do the work is empowering. This book outlines a writing plan for you so that you can return your focus to the aspects of your research that bring you joy.

Questions for Reflection

1. To identify your optimum writing/research schedule, think back to the last few times you sat down to write. When did it feel the most right? Were you home, in your office, at a cafe? Did the time of day factor into your productivity?
2. What kind of writer are you? Are you someone who tends to start with the easiest or the hardest part? Are you good at planning and keeping track of progress, or do you need support from others? Reflect on the aspects of writing that are most difficult for you and those that come easily to you.

Questions for Discussion

1. Talk to your peers, colleagues, or friends about what brings them joy when they are working on a complex task. It can be writing, but depending on their profession, it could be a different task. Either way, focusing on the positive and learning what motivates others and makes them feel good about their work could help you discover something about yourself.
2. Have a conversation with colleagues about how they keep writing even when they feel uninspired (if they do). The goal is to learn from each other's strategies.

Questions for Your Mentor

1. Your mentor has years of experience, so ask them what they do to keep track of their many projects and deadlines. How do they deal with delays or other issues that (inevitably) come up?
2. If your relationship with your mentor allows, ask them how they find joy in academic writing and how it has evolved throughout their career.

2   Mental Well-Being

Part of being able to write successfully and to thrive in academia is learning how to advocate for your health and mental well-being. Care for yourself first. Watch what you eat, how many hours you are sleeping, and how frequently you exercise. While most people pursue graduate studies and jobs in academia due to a passionate interest in teaching and researching their subject matter, academic life is often not easy. "University students – and graduate students in particular – suffer from higher rates of depression, anxiety, and suicidal thoughts and behaviors than their peers who are not students" (Bernstein et al., 2022). Those of us who work within academia experience multiple physical, mental, and emotional demands from colleagues, students, administrators, and families. If you suffer from depression, or other mental health issues, you should seek professional help. Most academic institutions provide some support, like campus clinics, or offer insurance that covers mental health care.

Your academic persona is just *one* part of your identity. If your experiences with graduate school and academia are similar to ours, you may have experienced guilt at times when you're trying to rest, perhaps equating your worth as a person to your level of productivity. While research and writing are crucial components of academic success, it's helpful to contextualize this part of your life within the bigger picture of everything else that makes you who you are. For example, if Heather had to make a pie chart of everything that she hopes to prioritize in her life, research would be a significant slice, but spending time with her family and friends, lifting weights, reading books, eating pie, and petting random cats would also comprise large portions of the chart. In other words, you're not going to function at your peak abilities if you're a few slices short of a whole pie. By allowing yourself to be well-rounded (something actual pies can help you with), taking those 15-minute breaks to clear your mind while speed-walking around the neighborhood and judging everyone else's landscaping choices, you put yourself in a position to bring your best self back to the keyboard.

2.1 Being in the Right Place

In Chapter 1, we talked about establishing a routine as creating momentum and writing frequently and consistently. A solid routine, however, encompasses so much more, from where you write to what you wear while writing, and we recommend having a routine that works specifically for you. This requires experimenting with different things to see how they work out for you. Because of this, you should not try to establish a new routine at the beginning of an important work project with tight deadlines. Ideally, you would have a couple of weeks in which you can try out different locations (the library? Starbucks? a shed in your yard? a closet? your kitchen table at 5:00 am?), time goals (write for twenty-five minutes and then take a break, as in the Pomodoro technique, or settle in for two-hour stretches?), times of the day, various forms of caffeination or lack thereof, type of light, combinations of clothing and temperature settings, noise-canceling headphones, and physical arrangements (a comfy oversized chair or a standing desk?). This may seem like a silly list of things that are ultimately irrelevant, but our point is that you should try to make your routine as pleasant and conducive to your work as possible. For example, Sal tried working in a "shut up and write" group, which met in a semi-public place on campus. While this is one of Hilal's preferred ways to write, Sal did not enjoy himself because of the distraction of having other people around. Could he pull off writing in that environment? Yes, but even if he were exactly as productive, he prefers writing at his desk in his home office at night. So, why not go with what works best for him? What works best for Hilal won't necessarily work best for Sal, and vice versa. You can probably write anywhere if you have to. The point is to find your ideal writing circumstances. Fuzzy socks, copious amounts of coffee, and a variety of pet co-authors seem to be quite popular preferences among this book's writers.

Action item!

Having a checklist to keep track of what works for you and what you need in order to be at your best is a useful strategy that will come in handy when you are overwhelmed, feeling stuck, or find yourself procrastinating. Take a few minutes to think about your ideal writing context and write it down. Use our suggestions above to get started, but make sure to think about your experience. And if you aren't sure yet, try out different options until you know what to write for each category.

Location (Where would you like to be?): _____
Time (What time is it, and how long do you have?): _____
Pace (Do you need breaks? Can you be interrupted?): _____
Drinks and snacks (What are you having?): _____

People (Who else is there?): _____
Device (What are you using to write?): _____
Clothes (What are you wearing – socks, blanket ...?): _____
Sound (What are you listening to?): _____
Distractions (Is your phone on silent? Is your inbox paused?): __
Others (What else is important for you?): _____

2.2 Writing Hurdles and How to Leap Them

The blank page can be terrifying. There are many reasons the page remains blank, but let's start with your disposition since our writing philosophy is geared toward enjoying your writing more. It's perfectly normal for people to have different attitudes toward and experiences with writing. Some people are confident writers, while others are apprehensive. The problem is that research, dating as far back as the 1970s, has shown that apprehensive writers write less and worse (Daly, 1985, pp. 56–59). Studies have shown that writing apprehension also correlates with procrastination (Onwuegbuzie & Collins, 2001). The nice thing about dispositions is that they are stable but not fixed. If you take sugar and cream in your coffee, you may switch to drinking it black, and eventually come to prefer it that way. The same can be true for how you view writing.

In the remainder of this chapter, we look at three of the most common holdups for academic writers and suggest ways to overcome them. At this point in the book, you probably suspect that our advice is going to be "find whatever works for you." Well, in a sense you'd be correct, but our advice is more simply that you are unlikely to experience writing hurdles if you follow our approach. The whole idea of demystifying writing, of breaking tasks down into smaller, manageable chunks and writing incrementally but regularly, is geared toward avoiding these challenges in the first place.

2.2.1 Writer's Block

Writer's block is defined as a competent writer's inability to write, even after you have made the time and sat down to do it. Google finds over thirty million hits on writer's block (apparently the people who wrote those were not blocked). Rose (1985) offers a classic review, while a more recent review of the research can be found in Ahmed and Güss (2022). There is a whole industry of consultants, advisors, therapists, and writing teachers with a variety of methods to overcome writer's block, such as freewriting (essentially brainstorming in writing), mind mapping, outlining, and so on.

One of the causes of writer's block is the idea that what you write should be perfect, or at least brilliant (Bloom, 1985, p. 127), which is a difficult expectation to live up to. Sal once famously said, "It's hard to be brilliant on demand." (He's very proud of having said that, so he repeats it all the time.) Fortunately, academic writing is not creative writing. Nobody cares if your methodology section is not sparkling with witty insight and well-rounded characters. You are describing statistical methodology and similarly unsparkling topics. Clarity, simplicity, and conciseness are the name of the game. You shouldn't worry about being brilliant in a methodology section. In fact, you should not be brilliant in that section. The place for brilliance is in your conclusions.

Rather than looking for perfection, embrace the Italian proverb that roughly states, "Better is the enemy of good." This is very true in many aspects of life, but it is extremely true in writing. Trying to organize an argument or state an issue in the best possible way may be a waste of effort, as a variety of organizational structures would most likely do the job adequately. Once you have achieved a clear and effective presentation of your work, there is little to be gained from belaboring that part of your writing. Some reviewer is probably still going to make you redo it, anyway. The passage you just spent hours agonizing over could also get cut by your editor or by yourself during a revision, which would make your finessing efforts a complete waste of time. You always have the option to go back and revise, so don't get too distracted by revision as you write. Consider Simon's (1956) statement that "organisms adapt well enough to 'satisfice'; they do not, in general, 'optimize'" (p. 129). To put it differently, trying to achieve maximum returns can cause us to waste more effort than it is worth. Schwartz et al. (2002) show that satisficers are happier than maximizers. Being content with what is good enough is one of the secrets of happiness – trying to maximize success leads to increased regret and depression.

We all hear those negative voices in our heads telling us that our writing needs to be "improved" or "fixed." Whether those voices are channeling the dreaded Reviewer 2 (see Chapter 13), former teachers, supervisors, or colleagues, if you listen to them, you will start editing as you write. That is a recipe for disaster. Rather than focusing on what you have to say and banging out your content, you will concentrate on how you say it or how you could have said it better, or how your reviewers will react to what you said, and so on, spiraling downward until the inevitable crash landing of throwing away what you wrote and starting from scratch (back to the blank page). The trick here is to silence the voices by convincing yourself that you are writing just for yourself. Remember the rule: no one sees your first draft but you. Editing starts much later in the game.

2.2.2 Procrastination

We sometimes procrastinate or fixate on small, writing-related tasks that aren't very important because some part of us is afraid to finish our research and send it off, exposing it (and ourselves) to potential rejections. Our writing is closely related to our self-image. If you've been working for years on a study, it is very likely that you are invested to a significant extent in the subject matter, your argument, and your findings. Being rejected is inherently hurtful, but having our writing rejected or criticized is particularly so. No wonder, then, that fear of failure, the threat of being evaluated negatively, or anxiety in a broader sense are some of the causes of writer's block. If you don't finish your paper/book/dissertation, you do not run the risk of having it rejected or criticized. It doesn't matter that this argument is irrational (as you *will* fail your PhD or not get tenure if you don't finish and publish your research); it reduces stress or averts the fear in the short term. Also, please bear in mind that academe is systemically flawed when it comes to rejections. If you belong to a marginalized group (due to your race, gender, sexual orientation, social class, ability status, etc.), you may experience rejection more frequently from your colleagues, advisors, and administrators than your more privileged peers due to implicit and explicit prejudices. While we don't have a solution for systemic bias, we hope it helps to contextualize rejection in this way. To learn more about power dynamics within academia, we suggest checking out Chela Sandoval's *Methodology of the Oppressed*.

If you are a procrastinator, we have potentially good news for you. While much scholarship on procrastination views it as a failure of self-regulation (Steel, 2007), there is also research (reviewed in Klingsieck, 2013 or Sirois, 2023, for example) connecting procrastination to managing stress and negative emotions. In other words, procrastination is not just a weakness or failure but a way to deal with stress or other unwanted emotions. For example, Sal has been procrastinating on writing the fourth edition of the book he coauthored with his best friend Steve Brown, who passed away during the COVID pandemic. It did not take a therapist for him to realize that even just thinking about the book brought up sadness and longing for his missing friend. No wonder then that he was reluctant to start working on the book. Less dramatically, one may procrastinate on finishing a paper because if the paper is not submitted, it cannot be rejected. It doesn't matter that rationally this makes no sense. Emotionally, avoiding rejection is all that matters. Of course, we also procrastinate on doing things we simply don't like doing.

If you procrastinate, you don't need to be too harsh with yourself about it. First, you are not alone. Studies have shown that up to 90 percent of students and academics procrastinate (the other 10 percent just didn't fill out the survey on time). Second, there is clear evidence that procrastination is a form of mood regulation, or managing stressful and negative emotions. For many of us, stress factors (including chronic diseases, financial worries, family problems, etc.) make it even more likely that we will turn to procrastination. We can reduce or eliminate procrastination by mitigating stress factors and adopting strategies like mindfulness training (Rad et al., 2023). You may not be able to totally eliminate your stress factors, but there are strategies to help put some distance between you and the issue. Third, not all procrastination is necessarily negative. Strategic procrastination (or delay) is the practice of putting off work because it may be more advantageous to do the work later. For example, you might work better under pressure from a deadline, or you may delay doing a task until you have a chunk of time free from other distractions. In fact, some research shows that moderate procrastination may lead to more creativity (Shin & Grant, 2021). However, this is a fairly rare phenomenon. By and large, most people find that procrastination is damaging or at least annoying. The difference between strategic delay and procrastination is that the latter is accompanied by negative consequences or at least negative subjective feelings.

Overall then, a positive frame of mind may help with procrastination. If you change your attitude toward writing, you will not procrastinate doing it because you will enjoy it. If you can eliminate the sources of stress, then the tendency to procrastinate will also diminish. A positive frame of mind necessitates self-compassion, which includes self-kindness (avoidance of self-criticism), recognition of the common humanity of our experiences (seeing ourselves as connected to others with the same experiences, rather than isolated), and mindfulness (accepting events and feelings as "happening" without endowing them with emotional significance [Neff, 2003]).

2.2.3 *Impostor Syndrome (IS)*

An important aspect of IS is the "impostor cycle" (proposed by Clance, 1985). It works roughly as follows: a task is assigned or selected, such as writing a paper. The IS sufferer reacts with anxiety and fear. This manifests in either overpreparation or procrastination, followed by a last-minute flurry of activity. The individual completes the task (the paper is submitted). The completion of the task is followed by relief and a feeling of accomplishment and possibly validation (positive reviewer comments, acceptance of the paper, etc.). These positive feelings do not last, however, as the IS sufferer attributes their success to hard work (and hence no particular ability) or luck. This causes anxiety and fear that the next writing task will not be successful, and so on *ad libitum*. What is important to notice is that not all steps of the impostor cycle need to be present or observable, but that the self-validating discounting of success, praise, and accomplishment is impossible to break from within the cycle. So, what can a sufferer of IS do?

The problem is difficult to tackle. IS does not exist in a vacuum: issues of class, gender, and race are obviously reflected in the prevalence of IS among marginalized populations. So many of us suffer from IS because of the way that society and academia are structured. It is not an internal flaw of any one individual but a natural response to living within systems that function in ways designed to make us question our authority and our right to have a seat at the table, even while we are succeeding in academia. In fact, speaking purely rationally, IS is a contradiction in terms for academics. Most of us who suffer from IS are high-performing individuals. Only about 1 percent of the US population holds a PhD, and about half of that group publishes. Yet, those of us dealing with IS at times think that we are frauds or impostors who do not deserve our success. Objectively, IS sufferers are pretty awesome people, with impressive accomplishments by any metric.

It is fairly clear that IS is connected to psychological issues such as fear of failure, perfectionism, the need to be the "best" or a "genius," but also to fear and guilt of success, and to being overwhelmed by too much work or too many commitments. In all of these cases, therapy can help, by recognizing the underlying causes of the behavior and taking steps to mitigate it. Unfortunately, not everyone can afford therapy. If your IS affects you significantly and you can get professional help, you should (some universities include a limited number of therapy sessions within their healthcare plan). Think about it this way: if there is an issue with your refrigerator, you call a service person. Mental health should be no different. However, if your IS doesn't warrant therapy or you can't afford it, then what? Fortunately, there are steps you can take on your own. Recognizing and acknowledging your feelings of impostorism is an important step forward, as this can help you to normalize the feelings, which you may then want to discuss with friends, trusted colleagues or mentors, a support group, or perhaps even your writing group, if you have one. Sharing such feelings with a group reduces the sense of isolation and normalizes the feelings, as you realize how many people truly are impacted by IS.

Other strategies to manage IS include redirecting your mind away from worry and toward a more positive place. Thought stopping is a self-regulation technique where you dismiss negative thoughts ("Everybody around here is so much smarter than me") as soon as you become aware of them. Ideally, you replace the negative thoughts with self-compassionate ones, but pretty much anything positive will do. Keeping a file of grateful letters from former students or complimentary comments from colleagues or reviewers that you can open when negative thoughts appear may be a useful strategy. Likewise, consider keeping positive-thought-inducing memorabilia displayed in a visible way in your office, such as your framed diplomas, awards, copies of your published books and articles, and anything else that makes you feel confident in your academic abilities.

When you're feeling down, you can also produce an objective evaluation of your successes. Most tenure-track academics are required to report annually on their accomplishments. To mitigate the effects of IS, ask a trusted colleague to help you establish a list of your accomplishments; they can make sure you aren't discounting any of the important work you've done. If this feels intimidating, you can ask your trusted colleague to share their annual report with you, as a way to see what they have included and spot anything that you might have left out of your own report. Once you have a complete report, you can use it to more objectively assess your successes and strengths. Add in any positive comments from supervisors, colleagues, and students to further bolster your confidence. As a nice side effect of this strategy, most of these materials are required for your tenure and promotion dossiers, so this is work that you will have to do at some point, no matter what.

> **Action item!**
>
> To remind yourself what you are capable of and fight back against IS (even just a little), find some positive feedback that makes you proud of your work and your writing. This could be a short note from a student who really enjoyed your class, a long letter from your annual review, or a heartwarming comment from a reviewer about an article you submitted. Whatever it is, print it and hang it in a place that is visible to you from your writing spot. When you are struggling to see or appreciate your professional worth, or when you are dealing with negative comments from Reviewer 2, you can look at the positive feedback and remember the positive impact you are making within your field.

Surprisingly, there is some evidence that managerial support can palliate the effects of IS (Crawford et al., 2016). Crawford et al. hypothesized that perceived organizational support "moderates" the impact of IS on work-to-family-conflict: "organizations can fulfill socio-emotional needs for impostors, such as the need for approval, esteem, and affiliation" (p. 379). Organizations can implement policies that support IS sufferers, as a personal, individual approach and reframing evaluations as formative rather than summative may lessen employee anxiety. Supervisors and mentors can offer praise and emphasize that an individual's successes are due to skill and hard work rather than luck. Those in positions of authority can help their colleagues who struggle with IS to set appropriate goals and seek adequate promotion opportunities, encouraging them to strive for goals that they may otherwise consider beyond their reach. If you are providing support for an IS sufferer, you might try asking them to answer the question, "What is the worst that can happen?" This helps differentiate between legitimate fears ("I will not publish enough papers and will not get tenure/promotion") and exaggerated ones ("Everyone will laugh at me"). In many cases, the worst that can happen is that you will need to submit your paper elsewhere. A bit deflating, in terms of fears, isn't it?

No matter which writing hurdle you struggle with most, being able to identify whether you're a perfectionist or a procrastinator (or both) is helpful. Once you know what you struggle with, you can work to remediate the issue, whether the solution is therapy, anti-anxiety medication, meditation, exercise, changes in diet, distancing yourself from the toxic people in your life (the ones you can, at least), dedicating more time to your favorite activities, joining a support group, or any combination of these or other strategies. Most of the writing principles in this book directly or indirectly help to reduce writing anxiety and create positive motivations. So, use this book as a guide. Another strategy you can use is to practice thought control: if you detect yourself engaging in negative or anxious thinking (e.g., by imagining what a negative reviewer might say about your work), consciously stop yourself and instead produce a positive thought (e.g., visualize hitting "send" for the final submission of your paper or holding the first hard copy of your book). Next, practice self-compassion (Neff, 2003) – avoid self-criticism and frame your experiences as part of a community of fellow scholars who undergo the same stresses you are experiencing – and mindfulness – keep some distance between your thoughts and your inner self, essentially meaning that you watch yourself be scared, anxious, or sad but accept that you can let the thoughts just pass you by; they don't have to stick around unless you hold on to them. Finally, you may want to try asking one of the many AI tools to produce a paragraph to get you going. Reacting to the AI's text is a completely different action than writing your own, emotionally speaking. The risk is that journals' and employers' policies about the use of AI are in flux (to be generous), so we advise extreme caution in using AI text for anything other than nudging you in the direction of writing or suggesting a topic to tackle. To sum up, taking care of your mental well-being is essential. Keep this book's principles in mind as you write: tomorrow is another day and another opportunity to write something, however little.

Action item!

To keep the positive thoughts coming, create or find something that makes you feel good and keep it close so you can see it when you write. This could be a picture of your advisor on a unicorn shooting rainbow rays, a Post-it note with a positive message, a drawing your niece made for you, a meme that makes you laugh, or a silly picture with some friends. The object is up to you, but the feeling it produces should be one of joy. If you find yourself engaging in some kind of negative thinking, looking at your object can help you get back to a place of positive thoughts.

No matter what is keeping you from writing – from impostor syndrome to negative self-talk to a mischievous poltergeist who keeps stealing your notepads – being aware of what is holding you back is the first step. Once you know what the issue is, you can fight back with positive self-affirmations, logic, support from your writing group, and any other strategies you have devised. Most importantly, give yourself credit for what you have already accomplished and use the routine you've established to get right back to writing as soon as you can.

Questions for Reflection

1. Acknowledging the effects of impostor syndrome is an important step for moving forward and overcoming it. Think of a time when impostor syndrome impacted you. Try to remember what happened and how you reacted. How could you have used the strategies shared in this chapter to react differently?
2. Pretend you are your academic bestie. What would they say about your work? How would you encourage yourself to keep going when you are feeling stuck?

Questions for Discussion

1. Sharing is caring, and it can also help you see what you are good at. Find a colleague you trust and exchange manuscripts (this could be an entire article or just part of it). Read each other's manuscripts and then share only positive feedback about it. What is particularly clear, well-written, thought-provoking, or inspiring? What are the strengths of your colleague's manuscript? What are the strengths of their writing in general?
2. Discuss the strategies for mitigating IS that are proposed in this chapter with your colleagues. What other techniques can they add to the list? How might they modify the strategies offered in the chapter to make them more effective for them personally? Compile all these ideas into a list that you can share with colleagues and students.

Questions for Your Mentor

1. Your mentor probably also has writer's block from time to time. How do they move past it?
2. If your relationship with your mentor allows it, ask them if they have ever experienced impostor syndrome. What strategies have been effective for them in dealing with it?

3 Getting Started

You're ready to get started with your writing project and commit to gaining some serious momentum. You have a fresh cup of coffee beside you, you're ensconced in your trusty snuggie, and a white noise machine is regaling you with whale songs. You have silenced your phone, shut down your email, and locked the door to prevent pets or family members from distracting you. You're ready to write. We promise you don't need to add more whipped cream to your Frappuccino or move that plant two inches closer to the window for feng shui. Here is our take on how to get going.

Set mini goals. Even if your output is merely incremental, it's important to keep going. If your writing sessions depend on waiting for the perfect opportunity when you will have several hours of unimpeded time to write, you will very probably never finish your project, because perfect writing time is a myth, much like the Tooth Fairy but without the spare change under your pillow. There will always be something in the way. That is why one skill you can add to your toolbox is learning to write, research, or take notes in the snippets of time that occur in your daily life. You can even dictate notes in your phone and transcribe them when you get home that evening. Shape your notes or ideas into a coherent paragraph, and you are 100 words closer to being done with your book or article. In our writing group, we celebrate all amounts of writing, even when it's under 100 words a week. It is better than no words.

Start wherever. Books, articles, and long projects in general are not written sequentially. To think otherwise is a common mistake that can result in unnecessary stress and wasted time. Umberto Eco has the best piece of advice: start from the topic you know best, the part of the subject you are most comfortable with. You don't have to start from the beginning; start with the part that comes easiest to you, whether that's the acknowledgments, bibliography, or keywords. And remember, writing is never a one-size-fits-all experience. Maybe, like Hilal, you prefer to start with the most challenging part of the book or article. This way, you'll get a confidence boost and you'll have the thrill of knowing the hardest part of your project is already completed.

Let go of the pressure of an immediately perfect manuscript. Regardless of where you start, remember that this is just your first draft. What's the worst that can happen? Your first draft can be crap – you are the only one who will ever see it, and then you'll revise it. You can show your revised draft to your trusted readers, but literally no one but you will ever see your first draft. So, don't worry about it; just put the words down. You may surprise yourself.

In any case, it's hard to be brilliant on demand, so you shouldn't worry too much about that. For academic writing, you only need to be clear and thorough. Most authors will have a moment or two of brilliance, but if you can explain your insights in your writing, this is good enough. Unless you are a poet writing lyrical poetry, the quality of your writing will not significantly affect the professional outcomes of your career. Aside from one or two scholars who are known for their delightful style, most academic writing is clearly not meant to have aesthetic appeal. Well-researched and clearly written academic writing is more valuable than perfectly crafted prose.

You may have heard the saying "A good dissertation is a done dissertation." Though this book isn't meant only for graduate students, this motto has a lot of wisdom to it. However, no one is suggesting turning in an underresearched dissertation, book, or article. Rather, the idea is that we all reach a point after which continuing to revise a piece of writing yields diminishing returns. In the case of the dissertation, your advisor will eventually schedule your defense and toss you out of the comfortable nest of graduate school. When it comes to professional publications, however, you could spend the rest of your life perfecting an opus magnum that will never see the light or building the largest ever bibliography on a subject but never publishing it.

Deadlines are a feature, not a bug. Often, what forces us out of the cycle of infinite revisions or the ever-expanding literature review is a deadline. Perhaps you signed a contract that states that your book is due on the publisher's desk by a given date, or your report is due to a supervisor, or the editor of a journal has already sent you a couple of increasingly firm emails about your resubmission. In short, you cannot dilly dally any further; the project must be completed and sent off, whether you are completely satisfied or not. This book is not the perfect book the authors would have wanted to ship to the publisher, either, but ship it they must, in order for it to appear in print. Deadlines can be your friends, as they can help you get over the futile quest for perfection.

3.1 Building Momentum

Writing a large project that requires more than a couple of days of work (say, a 100,000-word book) can only be accomplished through repeated sessions. If you can write 500 words a day (and that's a fabulous performance), it will take you 200 days to write a book. That's over six months. Again, assuming you can produce 500 words a day, and you are willing to write every day, you could conceivably produce an 8,000-word paper in slightly over two weeks. Both of these (very) hypothetical examples assume you sustain a production of 500 words a day for 16 or 200 days. Sustain is the crucial word here: you need to keep going until you finish. That's quite hard to do, as we will discuss in the next paragraphs, but that is where momentum kicks in. When you are working on a given topic, even while you're not writing, you are most likely still processing what you want to say next, even as you go about your daily tasks. When you get back to your manuscript, you should be able to get right back to work, writing down those ideas or copying the notes you've taken, because the project has never been far from your mind. In other words, writing will come easily because of the momentum. You need to stick with whatever action you hope to turn into a habit for quite some time: on average, it takes more than two months for a new behavior to become a habit, while some people need up to eight months (Lally et al., 2009). If you can get into the habit of writing regularly, this will make your job easier because you will have fewer words left to write after each day, and because regular writing creates momentum. Momentum can become a powerful ally, as writing begets writing.

However, momentum needs to be cultivated. The most important thing is never to space out your writing days too much. Some writing coaches recommend writing every day. We see the wisdom in that idea; zero days is the best gap between writing days, momentum-wise. However, as with most ideal visions, reality gets in the way, in the form of children needing your attention, spouses needing to be reminded of why they chose to attach themselves to your glorious writing-focused self, students needing to be taught, lab animals needing to be fed, emails needing to be answered within ten minutes of receipt, and the rest of the daily life of a busy academic. Inevitably, there will be days when you cannot write, not because you are weak or a bad writer but because it is humanly impossible to do everything that is on your schedule. Our advice is to accept that and even plan for it. If you are teaching all day on Tuesdays and Thursdays, on top of dealing with other obligations, accept that you will not be writing those days. That leaves five other days of the week. On Tuesdays and Thursdays, you still can be thinking about what to write on the other days. Always carry a notebook or, if you don't feel ridiculous doing so, leave a voice memo to yourself on your phone, recording good ideas. You can simply say, "Hey Siri, remind me to write xyz." Apple, you owe us for that one.

What if you can only squeeze out a couple of days each week? Perhaps you can only find time over the weekend. That makes things a little more difficult, but not impossible. First, check to see if you can reorganize your week cleverly, thus relocating some activity that takes your time during the week over to the weekend. For example, you could do the laundry on Saturdays, or cook a breakfast casserole on Sunday, to free up a half hour every morning for some predawn writing. We want to avoid a situation where you have to restart from scratch every time you get going. If you need to remind yourself of what you were supposed to be writing about every time you sit down to work, then you cannot have been thinking about your research while engaged in routine activities. (Elisa finds that playing mindless video games can be very conducive to thinking, for example.) Let's examine a worst-case scenario: your life currently only allows you to write once a week, for a few hours. You need to keep the momentum going, regardless of not being able to write more consistently. How can you accomplish that? For starters, use routine activities to think about what you will write. Always take notes (in writing if possible, but text messages to self and voice memos work, as well). Accumulate the notes, or their transcriptions, in a folder, white board, or document you keep open on your computer to help you to keep your thoughts focused on the project. Then when you get started, spend some time re-reading your book proposal, grant description, or the abstract of the paper to refocus on the work and reignite your interest in the project. After all, there was a time when you were excited about your great research idea. That spark is still there. What you need to do is fan the flames. Being part of an accountability writing group is a very good way of doing this, but in keeping with the philosophy of "whatever works for you," you may find another way of achieving the same goal. If you need more incentive to find your motivation, a writing streak helps decrease the chances of writer's block and procrastination.

3.2 Tracking Your Progress

Keeping track of your word count is important, albeit not the number itself. It doesn't make a huge difference if you wrote 245 or 250 words in a day. However, there are good reasons to keep track. First, having an actual number keeps you honest. It is very difficult to estimate the number of words you write in a session, let alone in a week. You may feel like you wrote a thousand words, while in fact you only wrote 400. Second, keeping a record of your word count is important when you are working toward a particular goal. If you set up a backward calendar and calculate your daily writing output, you can monitor your progress and determine if you are on track to finish on deadline or not. One advantage of knowing your word count is the ability to self-regulate. Suppose you find out that you need to produce 400 words a day, which will allow you to finish drafting an 8,000-word paper in twenty days, but in the first week, you are short of the 2,800 words you needed to produce (400 × 7). This tells you to pick up the pace. Conversely, if you banged out 3,000 brilliant words on the first day, booking a vacation may be in the charts. Third, seeing the overall total increase can be a powerful motivator. If you are writing a book, when you pass the 40,000-word mark, you know you are half done. This can boost your confidence and reassure you that you will make it.

Keeping track of your word count will also help ensure that you don't write too much. In our experience, cutting excess text is much more difficult than adding text, because we tend to get attached to the fruits of our labor, and it's wasteful to have to delete words you've already written. Furthermore, if you need to delete 1,000 words, for example, then you have essentially wasted a day's or week's worth of work, which could have been used for something else. That is highly inefficient.

Action item!

Consider this scenario: Bob Writalot had 6 months to write a 90,000-word book: $6 \times 30 = 180$ days of writing; $90,000/180 = 500$. If Bob wrote 500 words a day, he'd be fine, assuming nothing happened to disrupt his routine. You may want to give yourself a buffer if you have a hard deadline or to give yourself time for editing.

Now take a project of your own (an article, a chapter, a book, a conference paper, or whatever you're working on) and establish a backward calendar to track your progress and calculate how many words per day you need to produce.

How many words do you need to write? A _____
How many days until the deadline?   B _____

From B, subtract the time you will need to edit your manuscript, as well as some buffer days to account for unforeseen circumstances (e.g., one week every two months, depending on the length of the project and your commitments outside of work).

C _____

Now, calculate A/C = D _____ This is the number of words you should write every day to be able to meet your deadline.

Tracking your daily/weekly word count is a low-cost activity that only takes a few seconds. If you have yesterday's total, all you need to do is subtract it from today's total word count.

3.3 Defending Your Writing Time

It is not enough to set up a writing routine and build momentum. You also need to protect your writing time from possible interference. Famously, Virginia Woolf said that a writer needs "a room of her own." We definitely agree with her, and we would like to add that our room needs a sturdy, soundproof door that locks. Noise-canceling headphones at Starbucks work, too. Even when they're well meaning, spouses, children, colleagues, students, and even random

3.3 Defending Your Writing Time

strangers can easily interrupt your writing time. You can make yourself inaccessible and protect your writing time by working in a closed office, a remote cubicle in the library, or a corner of a coffeehouse with your back to the other patrons. Turn off or mute your phone, and switch your email and other notifications off while you're at it, so you won't be tempted to get sucked back into life's distractions. If silencing your phone or removing yourself from the reach of others is impractical, politely but firmly stating that you will address their problem at the end of your session (giving them a concrete end-time for your writing session) usually does the trick, unless you are dealing with children, in which case we suggest bribes, candy, or unfettered access to cartoons or the internet.

However, the greatest threat to your writing time is none other than you, dear reader. We are all too familiar with the temptation to take on another review, another committee, another interesting project. Heather agreed to review two articles while writing this chapter (sadly, no joke). The most important skill that a writer needs to develop is that of saying no to projects that will cut into your writing time. Under no circumstance should you agree to do anything that will require you to lose writing time for your current project. Here, you should distinguish between true opportunities and time suckers. A true opportunity is something like an invitation to collaborate with a major scholar in your field. You may want to rearrange your schedule to make that work. You can always agree to work on a project *after* you finish the current manuscript. Time suckers are anything related with assessment of courses, improving a perfectly fine course that could be taught as it stands, reviewing bad articles, and working on projects that will not result in a tangible output.

Action item!

It may be difficult to say no, but we can help you create a healthy(-er) habit. Print out the say-no punch cards you will find in Appendix A or make your own. Share them with colleagues or friends and pick a reward to work toward (write or draw your reward in the reward space). Say NO nine times, and then enjoy your reward for a job well done.

You cannot write or work on your project if you are doing something else. Remind yourself of this self-evident truth every time you are considering taking on another task that may compete with your writing. If it is possible and politic, defend your writing time. If you want to say no, but are second-guessing yourself, the following tips may help.

1. Assess where the request is coming from. If a top journal in your field comes knocking, or you have a request from your department head or dean, you probably should accept.
2. Make sure that you are well informed on exactly what the request is (nature of the project, page length, time commitment, due date, etc.).
3. Assess the amount of time that will be required to complete the potential new task, and then multiply it. Around four times that number is realistically how much of your writing time you will lose.
4. Consider any research or skills you may need to learn in order to perform the task. The time needed for this stage needs to be added to the previous total loss of work time.
5. Decide if you can afford to agree to the task or not based on the amount of time you can actually spare.
6. Once you have made your decision, thank the person asking for your time, politely tell them you cannot do it (without providing an explanation), and end the discussion as soon as possible. We find it's best not to offer an explanation, as impolite and manipulative people will debate your reasons and argue with you that you can or should do what they are asking you. If you simply say, "I am afraid I cannot do it," there is nothing left to discuss.
7. Avoid saying, "I can do it later," or playing games ("I could do it if you extend the deadline to X"). They may agree, and now you are stuck. You might be tempted to say something like, "I can do it in two years." While it may be true, it comes off as arrogant.
8. Free yourself from any feelings of guilt you may experience. You are standing up for yourself.

In conclusion, once you've gotten started, momentum will help you going on, but you can build your momentum by spacing your writing times strategically, keeping track of your ideas and bouts of inspiration, keeping a log of how much you write, and checking that you are roughly on schedule, and finally – and possibly most importantly – you need to defend your writing time from distractions, even if it means making some difficult decisions or saying no to interesting projects.

Questions for Reflection

1. What is the most difficult part of saying no? Go back to the list of eight tips in the "Defend Your Writing Time" section of this chapter and try to identify your own personal challenges to defending your writing time. Do you struggle to find the right words to say no? Do you always put your students or colleagues before yourself? Think of some strategies

you can use to defend your writing time from these particular challenges moving forward.
2. Part of being an effective writer is seeing the big picture. How does the project fit in with everything else you have on your plate? Can you schedule and defend your writing time for this project without sacrificing your other writing responsibilities?

Questions for Discussion

1. People have different strategies for keeping track of their work and building momentum. Ask some colleagues to share theirs. What project management software do they use, if any? How do they manage to keep track of larger projects?
2. People struggle with different aspects of a complex project. What challenges do your colleagues often face, and how do they overcome them? You can use the following topics to start your discussion: distractions coming from emails or social media, interruptions from people in the workplace or in your personal life, lack of motivation.

Questions for Your Mentor

1. As a way of defending your writing time, discuss your current projects and professional commitments with your mentor. One benefit of this is that it will be useful to get their perspective regarding how much time each project requires (daily or weekly). The other benefit is, if they get a better sense of your current commitments, they may be less likely to add tasks to your to-do list.
2. Create a list of projects you have committed yourself to and share it with your mentor. Ask them to help you discern which items are time suckers and which are genuine opportunities. What advice do they have to help you avoid time suckers in the future?

4 Finding a Writing Group That Works for You

Do you remember that exhilarating feeling of getting positive feedback on a dissertation chapter draft from your advisor? Or the sinking sense of despair when a professor returned a final paper to you, the margins marked with less-than-glowing commentary? Whether you always appreciated it or not, you most likely received a steady stream of feedback on your written work in graduate school, which can make it hard to transition to researching and writing as a professional, a process that can feel solitary. You might not feel compelled to share your research in progress with others, due to insecurities about your writing, lack of community, or decreased motivation to write. Remember that the best writing does not happen in a vacuum. As an emerging scholar, your writing will benefit from the constructive criticism of your peers, and you will benefit from the accountability aspect of being part of a writing group.

4.1 Types of Writing Groups

Writing groups can be organized in a multitude of ways with varying goals, so it is important to consider your writing needs in order to choose a group whose structure will allow you to thrive. It is OK to join (and leave) a couple of different groups before you find the one that is right for you. Maybe you are even considering starting a writing group of your own, so in the next paragraphs, we will discuss a few different ways that a writing group could be configured.

Some groups read each other's work and give feedback. By structuring a group in this way, you give yourself a deadline and an incentive to write. If the group is reading your chapter this month, they need to have something to read before they can give you feedback. This kind of group works well if you are connected to people with similar research interests. If your writing group consists of a sociologist, a mathematician, and a Spanish education professor, your writing buddies may not be the best equipped to evaluate your research, but they can help you with your writing or keep you accountable (and we're sure there's a joke in there somewhere about the three of them walking into a bar). If you do have connections to people working on similar research topics, this can be a great way to get validation for your research, as well as suggestions for additional secondary

4.1 Types of Writing Groups

sources. Even though peer feedback is great, do not stop trusting your own judgment when it comes to your writing. Your research trajectory is ultimately up to you, and you need to be confident about your expertise.

Other writing groups use their time together to write, a great accountability option if you need someone or something to force you to sit down and write. This type of group usually meets frequently, maybe once or twice a week, and is helpful for individuals who are struggling to make time in their busy schedules for their writing or who are dealing with writer's block. Scheduling the writing group meeting in your calendar can help you to not feel guilty turning down other requests, like student meetings or committee work, during this time. These types of groups can meet in person or online, working for a set amount of time and then taking small, structured breaks where they can talk and build community. By physically or virtually being in the same room with other academics working on their writing, you may be more motivated to focus on your work. If you are scrolling through Instagram while everyone else is writing, you are going to feel bad when it comes time to report on your productivity. Hilal has been part of a writing group like this for years now, and it has worked like magic. She just would not make the time to research or dedicate time to writing unless she had promised others that she would be there. Once you are there, physically or virtually, then you figure you might as well work. If this is the right type of group for you, though, you need to make sure you are with people who will respect session times, break times, or any other mutually agreed-upon activities during this time. Otherwise it is too easy to just chat away the hours, possibly being frustrated the entire time about this otherwise welcome social activity.

A third type of group may never write together or read one another's work. Instead, the group meets weekly to report the number of words they have written since their last meeting, creating an incentive to be productive. The beauty of this type of group is that the meetings will not take much of your time, but knowing that you have to report your numbers can be a powerful motivation to write something before the meeting. Then the rest of the meeting can be spent on academic or professional questions where a discussion might be helpful for everyone in the group.

This last one is the type of writing group that the authors of this book participate in together. The philosophy of our group proposes that academic writing can be joyous instead of onerous once you make it a habitual part of your week. By writing every day (even if it's just a couple of words), you eliminate the fear surrounding writing. Instead of allowing yourself to build writing up in your head as an impossible or terrifying task, you convert it into a daily routine or practice. Even if you don't feel like you have enough time to accomplish "serious" writing, if you put 100 words on the page daily, you will have 700 words in a week. Little by little, you will accomplish your goals and finish your projects. Whether you have a group to report your weekly numbers to or you are keeping track of them for yourself (or for your cat or your houseplant), watching those numbers grow is empowering. The Joyous Writing Group firmly believes in the joyous part. No one gets punished or chastised for reporting a week of low (or zero) productivity. We believe that you will come back to your writing group more consistently if the group supports and encourages you.

Action item!

To get started, pick a project and make a list of what you need to accomplish in order to finish it.

Project: _____

To-do list: 1 _____
2 _____
3 _____
4 _____

Which of these actions are the most difficult ones for you? Maybe you get bored when writing or reading and need a sort of support group to keep going, or maybe you find it difficult to collect new data and need more accountability to make sure you actually do it. Choose a type of writing group based on your current needs to help you overcome these difficulties.

4.2 Reasons to Join a Writing Group

If you are still on the fence about the benefits of joining or creating a writing group, trust us, we get it. Academic life is busy, and it can be tempting to blow off a writing group because you really do not need one more meeting on your calendar. As people who have joined and left several writing groups, let us elaborate on why our writing philosophy turned us into believers. Sal had already had a full career before he started the Joyous Writing Group, so he was quite set in his ways. The group was not meant for him: Originally, it was supposed to be a support group for dissertating students, but once they graduated, the group kept going. Some people dropped out, while others joined. Gradually, he stopped thinking of his role as a mentor, and it started feeling like it was a group of peers. The funny part is that he noticed that a couple of days before the meetings, he started making time to write, even if his schedule was hellacious. For Sal, having to report his weekly total was a good motivator to

4.2 Reasons to Join a Writing Group

write. He has completed two books while in the group, and they were the fastest books he has ever written. So you might say that writing groups grew on him.

Heather always considered herself a fairly self-motivated individual, and she was suspicious that a writing group might take up too much of her time or cut into her productivity. However, shortly after joining the Joyous Writing Group, she realized that even though she already maintained a productive research agenda, her time management skills needed some tweaking. During the tenure-track years, Heather thought she was too busy to write during the semester, so she would delay her research until the summer and then dedicate one very intense month to completing any articles or research projects to which she had committed herself. This method worked, and Heather successfully received tenure, but she realized that writing intensively for one month in the summer was a miserable experience. Heather wanted to establish a more enjoyable and sustainable research routine. By joining the group and challenging herself to write every week, Heather has made it more of a priority to write consistently, which in turn has made her feel more confident in her research and writing abilities.

Perhaps you are more like Hilal, who really needs the accountability of a full-blown writing group to make her get down to work. Therefore, she is in two groups, one with some colleagues in her department and the Joyous Writing Group. The first group meets twice a week for three hours each, six hours total. Just having those three hours down on her calendar is not enough for Hilal if she is alone. She will just focus on the more pressing to-do list items such as grading or teaching prep. Her writing group meets on Zoom; everybody is on their own computers in the comfort of their own home or office with access to all their physical resources. All participants in this group promise not to schedule anything else during those hours and to show up every time for the full three hours unless it absolutely cannot be helped. It is a commitment they take seriously; it is sacred writing time. They start their sessions with a little mindfulness activity to get themselves in the right frame of mind. A lot of the time they just write about what they want to accomplish in the next three hours, or what needs to get done. They find that research tasks are easily pushed to the back of one's mind. Slacking on your research has no short-term ramifications until it's time for annual reviews, so it helps to do this little mindfulness writing activity at the beginning of each research session to put things in perspective, to bring research back to the forefront of the mind that is encumbered with so, so many other, seemingly more urgent professional obligations. Hilal happily does research writing for six uninterrupted hours a week, and meets or exceeds her personal (or really, contractual) ten-hour goal through collaborator meetings, readings, time-sensitive research tasks such as IRB proposals, data collection, grant applications, and so on that are spread throughout the week. She then reports her word count during her second group, Joyous Writing, to come full circle.

Finally, you may be like Elisa, who, despite being initially a bit skeptical, has tried several different writing groups over the years, depending on what was going on in her life and the goals she wanted to achieve, and has enjoyed every single one of them. She has been in virtual writing groups during the pandemic with colleagues who would just turn their cameras on and write, with the microphones off, after having publicly shared what their goal for the day was, as a way to keep each other accountable. She joined an in-person group with junior colleagues, like her, who were writing their way to tenure, where half of the time was spent writing and half of the time talking about common challenges and brainstorming solutions. And last but not least, she joined the writing group that led to this book when she was faced with the task of writing her first single-authored book. The group kept her motivated and accountable and provided the much-needed support and encouragement she needed to keep going.

Obviously, the main benefit of a writing group is that it will help you to write more. By making a conscious effort to dedicate some of your time to writing, you will focus more, and the process will become demystified. Writing groups will give you feedback on your work; it's important to build a community of trusted peers who can do this for you, as you can no longer rely on your professors' feedback. Just as importantly, a writing group can become a support system (Moore, 2003; Penney et al., 2015; Dwyer et al., 2021). In the Joyous Writing Group, every week after we report our numbers, we open the floor for any writing or academic-related questions that group members might have. This is a great way to pool the expertise of group members and learn how the academic experience differs by departments, universities, and ranks of professors. Writing groups can also be an excellent form of networking. Whether you are reading each other's work or not, you will most likely become familiar with your group members' writing topics. You never know when this will come in handy; you might see a call for papers or hear from a colleague that they are looking for someone whose research expertise aligns perfectly with one of your buddies from the writing group. Some writing groups even take on collaborative writing projects, as noncompetitive writing groups have proven to facilitate collaboration (Badenhorst et al., 2013).

4.3 Considerations for Choosing a Writing Group

You may need to try out a couple of writing groups before you find the one that works for you. To find a good fit, you should be honest with yourself about your writing needs and the time commitment that you are comfortable with. Ask yourself the following questions: What aspects of writing do you struggle with? Do you feel unable to write unless others are there, literally forcing you into it?

4.3 Considerations for Choosing a Writing Group

Or do you prefer to be alone, with no distractions, when you write? Can you commit to weekly meetings, or will that add another stressor to your life? You don't want to add an unreasonable commitment to your to-do list. A writing group should be a resource, not a burden.

You should also consider the people who will make up your writing group. Depending on how the group functions, you will want to weigh the benefits of working with people in your discipline versus a more interdisciplinary group. Some writing groups are composed of individuals who all work at the same institution. This can be great for community building, especially if you prefer in-person meetings or if you're a newer faculty member trying to make connections across campus. However, if you're on the tenure track or hope to be, you may not want to join a writing group composed of members from your department. Writing groups should be a place to ask questions and get support, and you may not want the people who will be evaluating your candidacy for tenure to know about that particularly rough revise and resubmit you received. If your writing group is made up of individuals from various universities, you may not feel an immediate sense of community, but you are networking on a larger scale. Another thing to consider is the group members' levels of experience. You probably don't want to be the only full professor in a group of first-year tenure-track professors, unless you are looking for a mentorship opportunity and are OK with being the group's primary resource. Our writing group has a range of scholars, from full professors to graduate students. We have found this to be a nice blend of experiences and expertise. We suggest either looking for a well-mixed group or staying with a group where everyone is approximately at the same level. Forming a writing group with some of your friends from graduate school can be a great option, especially since we are all accustomed to taking meetings online now, making it easier to connect with colleagues in your field. It's important that you trust and feel comfortable with the individuals in your writing group, especially if you're planning to share your unpublished work with them.

Finding a good writing group is like finding a good therapist; the first one might not be a good fit, but this doesn't mean you should stop looking. Don't be afraid to leave a writing group that just doesn't work for you. As academics, we're often conditioned to never say no, but remember that joining a writing group should be a gift you give yourself. Maybe that one chatty person who doesn't respect time limits or wants to turn the writing group into a social hour is sapping your motivation to attend your writing group. Maybe it's that you're overcommitted, and the structure of your current writing group is too much investment with too little reward. Don't give up. You can keep leaving writing groups in the dust until you find (or create) the right group for you.

Finally, if you identify as part of a group with a history of oppression (pretty much everyone except cis white males), you may want to look for a group that is especially supportive of your needs. Your university may have such a group (e.g., the University of Arizona has a People of Color Writing Group). Numerous such groups can be found on the internet. Of course, you could also start one yourself.

Action item!

Do you know what you want (i.e., the type of writing group you need), but not how to get it? Reach out to colleagues at a similar stage of their careers, or with whom you have a good relationship, and ask if they would be interested in starting or joining a writing group with you. It could be just one person or many people, online or in-person. The beauty of starting a writing group is that you get to decide!

Questions for Reflection

1. What are some of the stereotypes, fears, or misconceptions about writing groups that have been holding you back from joining or creating a group? Instead of focusing on these negative thoughts, try to imagine a positive writing group experience. Can you list some potential benefits that joining a writing group might provide for you?
2. Imagine your perfect writing group. What activities does the group complete when they meet? What does the group not do? How often does it meet? Who else is in this group with you? Jot down some notes or take a mental snapshot. Now, ask yourself, how can you make this group a reality?

Questions for Discussion

1. If you already have a writing group or if you are planning to start one, discuss the goals of this group with the (potential) members of the group. What specific aims do you all hope to achieve through membership in the group? How will you help each other reach your goals?
2. With the members of your group, clearly spell out some guidelines for what the group will and will not do. How will the group spend its time together? What are the expectations that members should meet before, during, and after each group meeting? How will the group deal with members who do not respect deadlines, quiet work time, and so on? It is better to have discussed a plan of action for these types of situations before they arise.

4.3 Considerations for Choosing a Writing Group

Questions for Your Mentor

1. Ask your mentor to share one of their positive writing group experiences with you. If they don't have a positive experience to share, ask them why and discuss. (Even if your mentor doesn't love the idea of a writing group, a writing group can still be a great idea for you.)
2. One of the fears about writing groups that people may have is that it will take up too much time. If your mentor has worked closely enough with you to understand your writing process, ask them what type of writing group they would suggest for you.

Part II

The Mechanics

5 Ethical Considerations

Behind every high-quality manuscript is an airtight code of ethics. Or at least, there should be. So before we delve into how to produce a high-quality manuscript, we need to address how to do so ethically. You need to think about the ethics of your research *before* you start writing. Addressing ethical issues upfront is a must; it avoids having to waste time rewriting, or worse, redoing work. We are saying this in case this is your first time being explicitly exposed to ethical considerations in academic writing. In many academic programs, ethical issues are not taught to students directly. Students are expected to pick up on how to behave by osmosis. There is nothing wrong with being taught this way, and it can be very effective, but the things you don't know that you don't know (the "unknown unknowns") are what will get you when you strike out on your own. We would hate for you to complete an entire project and its write-up only for it all to come crashing down when the journal or publisher asks for, say, signed informed consent forms. Consider this all-too-real situation (inspired by actual events):

A PhD student in the US collects interviews with high school students (fourteen to seventeen years old) who are Students with Limited or Interrupted Formal Education (SLIFE), primarily from rural Guatemala where schools offer education up to second or third grade. After that, the assumption is that children will leave school to help their parents. Many of the students immigrated in their early teens to the city where the PhD student teaches, and most have problems with their English proficiency. As she prepares to defend her dissertation proposal, the PhD student is informed that her data are not acceptable because, while the student got consent from her school to conduct the interviews, she did not get informed consent from the parents or assent from the children. She is ordered to destroy her data. Her dissertation director, embarrassed by the situation, quits, and her dissertation is now in shambles.

This debacle could have been avoided if the student had cleared her study with the university Institutional Review Board, which would have spotted the violation of federal guidelines. The student had only a general idea of what permissions to secure, a problem she could have avoided by informing herself ahead of time of the full requirements of a study like the one she proposed.

First, let's keep in mind that research that involves humans in any form, including surveys or interviews, falls under the scope of ethical treatment of human subjects and, as such, is federally regulated by many countries. In the United States, research that involves humans in any capacity is regulated through federally mandated Institutional Review Boards (IRB), Institutional Ethics Committees (IEC), or Ethical Review Boards (ERB). In the UK, Research Ethics Committees are governed by the Central Office for Research Ethics Committees (COREC). In Australia, Human Research Ethics Committees are regulated by the national Health and Medical Research Council. In New Zealand, the Health Research Council oversees Institutional Ethics Committees (IEC). We limit ourselves to English-speaking countries, but all countries are likely to have such institutions. It is important that you familiarize yourself with the regulations that oversee research at your institution. If you collaborate with a researcher from another country, you may be required to abide by their regulations, as well.

Action item!

Figure out what the ethical rules and guidelines are at your institution. A few places to start your research include the library, the office for faculty affairs, and the office for research compliance or IRB. Keep in mind that the names of these offices may change slightly, but it's nothing a quick online search can't solve. Try using some of these keywords: "research ethics," "ethics committee," "research participants," "IRB" (if you are in the US), or "human subjects research." Alternatively, you can ask some senior colleagues, and don't feel like you need to limit yourself to people in your department.

The next step is to do some research with the professional associations in your field. Some, such as psychology and sociology, have elaborate sets of standards and recommendations. Other fields may be too small or too young to have those types of resources. In that case, a major journal or a sister organization may have guidelines that you can use. For example, the British Oral History Society (www.ohs.org.uk/legal-and-ethical-advice/) and the US Oral History Association (https://oralhistory.org/oha-statement-on-ethics/) have ethical guidelines for oral histories. Suppose you decide to collect autobiographies from some of your colleagues or from your students, in which you ask them to reflect on what attracted them to the field of comparative literature. Even though there may not be guidelines for literary autobiographies, those from the oral history field would certainly be useful, at least as a starting point. Ultimately, it's all about transparency and respect for your subjects. If someone questions your ethics, being able to point at best practices in a related field or in a major journal should be enough to establish your bona fides.

5.1 Resources on Ethics   41

If you know where your work is going to be submitted, download the publisher's instructions as well. For example, Taylor & Francis has a sophisticated website (https://authorservices.taylorandfrancis.com/editorial-policies/research-ethics-guidelines-for-arts-humanities-and-social-sciences-journals/) with specific instructions and links to organizations from several countries. Follow the publisher's guidelines as closely as possible to avoid giving them any reason to potentially reject your paper.

If you need more foundational resources, our next section should help.

5.1   Resources on Ethics

Unfortunately, due to historical reasons, very little training is provided about ethical matters in many fields. If you haven't had access to this type of training, fortunately there are plenty of free resources available that tackle human subject protection, in addition to all the kinds of ethical problems that we discuss in this chapter.

For example, the Committee on Publication Ethics (COPE), while geared toward editors, publishers, and universities, provides a host of helpful resources for writers. They lay out the recommended process for handling situations such as when to give authorship to a collaborator, how to handle suspected plagiarism or self-plagiarism, and how or why to remove or add an author after submission. Having access to the documents used to train editors to handle these situations can help you differentiate between acceptable, questionable, or plain wrong behaviors. Another similar source is the European Association of Science Editors (EASE), which provides a variety of resources, including guidelines for peer reviewing and a downloadable poster on Sex and Gender Equity in Research, which could be usefully posted in a lab or other public space. Within Applied Linguistics, both the American Association for Applied Linguistics and the journal *TESOL Quarterly* provide useful resources. The Modern Language Association has, among other resources, a Statement of Professional Ethics, which is available online. The American Psychological Association's Publication Manual (7th edition) has several valuable chapters on these issues. The European Union's European Commission released a document on Ethics in Social Science and Humanities in 2021.

Finally, we recommend that you check out the Office of Research Integrity's (ORI) case summaries. The ORI is part of the US Department of Health and Human Services, and it deals primarily with medical research, but it is instructive to see what can happen when people do not follow the rules. We don't mean to scare you, but as the saying goes, a stitch in time saves nine. It is better to think about these issues before you get in trouble, rather than after the fact.

Here are a few additional resources on research ethics that can help you:

- EASE, The European Association of Science Editors (www.ease.org.uk/wp-content/uploads/2016/09/Sager.for-web.pdf). We recommend you also check out the available resources about research integrity and publishing ethics at https://ase.org.uk/resources/.
- COPE, Committee on Publication Ethics (https://publicationethics.org). Its guidelines (https://publicationethics.org/guidance/Guidelines) include numerous practical resources and documents.
- ORI, The Office of Research Integrity (https://ori.hhs.gov/content/case_summary). This site includes summaries of cases of research misconduct (good examples of what you want to avoid). We encourage you to explore the many resources ORI offers through its webpage.
- European Commission (https://ec.europa.eu/info/funding-tenders/opportunities/docs/2021-2027/horizon/guidance/ethics-in-social-science-and-humanities_he_en.pdf). Check out the document *Ethics in Social Science and Humanities by the European Commission* (DG Research and Innovation).
- HHS, Health and Human Services (www.hhs.gov/ohrp/international/compilation-human-research-standards/index.html). It includes the *International Compilation of Human Research Standards*, searchable by geographic region (www.hhs.gov/sites/default/files/ohrp-international-compilation-2021-europe.pdf).

5.2 Avoiding Plagiarism and Self-Plagiarism

Nearly all scholarly and professional organizations, as well as universities, warn students and faculty alike against plagiarism. Indeed, there is a widespread belief that the problem has gotten worse recently due to the ease of finding material on the internet, the effortless process of copying and pasting a passage into a paper, and now the existence of AI tools that can generate grammatical text that is not easily traced back to a single source. Plagiarism breaks down intuitively into two categories: plagiarizing someone else's work and plagiarizing your own (yes, that's a thing). We will address them separately.

5.2.1 Plagiarism

There are many definitions of plagiarism, but they generally agree that plagiarism is the use of someone else's words or ideas without proper acknowledgment. Note that we've made no reference to the intentionality of the writer/plagiarist. The intention to deceive may differentiate between inadvertent and malicious plagiarism. An individual may inadvertently plagiarize if they forget to include quotation marks or paraphrase a piece of text too closely. There may

5.2 Avoiding Plagiarism and Self-Plagiarism

also be cultural differences about what constitutes acceptable "reuse," as some cultures may see reusing text as a form of reverence. Malicious plagiarism is when someone tries to hide the plagiarism by changing a few words and deleting references to escape detection by software or human readers. Inadvertent plagiarism is still plagiarism, however, and it will get your paper rejected just as fast as malicious plagiarism.

If you suspect you may be inadvertently plagiarizing, the first place to look for help is the countless plagiarism detectors available on the web, such as TurnItIn or, better, iThenticate (the latter is for academic writing). It doesn't really matter too much which tool you use, but such software will check your writing against available sources and can detect some cases of plagiarism (not all, of course). You can also ask friends, spouses, and colleagues for their help, especially if you provide them with copies of the sources you used. Be sure to thank them profusely, cook them a good meal, or buy them a small gift, as this is hard work. If need be, you can hire freelance consultants who will do editorial work for you, albeit for a fee, and will check that you did not plagiarize your references (again, you should provide them if possible).

Here are some strategies that might help you avoid plagiarism in the first place. Start by exhaustively documenting any citation or quote that you take from a text. If you cut and paste from a document, start by adding quotation marks before you paste the citation. Even if you should forget to close the quotation marks, the presence of the opening quotes will highlight that something went wrong. Using a different font color for citations that you cut and paste will help too. Next, use a clean room approach: When you are writing, hide the document you just read, or close the book. Paraphrasing from memory is harder to do but makes inadvertent plagiarism much less likely.

Action item!

Most (if not all) universities in the United States have a writing center, where students and faculty can get help with their writing across subjects. Some writing centers offer their services for languages other than English. If you need help with your writing, including strategies to avoid plagiarizing yourself or others, the writing center can help you. Make an appointment to visit them, and bring your paper, secondary sources, and questions along with you.

Let's note in passing that recent advances in AI can provide you with near-flawless prose and summaries and paraphrases of a given text. In our opinion, writers are better off not using them. However, if you use such tools, be extremely careful. Most journals require you to disclose their use, and some software claims to be able to detect whether a text was generated by AI. Keep in mind that current AI tools are completely unreliable when it comes to the content of what they write. Always double- and triple-check what AI produced, as it may be nonsensical, including imaginary sources or wrong information.

5.2.2 Self-Plagiarism

Self-plagiarism is a much murkier area. Fundamentally, it consists of an author reusing a piece of text they have published before. Since it's your own work that you are repurposing, so to speak, some may question why self-plagiarism is even an issue. Even though the work is yours, the expectation is that each new paper or book you publish should be original. Indeed, this is reflected in the way the APA, for instance, defines self-plagiarism as "the presentation of your own previously published work as original." By taking credit for a novel (original) idea twice, you create an unwarranted aggrandizing of your profile, as well as unnecessary work for editors and readers.

Publishing the same paper twice (or even more often) is clearly wrong, but issues of self-plagiarism can be much more complex. For example, using the same sources in different papers is entirely legitimate, but reusing the same summary of said sources is not. Likewise, it is reasonable that if you introduced a term in your previous work, you may reuse the term and its definitions. If you repeat an experiment, you can use the same methodology again. The issue boils down to quantity: It may be OK to reuse snippets of text (a term, a definition, etc.), but reusing full pages of a literature review is going to raise more than a few eyebrows. One reason for this is that, once you publish a piece with a commercial publisher, you generally transfer the copyright of your work to them. If you recycle three pages from a previous paper, you are violating their copyright. The fact that you wrote the text is irrelevant (welcome to capitalism).

To make things even harder to assess, the policies of individual journals and editors vary significantly. Some authors advise you to contact the editor or publisher in advance and inquire about the appropriateness of extensive self-citation. We advise against this option, for the simple reason that it may be counterproductive, as the editor or publisher may become suspicious of your motives. A far simpler solution is to paraphrase any part of text that is longer than a few words. After all, you wrote it in the first place, so you are capable of rephrasing it. In fact, summarizing a discussion or literature review, with a reference to the prior full discussion, may save otherwise-needed space. Another option is using a self-citation. It's a bit unorthodox, but it may be a good solution if the exact wording of the text is somehow significant.

Reprinting a paper you published in a journal (or in another venue) as part of a larger project (say, a book) is a separate issue. In this case, you need to obtain the permission of the copyright holder and provide the evidence of said permission to the publisher of the larger work. You will also acknowledge the fact that a particular chapter was previously published as a journal article (citing the specific journal's name), in a slightly different form, since you probably fixed a few typos and maybe made other minor changes.

5.3 Avoiding Conflict of Interest

In addition to plagiarism, conflict of interest is another ethical consideration. A conflict of interest can be defined as any situation in which someone's objective judgment may be affected by extraneous factors. For example, suppose that you are asked to review a paper written by your best friend. This situation has a built-in conflict of interest: on the one hand, you are supposed to be looking out for the interests of the journal, which wants to publish the best papers possible, but on the other hand, you are supposed to be looking out for your friend's interests. Another scenario is favoritism. Suppose you are the editor of a journal, and a former student of yours submits a paper. Can you be sure to be impartial and objectively assess the submission? Now imagine that this is the student who brought you Belgian chocolate pralines after attending a conference. How can you not be moved by Belgian chocolate? Finally, we all know those scholars who will reject a submission unless they are quoted, even in areas that are not relevant to their expertise. All of these are cases of conflict of interest. Let's now turn specifically to conflicts of interest in reviews.

There is no question that the assessment of a paper, book, or grant proposal should be based exclusively on its merits. Good journals and publishers have strong ethical guidelines that encourage you to voice your concerns when you detect a possible conflict of interest. The best policy is to contact the editor, funding agency, or other organization that has asked you to review the piece and make them aware of your situation. They can decide if the conflict of interest is enough to warrant finding another reviewer.

For those cases in which the conflict of interest is unavoidable, special workarounds can be found. Editors may recuse themselves and appoint an ad hoc editor to review a paper by their students, or several independent peer-reviewers can be brought in so that a panel of distinguished scholars guarantees the quality of the piece.

Naturally, there will be gray areas. For example, is it ever ethical to point out that an author should have quoted your work? As is the case for most interesting questions, the answer will depend on the situation. Is your paper foundational? Did it introduce a term now being used in the field? Did it establish some of the research parameters or methodologies in that area? Then it should be quoted, regardless of who wrote it. Conversely, if your paper is one of many that would fulfill the need to quote some source on the subject matter, then it would be unethical to demand that it be quoted.

5.4 Authorship Issues

An area where particularly acrimonious discussions and at times actual conflict arise is the decision of who to list as authors of a paper or book, and in what order. Despite the seeming triviality of the issue, these are serious matters. Many tenure and promotion committees consider author order to be significant, with first authorship being given a greater share of credit for the publication. If there are more than two authors, everyone else disappears in the gaping mouth of "et al." Some countries and publication venues require a statement in the paper detailing who was responsible for each part of the research. Sometimes, the authors state that they adjudicated order of authorship using amusing techniques such as dice tosses, bets, or by a bake-off (Duffy, 2016). Sal (whose last name is Attardo) insisted on reverse alphabetical order when coauthoring a paper with an author whose last name starts with Z. Such shenanigans are best left to senior scholars with nothing to lose. One pragmatic approach, discussed in Duffy (2016), is to put the coauthors who are closest to tenure and promotion decisions in the first positions.

On a more serious note, a natural approach is to put the author who did most of the work in first position. Another position that is fairly common is known as the "supervisory" position, in other words, dead last. This is common when a supervisor (the director of a dissertation, a lab director, or a grant's PI) co-authors a paper with one or more students or subordinates. By positioning themselves last, they give the students or subordinates the privilege of being first or second author, while still maintaining responsibility for the content.

It should be noted that practices are different in various fields. In the sciences, it is quite common for a lab coordinator or PI to have their name added to all papers produced by people employed in their lab or by their grant, regardless of whether they have actually contributed any actual writing, research, or even supervision to the work. An extreme example of such a trend of inclusion can be found in a famous particle physics paper about the Higgs boson that has more than five *thousand* authors. In the humanities and social sciences, authorship is usually restricted to those who actually wrote the paper and/or did the research. Whether someone who coded the data or ran a statistical analysis, for example, deserves authorship will depend on the substantiveness of their contribution. Did the data coding involve developing the coding tools? Did the statistical analysis help shape the study in some way? In those cases, coauthorship may well be warranted, but if the help was merely mechanical, a simple acknowledgment may be a better choice. Whatever your decision, always be upfront and clear in letting any collaborators know what

5.4 Authorship Issues

their contribution will be and how it will be acknowledged. Otherwise, people may drop a footnote on you exposing you, as can be seen in Recht et al. (2019), with "Ben did none of the work" (p. 1).

From the beginning of a project, ethical considerations give research a solid basis to stand on. Benevolent, fair, and respectful treatment of everyone involved in the project protects the integrity of your efforts, and can prevent a plethora of issues moving forward.

Questions for Reflection

1. Explore one of the online resources listed in the "Resources on Ethics" section (pick the one that seems most relevant to your field or geographical area). Do you feel confident that your research meets the necessary ethical standards? Highlight any area that you are not sure about so you can ask someone about it (colleagues or mentors).
2. Go to https://retractionwatch.com and look at some of the cases. What do you think happened? What lessons can you take away from these cases?

Questions for Discussion

1. Ethical guidelines often provide useful but generic advice that can be difficult to relate to your specific research project. With colleagues, discuss how one aspect of these guidelines "materialized" in their past research experience (what it meant, on a very concrete level). How can this help you approach your own research differently?
2. The introduction of AI has affected, and will likely continue to influence, academic writing. With your colleagues, discuss the impact of AI on their writing.

Questions for Your Mentor

1. Ask your mentor about any pitfalls to avoid in this domain. What examples can they give you of situations to steer clear of? Do they have any strategies for avoiding or navigating dilemmas related to academic ethics?
2. Discuss with your mentor how they deal with publishing multiple pieces about a similar research topic. What strategies have their experiences taught them? What risks do they suggest that you consider?

6   Outline

An outline is the initial step in writing, used for organizing your thoughts and crafting a solid argument that flows logically. For academic writing, it is where you put together the main themes and key points with the citations that support them. A manuscript without an outline is like a boneless arm, like the one Harry Potter had in *Chamber of Secrets* (Columbus, 2002; Rowling, 2000) when he broke his arm playing Quidditch and Professor Lockhart attempted to fix it by getting rid of the bones altogether. As the school nurse lamented, it's no problem to fix a few broken bones, but growing them from scratch is a very long and painful process. When you start a manuscript with an outline, you can easily spot where things don't fit at all or how things need to be rearranged. A few broken bones are no biggie when you have to fix them on an outline. If you just start writing, then you risk having to shuffle paragraph upon paragraph and page upon page to make it make sense. What's more, all your transitions that beautifully tie one section to the next will also stop making sense and will need to be rewritten after you're done reorganizing everything, assuming you can manage. Trust us, a full draft is a bear to tackle when it comes to organizational redos. Even worse, without an outline, you may not realize that your arguments are veering off course. It may all make sense in your head until a ruthless reviewer tears it to pieces. So do yourself a favor and start your next manuscript with an outline. Taking the time to create an outline is highly recommended for all types of manuscripts, but in this chapter, we focus on an article. We follow the example of an empirical journal article outline created at the onset and take you through it step by step. Though not all manuscripts will have the same sections, the outlining techniques and strategies presented here will apply.

The outline can look different for different people, but in essence, it should work to make your job less complicated, not more. Let's get started. You have about 9,000 words for an original article (depending on your discipline and the venue), so it helps to break that down into sections. You will also save yourself a lot of frustration later by assigning approximate word limits for each section. Knowing roughly how many words you have to cover your review of the literature, for instance, will help you decide how deep you can go and what needs to be the priority. Your discipline's style guidelines will have more information on what sections are expected to be in your paper and what they need to cover (see, for instance, the Journal Article Reporting Standards section in American Psychological Association, 2020). Here's a simple outline template you may consider following:

1. Tentative title: It doesn't have to be fancy at this stage, just functional. What is the paper about?
2. Thesis statement: What is the overall argument you will be making in this paper?
3. Research question(s) to be answered: Do not skip this essential part. A good research question will guide and shape your paper. It's the glue that holds everything together and protects you from going off on tangents.
4. Review of the literature: Noting your tentative word limit can be extra helpful here.
   a. Subheading 1: Your review of the literature will likely cover multiple concepts and/or phenomena in your field. What's the first one?
   b. Under the subheading, create a bulleted list of items that you know you have to cover. It's OK to just include words or phrases at this point, unless you already have full sentences in your mind. Add any citations you already know you will be using.
   c. Repeat as needed.
5. Methodology: How many words can you allot here? While the contents will be discipline-specific, here are some subheadings that would belong here: theoretical framework, analytical framework, data collection, participants, and so on.
6. Findings: You will need the majority of your word limit here. This is what matters the most; this is your contribution to the field. Which of the findings will go here? Remember that not everything you find is relevant for this specific article. Delineate based on your research question(s) and thesis statement.
7. Discussion: Remember to give yourself a word limit. List how your findings are connected to previous research. Are there any noteworthy differences that you can explain? Make points on how your results contribute to the theoretical discussion on your subject in the field.
8. Conclusions: How many words can you afford here? You will not need a lot of space for conclusions, unless the discussion is merged here. This is where everything comes together. Add a reminder to recap your thesis statement and major findings.
9. Bibliography: It is important to have this in your outline and give it a ballpark word count allowance. This will help you better determine how many words can actually go into the rest of the sections in the paper. It is easy to forget about the bibliography and write the rest of the paper to the limit, and when you finally add your references, all of a sudden you are way over the word count.

> **Action item!**
>
> Now that you are familiar with the components of an outline, we recommend that you find a published paper in a reputable journal in your field and use the outline template above to guide your analysis of it. Remember that each field has its own traditions and norms, so you may find that not all parts of the template above apply.
>
> - Can you identify all the parts described above? Are the parts labeled with titles or subtitles in separate sections or merged into one?
> - Which parts take up the most space? Is this common in your field?

6.1 Example Outline

To serve as an example, Figure 6.1 shows part of an outline Hilal wrote for one of her papers. It was later published in the *Journal of Pragmatics*.

True to the template we are working with, in Figure 6.1 Hilal has her tentative title listed up top, and then goes into the introduction section (as many research papers do). You will notice that this outline, meant only for the eyes of its author, does not have to have spelled out terminology or even full sentences. The first second-level bullet point talks about OCF, which is a very frequent abbreviation for oral corrective feedback, or correction suggestions on second language learners' oral language output. Toward the end of the outline excerpt, you notice she uses CA for Conversation Analysis, which is a type of discourse analysis. All Hilal needs are these letters; she does not need to go into what OCF or CA stand for or what they denote. She knows all that. There is a percentage that she listed as a question mark. She had that number, and she knew it was significant in terms of building a solid argument, but she didn't bother adding it there. What she is trying to do at this stage (it is the thesis paragraph of the introduction after all) is to get the main argument of the paper out, supported by her research findings. In the North American setting, that is what you do: state the idea first, then support it. She also does not worry about defining terms such as mitigation or teacher immediacy or face threat, because the outline is for organizing her thoughts about what goes where in the paper. Defining the terminology is part of the final writeup but is irrelevant in the outline because who would you be defining the terms for? Yourself? Another important thing she does in this introduction section is to organize all the prior research that helps her delineate the gap in the research (which then warrants the publication of her paper). She does not need to include much in this part of her outline because she's read the research and she has her

6.1 Example Outline

- Tentative Title: Smiling as a mitigating strategy in oral corrective feedback: An empirical study of three Turkish EFL classrooms
- Introduction (600 words)
  - Thesis: Smiling is a mitigating strategy used by language teachers to lessen the facethreat embedded in OCF
    - Research question: What is the role of mitigation during OCF provision, and how does teacher smiling factor in?
    - All OCF instances in the data are mitigated.
    - ?% of the mitigation co-occurs with or is done through smiling
    - Correlation between mitigation and smiling (immediacy)
    - Smiling here includes laughter
  - Smiling is an act of mitigation for OCF/in classrooms.
    - Mitigating instructional face threat – Cazden (1979), Cazden (2001), Kerssen-Griep et al. (2003), Kerssen-Griep et al. (2008), Trees et al. (2009), Witt and Kerssen-Griep (2011) on the interaction of facework and immediacy, Kerssen-Griep and Witt (2012), Hadden and Frisby (2019)
      - Face – Goffinan (1955)
      - Politeness – Brown and Levinson (1978, 1987)
    - Smiling in teacher immediacy studies – Andersen (1979) which is the first, Hyerdahl (1980) replication of Andersen, Sanders and Wiseman (1990), Witt and Wlicclcss (2001), Witt et al. (2004), Witt and Kerssen-Griep (2011), Sözer (2019)
    - Smiling in CA studies – Holt (2010), Sert and Jacknick (2015) for student smiles, Petitjean and Gonzalez-Martinez (2015), Looney and He (2020)

Figure 6.1 Initial part of a sample outline

notes and quotes on them in a separate document. In the outline, she just needs to see what citations to include in what logical order so they support her argument.

Note that the main section heading has a word count, but unlike in the template, it has lower-level bullet points to help organize subheadings, or to note the important ideas, citations, and concepts to include. You might even ask yourself some questions as they arise along the way. The questions in the outline, in fact, are proof that this exercise facilitates thinking and reveals what needs more attention.

The next part in the outline is the literature review. And while we have Chapter 9 dedicated to it, it's worth noting here as well that you need to write the outline of that section *after* you have steeped yourself in the extant literature. There are two main reasons for that. First, what is and isn't already out there is going to significantly change how you will present your research, from the justification of your research to the relevant findings to the discussion of the findings. Second, your methodology will be significantly dictated by the literature. Sure you're familiar with it to some extent, because you conducted a study. It would be quite counterproductive to conduct a study without knowing that it's worth your time and efforts. Conducting the study also likely required you to apply for various things like ethics board approval, a grant, or a paid leave of absence, all of which would have asked for some background. None of those reviews of literature was meant for the perusal of other experts in the field, though. If you now make incorrect claims, you risk losing your credibility. So even if you are confident in your knowledge of the literature, do another sweep and make sure your arguments are all based on solid ground. Let's now take a look at the rest of Hilal's outline, in Figure 6.2, starting with the review of literature.

- Mitigating oral collective feedback (1,000 words)
  - Oral corrective feedback
    - OCF is an important component of language teaching and learning.
    - What is OCF?; it's good for SLA
    - The structure of error correction sequences and where mitigation can be expected
  - Mitigation
    - OCF is inherently face threatening and requires mitigation
    - Linguistic sources of mitigation – Caffi (and what else is new?)
- Methodology (600 words)
  - Data
    - Private language school in northwestern Turkey
    - Seven EFL teachers, three intact classrooms of adult EFL Learners at the intermediate level
    - Video recordings of six days in three weeks, sixteen hours of data, ELAN
  - Analytical framework – explain the error treatment sequence and the revised version.
- Results and Discussion (5,000 words)
  - Explain mitigation was investigated to see how smiling reacted with it.
  - Provide numbers and examples of each mitigation strategy
    - Phonological; Lexical – Seedhouse (1997) the case of the missing "no"; Morphological; Syntactic; Textual; Phrasal
  - There's been NO instance of unmitigated feedback. It seems an INTEGRATED PART OF OCF PROVISION
    - Correlation between smiling and mitigation: Report Spearman's correlation coefficient between smiling and mitigation and the power analysis
  - What explains nonsmiling mitigation?
  - Mitigating smiles – Polite smile (nonfelt; non-Duchenne) and Felt smile (Duchenne) and Nonmitigating smiles – Schadenfreude, Aggression, Masking negative emotion, etc. (Cite your own OCF and smiling research!)
- Conclusions (300 words)
  - Smiling acts as a mitigation strategy.
  - All OCF involves mitigation
  - Smiling should be part of the OCF conversation in SLA
  - Talk about the coexistence of multiple mitigation strategies?
- References (1,500 words)

Figure 6.2 Remaining parts of a sample outline

The rest of the outline in Figure 6.2, true to our purposes and the template, encapsulates what needs to be discussed in the paper and in what order. The word count allotments are there, as well as the main and supporting points. Hilal listed all her relevant findings bearing in mind how they relate to her overall argument and research questions, minimizing the risk of rambling or going down rabbit holes at any point in the paper. She also made notes to herself and asked some questions to answer later. Some things you can leave for the writeup stage because this is just the skeleton.

6.2 Reverse Outlines

A reverse outline should never take the place of writing that initial outline; it's an additional technique that may come in handy for those papers where you're really struggling to organize your thoughts. After you have completed your outline and written a draft of your paper, take out a blank piece of paper or open a new document on your computer. Go through your paper, paragraph by paragraph, and summarize the topic sentence or main argument of each paragraph in a few words. Once you have done this for each paragraph, you will have a concise summary of the actual structure of your paper that you can compare to your original outline. Often, when you see the organization of your paper written out in this way, it becomes easy to find repetition of ideas, tangents, and paragraphs that need to be moved to other sections or eliminated. Heather often assigns this task to her students as a way of checking whether they are truly communicating the information they had intended to share when they conceptualized their papers. Keep in mind that, while you should always write an outline, reverse outlines are not a necessary part of all academic writing. When you are struggling to fit all the puzzle pieces together, though, they can help you to see the structure of your paper in a different way.

Action item!

Do you have a paper you've been working on, but you seem to be repeating yourself, or having difficulty connecting the parts? Maybe you can't figure out how to separate the points you want to make? Grab that draft, as well as a blank piece of paper (or open up a new Google Doc).

1. For each paragraph, write the main argument or point of the paragraph in a few words. Read the paragraph, but then look away from it while you summarize its main argument. This will help you to not copy directly from your writing but instead rephrase the most important elements of the paragraph as you remember them from reading the paragraph.

2. Once you have done this for each paragraph, examine the reverse outline as a whole. Where do you see repetition? Can you identify areas where your arguments abruptly change with no transition? Are there sections or parts of sections that would make more sense elsewhere in the paper? One technique you can try is to mark different themes, ideas, arguments, or sections with different colors of highlighters. This will make it quickly apparent if you are dedicating too much or too little time to a specific topic, or if you have one paragraph that is out of place.
3. Finally, you may want to compare your reverse outline with your original outline. It's OK if the paper you wrote varies from your original outline (honestly, we would be surprised if you were able to stick exactly to your original outline), but there may have been important topics that you planned to address in the outline and then forgot about or didn't fully develop. By comparing the outline and reverse outline, you can catch those omissions.

The outline might evolve later in the writing process, which is OK and to be expected. The paper will further evolve based on many revisions and editor and reviewer comments, which is also OK. The outline is only the first step. It is a tool for a strong start and logical flow for your initial draft. It helps keep you sane when there is so much going on in your head and in your findings that you don't even know where to start, aside from a rough idea. The outline helps you pick a thread and build strongly around it. The rest is the purview of the writing gods.

Questions for Reflection

1. Think back to a time when you wrote a paper without an outline. How easy was it to organize your argument? How could your experience have been improved by starting with an outline?
2. Breaking down a topic into smaller sections and subsections helps reduce the "stress factor" of writing a paper. What seems easier to do, write a paper on oral corrective feedback or write a description of three schools in Turkey? Do you think an outline might help you with stress management?

Questions for Discussion

1. After you have tried outlining, note any challenges you face and discuss them with peers. Talking them through can help overcome them.
2. Ask your peers if and how they outline their papers or books. One approach would be to ask them to share one of their papers and discuss its organization. How standard is it?

6.2 Reverse Outlines

Questions for Your Mentor

1. Does your mentor write outlines for their manuscripts? What can they tell you about the process (or lack thereof)? Has their practice changed with time?
2. Ask your mentor if there is a standard or preferred structure for papers in your (sub)discipline.

7 Abstracts and Keywords

The most important thing about abstracts and keywords is that they are meant to stand alone, apart from your work, representing it. They may appear at the top of your article or sometimes on the back of your book, but they are meant to be used in a context in which your work is not available, because either your reader has not purchased access to it or because they have not yet found your article (or book, book chapter, etc.). This makes writing effective abstracts and keywords rather difficult for a human (we will discuss using AI to do so below). We know what is in the paper (and we like it, to boot), so it's very difficult to pretend that we don't know what the article says and write from the perspective of an outside observer.

7.1 Writing an Abstract

To get started, the abstract (along with the keywords) is the last thing you should write. Until you have written the paper, you don't really know what will go in it. Sure, you planned it, outlined it, and drafted it, but it's not until you finish writing it that you will know what actually went into the paper. Often you have already written an abstract before writing the paper (e.g., if the paper started out as a conference submission or as a submission to a special issue of a journal), so it can be tempting to just copy and paste that abstract into your final paper. If you do so, you should re-read it carefully and weigh how much the old abstract matches the paper you just finished. We have seen enough abstracts that make claims that are not in the paper to tell you that it's not an uncommon mistake. In what follows, we will assume you are not recycling a prior abstract.

At its most fundamental level, an abstract is a summary of the paper. The problem is that you have anywhere between 100 and 500 words, but usually 250 or 300 words, depending on the publication, to summarize a 9,000-word paper. This means you will need to be very selective as to what information to include.

You should start by describing the general field in which the problem is located. This will help your potential readers to determine if they should keep

7.1 Writing an Abstract

reading or not. A paper on smiling in dentistry is generally of no practical use to a researcher on facial expressions, except perhaps to document societal perceptions of smiling.

Next you should describe the problem or question that the paper addresses. This is not quite your research questions but rather a general statement of where the research questions fit in within the field. This should be specific enough that your readers can situate your work in a general approach or discussion. Only then you will address exactly what your research questions are. The idea is to provide enough context for the reader to appreciate your work's originality and significance, but no more than needed.

Finally, you should close the abstract by describing your findings, which may be followed by conclusions, especially in experimental papers. If you are wondering what the difference is between the two, findings are contingent and specific to your study, whereas conclusions are more general and relevant to the field at large. If you have any space left, you may cap your abstract by mentioning implications for further research and limitations of your study, but in our experience this is unlikely. The example from Feng et al. (2023) in Figure 7.1 does this admirably clearly.

Notice that in the abstract in Figure 7.1, only two words are dedicated to the methodology: "empirically quantify." This is all the reader needs to know: this is a quantitative study, based on data collected somehow. The abstract is not the place to discuss what statistics tests you used or what theoretical models you

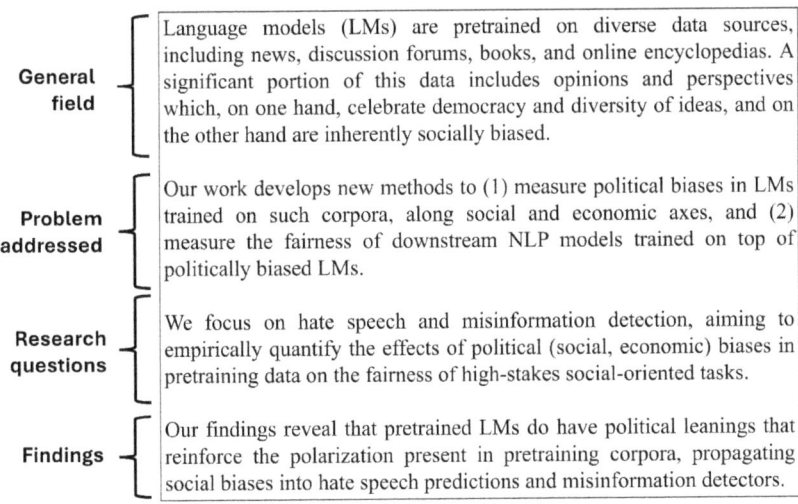

Figure 7.1 Sample annotated abstract

deployed. If your study is experimental, you may need to spend more time on the design of the experiment and related methodological matters. Some recommend that up to 25 percent of an experimental paper be dedicated to methodology.

> **Action item!**
> A good strategy to familiarize yourself with the different components of an abstract, which we also used for the outline, is mapping. Choose either a published abstract or one of your own and map its contents according to the four parts described in Figure 7.1. Notice how much space each part takes up, how these parts are organized (is the order the same?), and if anything strikes you as odd or different (Maybe some of the findings are anticipated when addressing the problem? Maybe there are no clear research questions?).

7.1.1 Writing an Abstract for a Conference

An abstract for a conference is not a radically different genre. Most of the advice on writing an abstract for a paper applies to conferences as well, but there are a couple of differences worth mentioning. First, at least for some conferences, there is the assumption that while you will have designed your experiment and/or gathered your data, the analysis may not be finished, so it's OK if your results are presented in a rather hypothetical way. Second, since the audience of a conference is broader, you may need to provide more context and cite a few references to show that you know what you are talking about, as well as to locate your work within a framework. Most conferences will accept textual references like (Chomsky, 1965) without the corresponding bibliographic entry. Third, many conferences allow a full page of text (250 words) or more and sometimes even a second page for references and examples. Take full advantage of this and use the extra space to present your argument as cogently as possible.

7.1.2 Things You Should Not Put in an Abstract

The abstract should be as objective as possible, so you should avoid language that is evaluative ("important," "crucial," "compelling") or editorialized ("thorny problem," an example of judgmental or opinionated language). You should strive to be balanced, so avoid making unjustified claims, such as "this paper solves the problem of X" when all you've done is propose a different approach to it.

You should also avoid too many acronyms or technical terms. If they are necessary or common in the field, it may be OK. For example, in the abstract we looked at above, we see that LM is defined upon first use, but NLP (Natural Language Processing) is not. This is because Feng et al. assume (correctly) that if you are still reading after the first sentence sets the stage for a paper about Language Models in AI, you will know what NLP stands for. Technical terms should be defined, again, unless they are common in the field. You would not define "sonnet" or "phoneme," but you must define "cento" (a type of poem created using lines from other poems).

Finally, references to sources should be avoided (unless it's for a conference). If unavoidable, they must have a full bibliographic entry within the abstract. This alone should dissuade you from including a reference in your abstract, as this will take up valuable space (remember, you have maybe 300 words, do you really want to waste 10 percent of them on a reference?). Unnecessary citations are one of the tell-tale signs of inexperienced writers, which is another reason to avoid them.

7.1.3 Formatting

Follow your publisher or editor's instructions very carefully. If the instructions say 300 words, don't turn in a 400-word abstract. Generally, there are no special formatting rules for abstracts. Some sources recommend that it be a single paragraph, but there seems no special reason for this. An easy solution would be to look at some samples from other articles in the journal or other books in the same series. If you have no samples available, just do what is easier, but be prepared to revise on very short notice. Usually, there is little time for that sort of fine tuning because, generally speaking, submissions are often last minute. If the editor asks you to revise, you may not have a leisurely window to do so.

7.2 Keywords

The purpose of keywords is to facilitate the work of search engines. It is quite possible that with the advent of AI-based search engines, keywords will become obsolete, but for now, they are still useful. Keywords make your article findable by scholars who are interested in your topic but do not know that your paper exists.

There are two kinds of keywords: core ideas and synonyms. The core ideas are relatively simple to identify. If you write a paper about Cervantes, "Cervantes" will be a core keyword. If your paper is about his theatrical work, then "theater" will also be a keyword. If instead you had written about his farcical interludes, the Spanish term for this ("entremeses") would be a core keyword, but "interlude," "farce," and "comedy" would also be synonyms that might steer a reader toward your paper, even if they don't know what an "entremes" is. Your knowledge of the field will help you think of synonyms. If you're struggling to get started, check out previous issues of the journal and look at the keywords in those papers. Yours will be different, but the keywords should give you a general idea of what you need to accomplish.

Note that in our Cervantes example we used multilingual keywords. This is natural if your topic concerns material outside of the English-speaking world, but you may want to add translations of key terms in other languages, as well. Do not rely on dictionaries or translation software if you do so. You need to validate the translation with an expert in the field in that language.

Keywords should be ranked by importance, with the least important last. There is a lot of variation as to how many keywords individual journals and publishers ask for. It's usually between three and eight, but you should follow the instructions you received. If they did not specify, five keywords seems like a good compromise. This is also why you need to rank your keywords. If you provide six keywords and the editor has to cut one, they will cut the last one, assuming it is the least important.

Some final tips: Omit any keywords that appear in the title of your paper. They are submitted to search engines anyway. If you use a word in the title, you may use a synonym in the keywords. It's useful to try to do a search with the keywords you've come up with to see what it brings up. You may be surprised and want to adjust your choices accordingly. Some disciplines, such as psychology, have a controlled vocabulary (a list of accepted keywords). For example, in the 2023 update, the APA lists the following new search keywords: "Artificial Intelligence – Chatbots, Emotion Detection (Artificial Intelligence), Facial Recognition (Artificial Intelligence), Intelligent Personal Agents" (www.apa.org/pubs/databases/training/thesaurus-update-summer-2023.pdf). If your discipline has a controlled vocabulary, you should use it.

Action item!

Choosing the right keywords is an art that can be learned and improved. Choose one of your papers and use it to practice:

- Choose the most important nouns as your keywords. Pick them from the title or abstract of your paper.
- For each noun, think of synonyms that could be used and write them down.
- Search online for each noun within quotation marks to limit the search to that exact noun. Compare the number of hits you get for competing nouns. If one is more widely used than the other, it would make a better keyword (because this is the word people search for and use more).
- Search in one or two journals where your paper could potentially be published using each noun. Make a note of which ones are used more often and what other keywords authors used (you may discover some good ones).

7.3 Using AI

This is one of the tasks at which AI is rather good. You can upload your paper to an AI system and ask it to provide an abstract or keywords, specifying the length. However, before you start celebrating, you need to consider the following issues. First, are you comfortable with the company running the AI site having a full copy of your paper, which they may use pretty much in any manner they desire? If you think that your copyright will stop them from doing so, read the user agreement carefully and weep. Second, you should always check AI's output very carefully. Is all the really important information we reviewed above included? Remember that AI is prone to errors and made-up information ("hallucinations"), which you would need to correct or remove. Third, many journals require you to disclose any use of AI in the process of writing the paper. This may have an impact on the likelihood of your paper being accepted.

In conclusion, abstracts and keywords, while seemingly banal, are an important part of the process and can help get your paper published and, more significantly, read by the scientific community you seek to reach.

Questions for Reflection

1. Think back to an example of a great abstract that you read that convinced you to keep reading the paper. What elements of the abstract made you want to keep reading?
2. Have you ever come across a really bad abstract? What were the problems you saw? How could the abstract have been improved?

Questions for Discussion

1. With your colleagues, discuss the advantages and disadvantages of using AI to generate keywords and abstracts for your papers.
2. In a writing group, workshop an abstract and see if you can identify its parts.

Questions for Your Mentor

1. Discuss strategies to select the most effective keywords, such as doing an internet search for synonyms to identify the most popular ones or considering terms used in different geographical areas.
2. Some people follow a pretty set outline for their abstracts (importance of the issue, purpose of study, data source, findings). Does your mentor have such a template?

8 Introductions and Conclusions

You conducted your research, organized your findings, put it all in writing, and contributed something interesting to the field. Finally, a well-deserved vacation awaits ... oh, no, you need an introduction, what? And a meaningful conclusion? God, why me? I should have been a yoga instructor instead, but since my yoga pants don't fit anymore, here we are ... Fear not, fellow researcher, help is on its way. For many of us, creating effective introductions and conclusions can be challenging, and we often put these sections off until the very end of the writing process. With a few suggestions and guidelines, this doesn't have to be such an onerous process. In this chapter, we review content and structure for introductions and conclusions. For introductions, we offer suggestions for different ways to capture your readers' attention and outline your key arguments succinctly. For conclusions, we address strategies for avoiding repetition when summarizing the main points of your research.

Although introductions and conclusions comprise a small percentage of the paper itself, they are important components of academic writing that should be carefully crafted. The introduction sets the tone for the whole piece. After the abstract, savvy readers will turn to the introduction (and maybe the conclusion) to learn more about the contents of the paper and decide whether to keep reading. The conclusion is your last chance to leave an impression on your readers and reiterate the biggest take-aways from your research. If you're feeling uninspired about how to start your introduction or unsure as to how long your conclusion should be, we suggest you read several articles from the journal you're hoping to publish in to get a sense of the length, tone, and content the journal expects. Introductions and conclusions contain valuable information for your readers; they may be the only sections of your paper that certain readers actually read, or they may be re-read several times by someone wanting to cite your work.

8.1 Introduction Structure

A complete introduction accomplishes the following three things, in this order: gives an overview of the area of investigation, situates your research within that field, and presents your argument or research question (Swales, 1990). Think of

8.1 Introduction Structure

the introduction as the readers' roadmap, which should clarify the article's structure and guide readers as they journey through your paper. And we're not talking about a circa 1996 Mapquest roadmap that you had to print out in twelve pages of confusing instructions, crossing your fingers that a page didn't blow out the window along the way. Your introduction should give Google Maps vibes: no surprises, intuitive, and taking the readers from point A to B via the most direct route possible. It may help to imagine your introduction as an inverted pyramid, starting with more general information and narrowing to more specific content, as shown in Figure 8.1.

The overview of the area should give your readers a broad sense of the conversations and research topics related to your subject that are occurring now. Before the overview, the introduction should begin with a brief attention getter or hook, which we'll skip over for now, as we dedicate an entire section to this later in the chapter. Let's say your paper is about a particular author's impact on contemporary lesbian detective novels in Spain. You will need to familiarize your readers with the genre, noting key players both in production of lesbian detective novels and in scholarship on this literary production. Be careful not to inundate your readers with too many specific details, quotes, or statistics in the introduction, though. You will have space later in the paper to expand on these ideas. For the introduction, you want to give your readers a general sense of what is happening in the field so that you can then point out how your research fits within the larger panorama.

After providing readers with the context of research being done in the field related to your topic, the introduction should then situate your work within those conversations. The goal is to pinpoint your specific contribution to the field, balancing the need to assert the aims and importance of your research

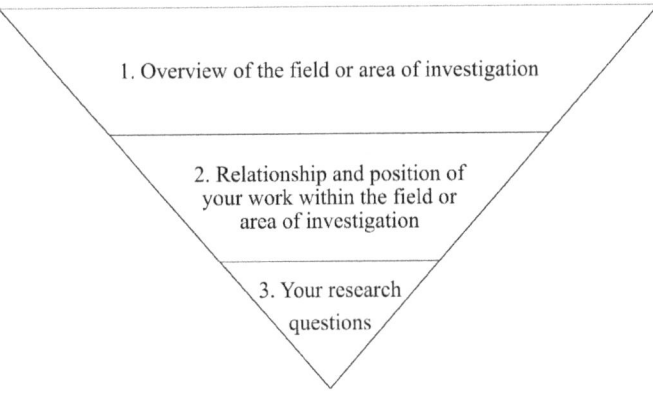

Figure 8.1 Parts of an introduction

without overinflating your contribution. Be cautious of using editorializing words like "groundbreaking" or "revolutionary," as reviewers and readers might find such claims arrogant or simply think you're out of touch. It's a "show, don't tell" situation. However, you do need to make the argument that your research is adding something new or unique to the field. Keep this part of the introduction concise, without diving into your analysis or a discussion of your results. You want to give your readers enough to entice them to keep reading, without revealing all your results and arguments.

The introduction usually ends with research question(s), your thesis statement, or your hypothesis, depending on the type of article you're writing. You should clearly explain your argument and lay out the structure of your paper so that your readers will know what to expect and exactly where the paper is headed. Here's an example sentence that puts forward a thesis statement and then clarifies the article's structure: To demonstrate that lesbian detective novels are subverting patriarchal conventions of the genre (your argument), this article will establish a trajectory of difference between traditional Spanish detective novels and contemporary lesbian detective novels, examine shifts in literary conventions, and demonstrate how protagonists render the male gaze irrelevant. An effective roadmap is straightforward, uses active verbs, and clearly defines the path of the writer's arguments.

Now let's look at Figure 8.2, which includes a sample introduction from an article that Heather cowrote with Dr. Allysha Martin about the use of Twitter (now X) as an educational tool in the second-language classroom, published in *Foreign Language Annals* in 2021.

8.1.1 Attention Getters

Returning to the beginning of the introduction, this is your opportunity to let your creativity shine. The first few sentences (or paragraphs, depending on the length of your introduction) are meant to draw your readers in, piquing their curiosity or raising interesting questions. Attention getters, or hooks, are meant to convince the reader to keep going, while introducing the article's topic in a thought-provoking or entertaining way. In the introduction example below, the attention getter introduces the topic and alludes to possible future iterations of technology in the classroom. Hopefully, the first sentence makes readers wonder about how possibilities for educational online community building have expanded. You have many options for attention getters; choice paralysis may be one of the reasons writers often find it difficult to start introductions. In the next paragraphs, we list some options for your attention getters that should be more effective than just writing the entire first paragraph in all caps.

Through the advent of social media, the possibilities for online community building tied to education have expanded extensively. More educators are experimenting with the role of social media in the classroom, often with the intentions of a one-way communication (instructor relaying information to students) instead of considering the concept of community building.	The authors give an overview of the use of social media in education.
1. Overview of the field or area of investigation	
While existing studies on social media in the classroom focus on topics such as student engagement and providing authentic content in the second-language classroom, the few studies that examine online community building do so in the context of alleviating students' feelings of isolation on campus (Eikenberry, 2012; Journell et al., 2014; Nicholson & Galguera, 2013; Roach & Beck, 2012). For language educators, the fifth "C," Communities, of the American Council on the Teaching of Foreign Languages' (ACTFL's) World-Readiness Standards for Learning Languages further guides their pedagogy of community formation.	They reference some scholarship on the topic, acknowledging trends in the field without presenting an overwhelming amount of information or details.
2. Relationship and position of the work within the field or area of investigation	
Meeting this standard has proven challenging beyond the classroom when students are asked to 'interact and collaborate in their community and the globalized world' (National Standards in Foreign Language Education Project, 2013). Apart from service-learning opportunities, educators have traditionally been equipped with limited means for extending the language-learner community beyond the classroom (Lear & Abbott, 2008).	Then, they situate their work within the already established conversation, showing that little research has been conducted on the specific topic / area of this article.
3. Research question(s) or argument	
As very little research has addressed the sue of social media for community building in the second-language classroom, this action research project explores the use of Twitter in two Spanish as a second-language literature classrooms and its use in creating an online educational community for Spanish-language learners, fulfilling ACTFL's standard of school and global communities through a qualitative study of student survey responses to assess the Twitter projects assigned in class.	In the last sentence, they further situate this article in relation to established research, present the research question, and establish how they conducted their research.

Figure 8.2 Sample annotated introduction

HELLO! COME READ MY ARTICLE PLEASE. You have to admit, this strategy is eye-catching.

A surprising fact or statistic: Recent studies have shown that 62 percent of teenagers report belonging to some type of recreational online community (Discord chats for video games, Twitch streamer chats, etc.), but only 23 percent self-identify as part of an online educational community.

An anecdote: During Carmen's first semester at the university after finishing high school online due to COVID-19, she felt shy and uncomfortable in many of her classes. That all changed when one of her professors required everyone in the class to create weekly posts related to the course content on Instagram. By following classmates' accounts and interacting with them online, Carmen grew to feel a connection with her peers that she had not achieved in the physical classroom.

A problem or question: How many hours a day does the average student spend on social media? Although they are surrounded by technology, how many of them are technologically literate enough to find and assess the value of educational content online?

A contrast: Education today looks very different than it did twenty-five years ago, when technology and social media was absent from pedagogical planning. We have the technology now, but are we utilizing it to the full extent of its educational benefits?

An idea to refute: Some scholars argue that social media has no role within an educational setting and is nothing more than a distraction.

A quote from an expert: (Respected scholar in the field) advocates for the value of social media in the second-language classroom, noting that "(quote)."

These are a few options you can use to hook your readers from the first line. The type of attention getter you choose will depend on how many words you can dedicate to it, the tone of the journal you're aiming to publish in, and the type of reaction you're hoping to elicit from readers, among other factors. Of course you may choose not to have a hook at all. Sal's most quoted article (written in collaboration with his mentor Victor Raskin) starts with the deadly sentence, "The goal of this article is to outline a general theory of verbal humor as represented by verbal jokes."

Action item!

Take a piece of research that you're currently working on and write a couple of different attention getters, using the strategies presented in Section 8.1.1, to see which one you like most.

8.2 Conclusion Structure

While it can be difficult to build the momentum required to write a good introduction, conclusions come with their own set of struggles. You're probably mentally exhausted by the time you get to the conclusion, and the idea of presenting your arguments one more time can feel overwhelming. The conclusion is an extremely important section of your paper, though, as it is your last chance to impress your findings upon the readers and leave them with a clear and positive understanding of your work. Our advice is to start writing your conclusion on a fresh day, when you are well-rested and full of energy. Just like introductions, conclusions should fulfill three main functions: repeating the topic and argument, synthesizing your main points, and indicating the significance of the research. While we asked you to think about introductions as inverted pyramids, you can go ahead and flip that pyramid back around for conclusions, where you will start with more specific points and then broaden your discussion, as shown in Figure 8.3.

First, you want to remind readers of the paper's topic and your argument. Avoid the temptation to simply copy and paste the thesis statement from your introduction. Our suggestion is to open a blank document and, without looking at your paper or notes, write your argument from memory. Double-check it against the thesis statement in your introduction to see if you have forgotten any crucial points or written something too similar, but odds are, you will have come up with a different way to state your argument. In her teaching, Heather has read many student essays where the introduction left her wondering if the paper even had an argument, only to find a beautifully articulated thesis

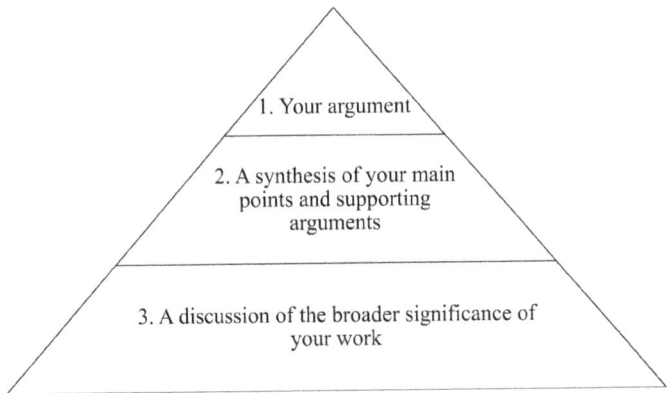

Figure 8.3 Parts of a conclusion section

statement in the conclusion. This makes sense, since conclusions are usually written last; the writer has had the time necessary to fully think about and articulate their argument. Heather now advises her students to come back to their papers a few days after writing them and identify the thesis statement both in the introduction (if they can) and in the conclusion. If the second thesis statement is better, she suggests moving it to the introduction and crafting a new sentence for the conclusion.

Next, synthesize your main points and create connections between your supporting arguments. Again, this doesn't have to be lengthy, but you want to demonstrate how your findings relate to one another and work together to support the overall conclusions of your research. This is also a good place to remind readers of the significance of your research and why you conducted it in the first place.

Finally, expand the conversation even further by highlighting the broader significance of your research for the field. This can be done by mentioning topics that your paper addressed that require further research and exploration, giving recommendations for best practices in applying the findings of your research, or perhaps indicating the limitations of the study (depending on the type of paper you're writing and whether you did that earlier in the paper). The conclusion is not a place to add new information, sources, or statistics, but it is appropriate to look toward the future and how this type of research might evolve. Let's look at the conclusion from Allysha and Heather's article in Figure 8.4.

Action item!

Take a look at your most recent publication or, alternatively, a recent one you read, and try to identify the three parts of the triangle discussed in Section 8.2.

- Can you divide your introduction and conclusion into the three parts of the triangle?
- Are there aspects of the triangle that are missing or underdeveloped?

8.2.1 Conclusion Strategies

Here are a few strategies that you can use to broaden the conversation in the conclusion.

A call to action: We know that second-language learners in rural areas often have limited access to in-person language communities. Therefore, we must

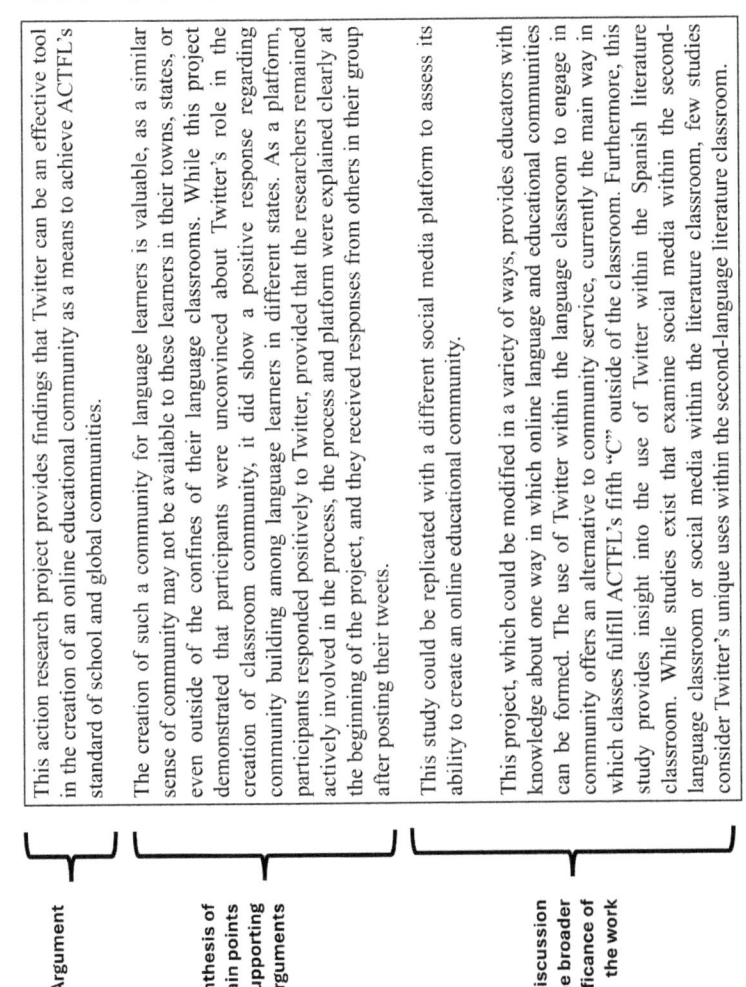

Figure 8.4 Sample annotated conclusion

continue to research online language communities as an effective alternative for these language learners.

A prediction and a recommendation (can be used separately): As we live in an ever more globalized world, individuals will continue to search out social and educational communities online in increasing numbers. Because of this, educators need to continue researching online communities in order to provide the most effective experience possible.

A question: What will the language learning classroom look like in twenty years? In fifty? As educators and researchers, how do we ensure that we continue to meet the needs of our students in an evolving classroom environment?

Now you have a few strategies for writing introductions and conclusions, but at what point in the writing process should you complete these sections? We weren't kidding when we said that we put them off until near the end of the process. Ultimately you should do whatever works for you, but here's a strategy that we use. At the beginning of the writing process, start with a bare-bones version of the introduction that has, at the very least, your initial attempt at the thesis statement. If you have an idea for an attention getter and some other introductory content, add it in. Don't let yourself spend too much time on the introduction during the initial writing process, as your ideas will most likely evolve and your introduction will change to reflect that. We can tend to get stuck trying to put together a perfect introduction instead of just moving along and getting ideas on paper. Once you have a draft of the body of your paper, come back to the introduction. It should now be significantly easier to fill out the introduction with all the necessary details and update your thesis statement. We then suggest drafting the conclusion.

THANKS FOR READING THIS CHAPTER. BYE!

Just kidding … Talk about pressure, though, writing a conclusion for a chapter about conclusions. Even though introductions and conclusions can be frustrating, they are crucial parts of your paper, both for setting the tone and providing information that readers will use to decide whether to read your article. Readers are more likely to come back and review your introduction and conclusion instead of reading the whole thing a second time, or they may only read your introduction and conclusion while skimming the rest of the article, depending on their motivations. For all these reasons, you want to put your best foot forward and produce introductions and conclusions that make your readers think, spark their interest, and clearly establish the place of your research in the field while describing exactly what your article does.

8.2 Conclusion Structure

Questions for Reflection

1. Look back through your publications (or those of others) to find introductions that you especially liked. Can you identify elements of those introductions or techniques that made them particularly effective? How can you replicate these strategies in your future writing?
2. Have you been giving yourself enough time to reflect on your writing before tackling the introduction and conclusion, or do you try to crank them out on the same day that you finish the body of the article? Reflect on how and when you approach introductions and conclusions, and try to build enough time into your schedule that you can let a few days pass between finishing the body of the article before moving on to these sections. This way, you'll have the time you need to mentally process your writing and come back refreshed to write these important sections.

Questions for Discussion

1. Have everyone in your writing group bring a conclusion they're working on to your next meeting. Workshop conclusion strategies together. Can the group think of additional strategies for conclusions that aren't listed in this chapter?
2. Pick a few iconic papers in your discipline and look at their introductions and conclusions. What can you gather from their practices?

Questions for Your Mentor

1. Your mentor will probably have good ideas or suggestions for hooks. They may remember some memorable ones they will be happy to share.
2. Some of us have pet peeves when it comes to introductions (think overgeneralizations, untestable claims). Ask your mentor if they have any to warn you against.

9 Literature Review

Literature reviews are important components of many types of academic writing. They are often a section in a larger research paper, but in some fields, literature reviews can be published as freestanding works. A literature review is not simply a summary of several articles you have read, but rather a comprehensive compilation of research on a specific subject that organizes and creates connections between scholarship on a particular topic. Although literature reviews require a significant time investment, they demonstrate your knowledge of the topic, establish context for your research, and allow you to pinpoint exactly how and where your research fits within the field. A well-written and comprehensive literature review is also a service to your peers, as academics with similar research interests will benefit from reading your literature review. Some fields critique and interpret the literature they are reviewing more than others (looking at you, humanities), so you should ask colleagues or mentors about any field-specific requirements or conventions for literature reviews. This chapter offers a step-by-step explanation of how to write a basic literature review, including advice on how to choose secondary sources; discussion about ways in which a literature review can be structured; and suggestions for how to synthesize large quantities of information and present it in your own words. While this chapter aims to give you a general overview of literature reviews, if you're searching for more in-depth resources on the topic, there are several books dedicated entirely to this subject (Feak & Swales, 2009; Fink, 2019). The information in this chapter about literature reviews will be helpful, whether you're working on the literature review section of a larger paper or whether your entire article is a literature review (see also Chapter 18).

9.1 How to Write a Literature Review

The first step in writing a literature review is to establish your topic and the research question(s) you are investigating. If you're struggling with a research question, you might start working on a literature review with just your subject, allowing the research process to reveal underdeveloped aspects or to help you find a question that piques your interest.

Once you have your topic, brainstorm a list of keywords associated with your investigation. At this point, it's OK to cast a wide net. Your list will very likely change as you research and discover additional themes that are relevant and/or discard issues that don't relate as directly to your research, but you can't foresee exactly where the research process will take you at this point. It's good to give yourself several possible pathways to propel your research forward. We suggest that you create a word cloud or a list of keywords that you will use to guide your literature search (see Chapter 7 for more on keywords).

Now it's time to start finding your sources. For many literature reviews, you will want your sources to be as current as possible, to demonstrate that you are aware of conversations that are happening in the field at the moment. When you are referring to theories and approaches that have been around for a while, you should always reference the original source. You wouldn't quote Jarin and Zahin (2023) on gender performativity rather than Judith Butler, who came up with the idea in 1990, just because the former is more recent. For other types of literature reviews, such as a chronological study of how a theory or pedagogy has changed over time, you will want to include a wider range of sources. If you're writing about the critical reception of a nineteenth-century author, you may wish to start with reviews by their contemporaries and work your way to the present. For a topic like the impact of smartphones on adolescent learning, though, the more current the research, the better. The date range of research acceptable to include will depend on your aims and intentions for the literature review.

You might be wondering where to find the research to include in your literature review. You're most likely familiar with the usual suspects, such as Google Scholar, EBSCO, JSTOR, Scopus, PubMed, and Web of Science. These are great places to start. If your searches in these databases aren't pulling up what you need, or if you're not sure that you're finding a good variety of relevant information, you can try some other strategies. When you find an article that's extremely helpful, or if you know of an author who specializes in the subject, check out their bibliographies. One good study or researcher will often lead you to others. If a name or concept comes up repeatedly in your reading and searching, look up that concept or person and their work. Finally, if you want to be sure that you're tapping into all the relevant resources, consult with a librarian. Most universities have research librarians who are dedicated to a set of departments. In our experience, they are treasure troves of knowledge who are happy to collaborate with faculty members in this way.

> **Action item!**
>
> Try out Connected Papers (www.connectedpapers.com/) to visualize the relationship between publications in your area. This feature works best in certain fields, but it is worth a try as it can help you find new sources and understand how a study fits in a larger body of research. Follow these steps:
>
> - Identify an important publication, one that is widely cited that sets the basis for the area or research question you are working on.
> - Use this paper as the pivot, the key paper in your search.
> - Let the algorithm build a graph for you.

An important aspect of assessing your sources is to determine their quality. This is a complex process, with a good deal of subjective judgment involved. You should first determine that the paper appears in a reputable, non-predatory publication (see Chapter 15). However, a reputable publisher does not necessarily guarantee the quality of the research. Peer reviewing is not an exact science, and some low-quality papers are bound to slip through. One way to establish quality is to compare a paper to other sources of known good quality (maybe your advisor can recommend some high-quality papers for comparison). If the methodological detail, depth of the analysis, quality of the findings, and other parameters match or exceed those of the sources you have as benchmarks, then you can be reasonably sure that the paper you are assessing is of equal quality. Often, low-quality papers can be detected by carefully reading the methodology. A quantitative study based on only one or two participants is probably not very good, unless it's labeled as a case study. Another cue is the number of citations (available in various bibliographic tools, such as Google Scholar): more citations indicate more interest from your peers, all other things being equal (of course a paper published last year will have fewer citations than one published ten years ago). Originality, breadth of the literature review, cleverness of the analysis, and writing style are all indicators of the quality of a paper. If all else fails and you are unsure of the quality of a given source, ask your advisor. That's their job, after all. Just don't try to run your entire bibliography by them!

Next, create a folder specifically for the articles you have downloaded for the literature review. With literature reviews, but also in all academic writing, to enjoy a smooth writing process, so much depends on preparation. Set yourself up for success by carefully reading the articles you plan to cite in your literature review and taking detailed notes now so that you don't have to waste time re-familiarizing yourself with the articles once you start writing.

9.1 How to Write a Literature Review

The trick to writing a good literature review is being a patient reader. You should also know that nowadays there are several programs and applications that can help you organize your sources and notes and make your life easier. They allow you to save digital copies or articles together with their bibliographical information, notes, and keywords and can be used to create a list of references in any given style, share a project library with colleagues, link the same source to different projects, and much more. We are listing some of these programs below with their notable features, but you can and should find out more about research management software (or reference management software) online or through your institution's library.

- Zotero (www.zotero.org/): free software with a useful web browser integration to add sources to your library in a click.
- Mendeley (www.mendeley.com/): free software that can be easily integrated with office tools.
- EndNote (https://endnote.com/): software with lots of functionalities but it's expensive, so we recommend checking if you can get a license through your institution.
- RefWorks (https://refworks.proquest.com/): this product allows you to import references from online databases, but you need institutional access.

The fifth step is to create a document where you will write notes about your sources. We suggest using one document for all your notes. Before you start to read an article, take the time to write the citation (APA, MLA, or whatever style you use) in bold for each article in the document. This way, if you use the article in your literature review, you have saved yourself some time by creating the bibliography entries as you go. If you use one of the applications we listed above, they will helpfully generate the citation, in the correct style, for you. You can even take your notes within the application if your chosen software allows it. As you read, take notes and include any quotes you might find relevant in this document. Figure 9.1 shows an example from a note-taking document that Heather created as she was researching for a literature review on the intersections of gender and Spanish postcolonial presence in Equatorial Guinea.

Once you have taken notes on your sources, it's time to think about how you will organize your literature review. There are several different ways to go about this.

Chronological: This is especially effective if you are studying how the scholarship on a topic has changed over time. For example, maybe you're interested in how the scholarly community's conversations, debates, theories, and word choices have evolved through the years on a particular point, such as the ethics of translation. In this case, it makes sense to begin your literature review with older research than you might typically

Connolly, Kathleen. "Efún: 'White Love' and Modernity in Guinea." *Arizona Journal of Hispanic Cultural Studies*, vol. 19, 2015, pp. 33-54.	For each source, Heather included a bolded MLA citation to keep her notes organized. This will save her some time if she decides to use the source, as she can copy and paste the citation to her Bibliography page.
"For Masoliver, colonialism must be undertaken with the proper guidance of National Catholicism, in order to protect Spaniard's 'whiteness,' and moral integrity. Efún's unease about mixed race, dangerous mestizos, and insinuations of Catalan racial purity all form an integral part of Liberata Masoliver's education of desire" (35)	
All about miscegenation in EG and Catalan identity in EG, EG as a Catalan space, the prioritization of whiteness for women and what that means.	
Mestiza character: "Part of Obama's dissatisfaction is due to the fact that she is self-aware and intelligent, unlike 'native' women without white blood, whoa redescribed as having soulless gazes. Obama's ('white') pride makes her dangerous; she can't be disciplined like a native and she gets angry like a white woman and seeks revenge ('se enfada como una blanca')" (Masoliver 16)" (46)	Her notes include a mixture of direct quotes (that she may or may not use in their entirety) and notes about the articles' content.
Maybe look up Nash's "Social Eugenics and Nationalist Race Hygiene in Early Twentieth Century Spain" *History of European Ideas* 15, 1992 pp. 741-8	The notes also include reminders to herself to look up other sources that the articles have mentioned.
Montuori, Chad. "Representing Gender on the Move from Africa to Spain: Donato Ndongo's El metro." *Black Women, Gender + Families*, vol. 5, no. 2, 2011, pp. 44-65.	
"Traditionally, many West African societies scorn childless individuals and view those women who are infertile as the ultimate betrayal. In 'Whose "Unmet Need"? Dis/Agreement about Childbearing among Ghanaian Couples,' Akosua Ampofo asserts that 'the importance of children makes childlessness an important reason for divorce, although husbands are more likely to seek an additional wife or have children outside the marriage than to choose this option' (2004, 122)" (49)	

Figure 9.1 Sample secondary source notes with annotations

include in a literature review and work your way to the present, noting moments of significant change.

Thematic: This is a common way of organizing literature reviews, grouping together articles that address the same theme.

Methodological: This structure is particularly useful if you're interested in the ways in which studies were organized and conducted. For example, you could divide the literature review into qualitative versus quantitative studies.

Theoretical: You can organize your literature review based on different theories or trends among thinkers in the field, dividing the literature review by arguments.

Once you have chosen a structure for your literature review, reorganize your notes document to reflect this structure. For example, if you chose the thematic structure, add the most relevant themes to your document, which will become the subheadings for your literature review. Then copy your notes and quotes and paste them under the appropriate themes. One article may be referenced under multiple headings. If you prefer, you can create a new document for this organizational step. Now you have an outline and possible quotes for your literature review before you even start writing.

The last step is to start writing. See how many steps we went through before getting to writing? We can't stress this enough; painless, dare we say joyous, writing is born from a thorough preparation process. A literature review follows the typical structure of most academic writing: introduction, body, and conclusion. We suggest starting with the body section of your literature review, creating paragraphs or subsections based on the organizational structure that you've already decided on. The introduction and conclusion don't need to be long, especially if the literature review is a section of a larger paper. In the introduction, you should give a general overview of the topic, highlight overarching themes or theories you'll be discussing, and inform readers of the structure of the literature review and the rationale behind it. The conclusion should synthesize some of the main take-aways of the literature review, remind readers of what you'll be contributing to this body of scholarship and the impact of your research, and demonstrate the need for your research within this larger context (for more information on introductions and conclusions, see Chapter 8).

9.2 Synthesizing Information from Various Sources

Admittedly, the last step of our literature review instructions is a big task. Your goal is to *synthesize* the information, not just summarize it. Even when you have a structure and a plan, how do you combine so much information from different sources without just copying and pasting? This means putting the various sources in conversation with each other, rather than just listing off the sources' findings. You are creating connections between ideas, pointing out differences, and searching for parts of the conversation that other scholars have underdeveloped or completely neglected. Here are a few examples of the types of sentences that are useful in a literature review.

Creating connections between ideas: For optimal plant growth, Sources 1, 2, and 3 demonstrate the value of incorporating fertilizer into the care routine. Source 4 advocates for the positive effects of classical music on plant growth. While no research studied the combined effect of fertilizer and music, this technique could result in greater success.

Sources that build on one another: While Source 1 and Source 2 both agree that fertilization is beneficial for houseplants, Source 2 provides an in-depth analysis of the pros and cons of seven specific fertilizers.

Pointing out and analyzing differences: Source 2 found MiracleGro to create a 24 percent quicker growth rate in plants, while Source 3 reported that MiracleGro caused no significant effects. This difference in findings could be attributed to the fact that Source 2 was studying hydrangeas, while Source 3 researched calatheas. Source 3's sample size was significantly smaller than Source 2, which could be another reason they did not find MiracleGro to be as effective.

Highlighting underdeveloped areas of research: Both sources, however, neglected to discuss the impact of sunlight on houseplant growth, a clear area for future research.

In the literature review, yes, you are reporting on what other studies have found, but don't be afraid to give your interpretation of the sources. What do they do well? Where are their blind spots? Do contradictory studies exist? If so, why do you think they have come to such different findings? As the writer of the literature review, it is your job to contextualize this research for your readers, largely in your own words. Use direct quotes sparingly and try not to get too wrapped up in minute details or statistics from the sources, unless they are especially relevant to your discussion. You should be focused on conveying the bigger picture and broad arguments from the sources to help your readers see patterns and trends surrounding the topic. Finally, although writing a literature review can feel constraining, you still need to write well, including transitions between paragraphs, topic sentences, and clear writing throughout the literature review. By following these step-by-step guidelines, you can eliminate the guesswork from literature reviews and produce a well-structured and comprehensive piece of research.

Questions for Reflection

1. Think back to a literature review you have read that you found particularly beneficial (find it, if you can). Identify different aspects that made the literature review so helpful and reflect on how you can incorporate something similar into your literature review.
2. How do you usually structure your literature reviews? Consider trying one of the other structures we mention in this chapter for the literature review you're working on. Write out two quick potential outlines for your literature review, each one using a different structure. What are the strengths and weaknesses of each structure for your current project?

Questions for Discussion

1. Does anyone in your writing group have a different strategy for note-taking during the research stage of the literature review process? Share what you do with the group, and think about ways you might modify these methods or the method suggested in the chapter.
2. Do some searching on the internet and you will come up with countless videos and webpages advising you on how to take notes. Pick two or three of the more promising ones and invest a few minutes in watching or reading it. You may gather some tips you hadn't thought about.

Questions for Your Mentor

1. It can be difficult to know when it's time to stop searching for and reading secondary sources and start writing. Ask your mentor if they have advice on how to balance these two important components of writing literature reviews.
2. Are there field-specific elements of literature reviews in your area? Discuss this with your mentor.

10 Data Visualization

Even if your field is more qualitative and you don't typically deal with a lot of numerical data or variables, we figure (pun intended) that data visualization can be helpful if you want to communicate complex relationships and help your reader follow along as you tell your story (or better, as your data tell your story). In this chapter, we describe different types of graphs and charts available (from common ones such as bar charts to novel ones such as circular visualizations) and discuss strategies and considerations for choosing the best visual display to compare, illustrate, and show trends and relationships in your data. Our goal is not to tell you how to create these visualizations or to explain any kind of visualization type since you can easily Google them. Here we offer you some guidance regarding how to choose and design the best visualization that fits your goal and data. We also discuss some tips to avoid common mistakes, such as being redundant with regard to the combination of visuals and text in academic writing or trying to cram too much information into one single chart. Before we move on, please know that all the data we are using in this chapter are made up for the purpose of illustrating different types of visualization. While there are many types of visualizations that may be included in academic research (from processes to hierarchies, or from syntactic trees to infographics), here we are limiting ourselves to *data* visualization.

10.1 Data Visualization with a Purpose

Data visualization can help make any kind of information easy to communicate and understand, but it should only be used if you have a clear purpose for it and something to say with it. Before you do anything else, know what you want to show, to whom, and why. What is your goal? What is the argument your data visualizations will make or support? What is your point? We know that answering these questions is easier said than done. To help you get a clear(er) sense of what you want to do, here is a list of the most common uses of data visualization, but keep in mind that you can accomplish more than one use at the same time (compare *and* show change over time).

- *Better understand your data and their distribution*: Yes, data visualization can also be helpful when you are trying to make sense of your data and won't necessarily make it into your published paper. For example, you can use boxplot graphs to identify outliers in your data.
- *Compare two or more pieces of information*: For example, you want to compare the use of a certain linguistic feature across groups, the literary production of two authors, or two perspectives about the same topic.
- *Show changes over time*: For example, the use of a linguistic feature, people's opinions, income, and so on.
- *Emphasize a specific point*: This can be done to make it more visible or memorable by noting, for example, a percentage, a group, or an idea that stands out from the rest.
- *Understand and show the relationship between two or more pieces of information*: This can demonstrate how they relate to each other, by showing how one item affects the other or how a set of values interacts with another set of values.

10.2 The Right Visualization for the Right Purpose

Once you know what you want to do with your data and how a visualization may help you, you are faced with the task of choosing the best graph or chart to do the job. This is an extremely important decision because each type of visualization has its own purpose, strengths, and weaknesses that affect how people will perceive it. There are many options to choose from and a variety of programs you can use to create your visualization. In the next few paragraphs, we summarize the most common and traditional types of data visualization according to what they are good for. We are only listing *static* visualizations here that can easily be inserted in a written paper and are easier to read because they don't change. If you are working on a conference presentation (see Chapter 14) or an alternative type of publication such as a blog (see Chapter 17), you may consider *dynamic* visualizations, as well. Dynamic visualizations are linked to the data source and can change (when the data set changes, for example), allow for interaction with the audience, and display many different pieces of information. The data offered by the US Census (https://data.census.gov/map) is one example, where you can select which variables to display.

Before moving on to discuss what charts are best suited for each goal, we want to point out the importance of charts' readability for your audience. Effective charts are easy to understand and remember, and they should be difficult to misinterpret. Cleveland and McGill (1984) researched how people perceive and understand different types of graphs and created a hierarchy, from easiest to understand (such as scatterplots that show the position of a set of items on a scale) to most confusing (such as pie or donut charts, because, as it turns out, people are pretty bad at interpreting angle and curvature in graphs). So, if you thought a pie chart was the way to go, you might want to rethink that. To have some fun and learn from other people's mistakes, have a look at some visualizations that make no sense (https://viz.wtf/). Speaking of memorability, a large-scale study (Borkin et al., 2013) found that people tend to remember visualizations with attributes like color and a recognizable object (icons) and unique visualization types (like those we describe later in the chapter) versus classic ones.

Action item!

It may be difficult to choose the best type of visualization for your data, and you may end up with two or more options that seem a good fit. If in doubt, find a couple of papers that use similar data and have a look at how they present them (it's always easier to take a critical look at other people's work):

1. Are they using visualizations? If not, would it have been a good strategy to use one? If they are using visualizations, do they feel redundant compared to the information in the text, or do they complement the text well?
2. Is the visualization easy to read? Do you need to go back to the text to understand what it's telling you, or is it readable as a stand-alone?

Now, let's talk about purpose. If your main goal is to start getting a sense of what your data looks like and identify outliers, trends, and ranges, you should consider using box plots, histograms, or scatterplots. We show an example of the first two types in Figure 10.1 and scatterplots in Figure 10.5.

If you want to emphasize a single piece of information (mean, frequency, ratio, count, progress), a few options you could use include waffle charts (that show a completion percentage), isotype charts (that show small counts and use icons or images to represent the type of data), pie or donut charts (which can be hard to interpret), and progress charts (that show performance in comparison with a set goal), some of which are exemplified in Figure 10.2.

If you would like to show change over time, for example trends and tendencies, your best bet is a line graph or, as an alternative, a column chart. Keep in mind that a line chart is easier to read, and people tend to interpret line charts in terms of change over time. You can also compare change over time by simply adding more lines or more sets of columns to your graph, as shown in Figure 10.3.

10.2 The Right Visualization for the Right Purpose

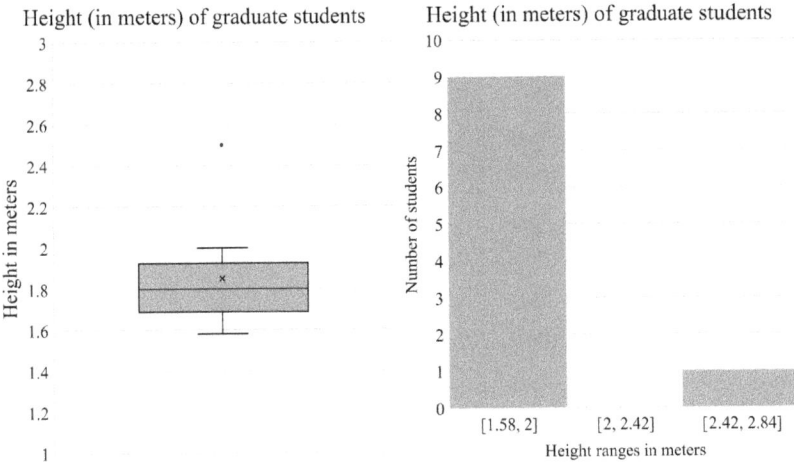

Figure 10.1 Sample box plot (left) and histogram (right) showing suspiciously tall graduate students (outliers)

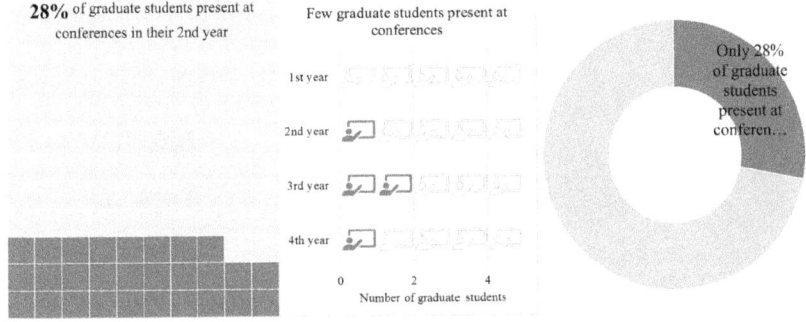

Figure 10.2 From left to right, sample waffle chart, isotype chart, and donut pie emphasizing a single piece of information (percentage or count)

Instead, if you want to compare different pieces of information, you can do so by using column or bar charts, although column charts are easier to read and understand or, as the title of a published article says, "Bars and pies make better desserts than figures" (Annesley, 2010). Other options that can be more or less effective depending on your data include area charts, Mekko charts (also known as mosaic plots), slope charts (again, be careful because people tend to interpret lines as change over time), and tornado charts, some of which are represented in Figure 10.4.

84   10 Data Visualization

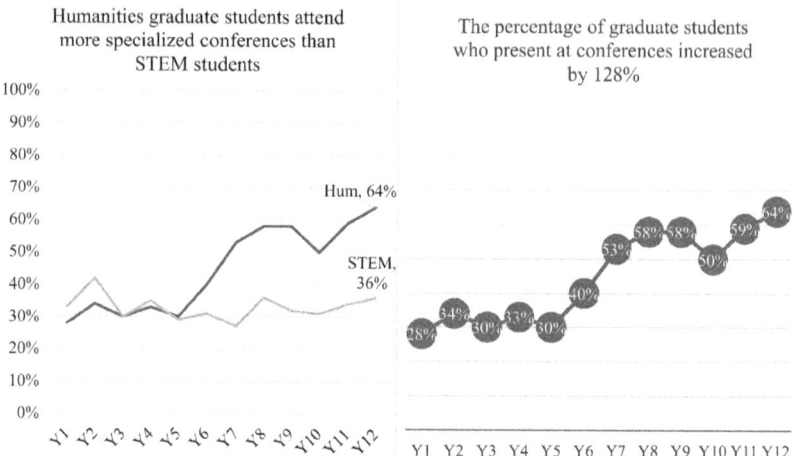

Figure 10.3 Sample single line chart (left) and comparative line chart (right) showing percentage change over time

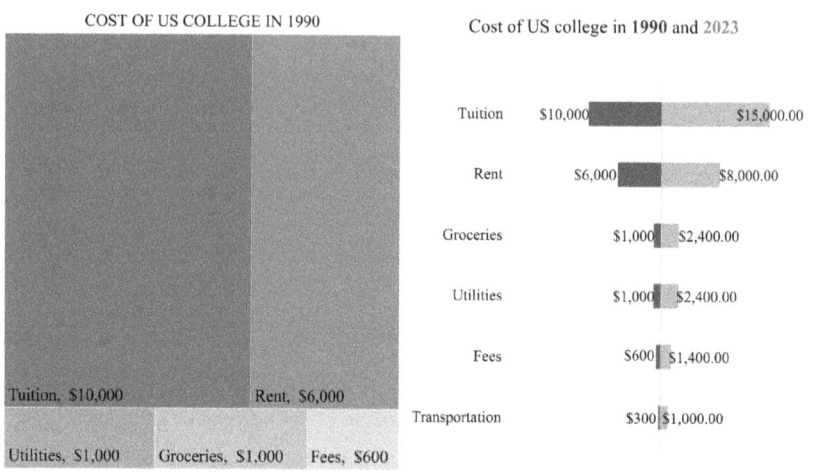

Figure 10.4 Sample Mekko chart (left) comparing variables within a data set and tornado chart (right) comparing two sets of data across different variables

Last, if you want to show the relationship between two or more variables, a common solution would be to use scatter plots, line graphs, or bubble charts (although these are easily misinterpreted and difficult to read, as shown in Figure 10.5). However, since relationships are complex, these may not be adequate for your data set or purpose.

10.3 Some Tips to Avoid Common Mistakes

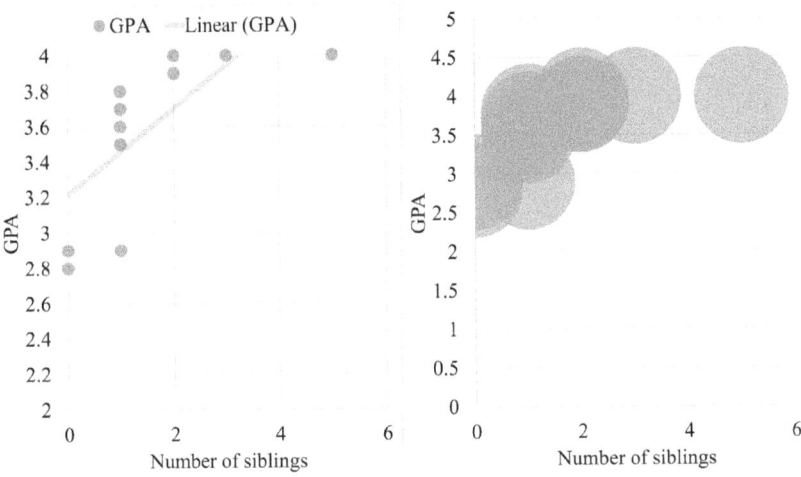

Figure 10.5 Sample scatterplot (left) and bubble chart (right) showing the positive relationship between number of siblings and GPA

So far, we have discussed some pretty common types of data visualizations, considering their purpose as well as their strengths and weaknesses. If you don't think a more traditional visualization will serve your purpose, you can search online for alternatives. Among the alternative forms you can use to present your data, some popular ones include *word clouds* (www.wordclouds.com/), which can be used to show what words are frequently used in a set of texts, and *word trees* (www.jasondavies.com/wordtree/), which allow you to visualize text sequences. Less popular, but not less useful, types of visualizations include *circular visualizations* like chord diagrams (http://circos.ca/), often employed to show complex relationships between different sets of data, and *mandala visualizations* (https://voyant-tools.org/docs/#!/guide/mandala), which are useful for showing the relationship between texts and terms. We cannot possibly cover every single type of visualization but have a look at this useful resource, searchable by function: https://datavizcatalogue.com/.

10.3 Some Tips to Avoid Common Mistakes

As you keep exploring new forms of data visualization and consider which ones would best present your data, keep these suggestions in mind to avoid misinforming your readers or misrepresenting your data and results.

1. Use colors and patterns to facilitate the interpretation of your chart. Be consistent (choose one color for women and one for men, and don't swap colors) and make sure the colors you are using are easy to differentiate and identify. Consider using a color-blind-friendly palette (Okabe & Ito, 2008). If your chart is going to be published in an academic article, check their guidelines, as colors may not be allowed (use grayscale or patterns instead).
2. Be objective. It can be easy to mislead your readers with a visualization. Sometimes this happens because you trust the default setting or the software you are using, which may or may not be meaningful for your specific goal and data set, while other times you may just make the wrong choice and lead your reader to infer something that is not in your data or is not an accurate interpretation of it. So, use labels and titles, and keep the point you want to make with the chart in mind.
3. Keep it simple. Listen to Occam, and choose the simplest type of visualization that allows you to convey your message. Avoid fancying-up your chart (no 3D, no special effects, no fonts that can be difficult to read, no Loch Ness monsters dancing the macarena) or cramming in too much information.

The old saying that a picture is worth a thousand words may be an exaggeration, but the nugget of wisdom is that a visual support can tell a story or make a point in a more accessible or direct way than an explanation, however clear. If your pictures and graphs make a point and convey an idea, adding an extra modality can only help you.

Questions for Reflection

1. Do you have go-to visualizations that you keep using over and over (line graphs, bar charts)? Evaluate their appropriateness based on the information presented in this chapter.
2. If you don't use visualizations, could it be that you're avoiding it? Consider how the incorporation of visualizations could enhance your research.

Questions for Discussion

1. In a writing workshop, bring images or charts you're working on so you can see how everyone interprets them. You may be surprised by what you hear.
2. Discuss your favorite software to generate charts and diagrams. What features do your colleagues find helpful?

10.3 Some Tips to Avoid Common Mistakes

Questions for Your Mentor

1. Ask your mentor if they have a favorite visual presentation tool, either a specific software or a type of chart. What specifically do they like about it?
2. Has your mentor ever received reviewer feedback about visuals? What helpful insights did they take away from that feedback?

11 Reproduction of Images and Copyright Issues

Using material from existing sources, such as visual support or extensive citations, requires copyright clearance. So, if you want to include an image of the Korean band BTS photoshopped with your cat in your next book, start saving your money now. To avoid last-minute problems with your publisher, we recommend thinking about this early on in the process. Doing so requires understanding a little bit about copyright law and the way publishers handle copyright issues. We will discuss these topics, as well as text and image reproductions. Our goal in this chapter is to provide you with all the information you need to deal with these topics calmly and confidently. Our discussion will be based primarily on US copyright, but take into account that different countries may follow different rules.

11.1 Basic Concepts of Copyright Law

11.1.1 Copyright

Copyright means that the person holding it owns the intellectual property to a work (e.g., a book, or a song). This means that the copyright owner can make copies of the work and distribute them for profit, perform a musical composition, display artwork, and so on. Usually, copyright is limited to the length of the life of the author plus fifty or seventy-five years, but recently some large companies have managed to extend the copyright of works that should have expired. So, when you want to reproduce someone's copyrighted work, you need to either secure the permission of the copyright owner (this may entail paying them) or determine that the use you wish to make of the copyrighted work is "fair use," which we explain in the next section. The work can also be in the public domain (works that are no longer under copyright because the copyright has expired or because the author has put them in the public domain), or it can fall under other forms of copyright such as "copyleft," which grants *some* rights (e.g., you may be allowed to reproduce and distribute the work, but not to modify it).

11.1 Basic Concepts of Copyright Law

> **Action item!**
> The Open Research movement promotes sharing and making your research (data, products, findings, publications, instruments, textbooks, etc.) freely available and accessible to anyone and is often supported by a Creative Commons (https://creativecommons.org/) license.
>
> - Read about the different licenses available to learn more about your options (https://creativecommons.org/share-your-work/cclicenses/). Are any of these suitable for you and your work?
> - Follow the steps of the "license chooser" to get some additional guidance about what each different type of license does (https://chooser-beta.creativecommons.org/).
> - Search among the many available resources (https://search.creativecommons.org/). Are you able to find images that you could use for your project?

11.1.2 Fair Use

So, what exactly is fair use? Fair use is defined by section 107 of the copyright law (see the US government website copyright.gov/fair-use, which provides helpful information), based on four criteria:

1. *Purpose and character of the use*: Commercial use is less likely to fall under fair use, whereas non-commercial uses are more likely. Likewise, transformative uses (uses that add some new information or significantly change the text, such as parodies) are more likely to fall under fair use. Another aspect is whether your reproduction replaces the use of the original. If it does, it is less likely to be fair use.
2. *The nature of the work itself*: Fictional or creative work (films, songs) are more protected than factual material (news items, technical articles). Another factor is whether it is published work or unpublished work. The latter is less likely to fall under fair use.
3. *The amount of the work you reproduce*: While it matters, there are no absolute rules. If the portion of a work you reproduce is crucial to the work, it may not be protected by fair use. Conversely, in some cases, reproduction of entire works has been found to be fair use.
4. *Effect on the market*: If your use of the work affects the market value of the copyrighted work, this may fall outside of fair use.

The vague and underdetermined nature of the law leads publishers to err on the side of caution. The determination of whether something is fair use or not cannot be based on a fixed formula (such as 10 percent of the original, for example); the courts take the above factors (and more) into account in order to make a case-by-case determination. Publishers are risk-averse, as they want to avoid costly legal disputes (penalties may be steep). Since there is no absolute way to determine fair use, they may ask for copyright releases even in cases that are obviously fair use.

11.2 Reproducing Copyrighted Products

11.2.1 Text

Having considered copyright and fair use, you can see that the less you reproduce, the better. As we discussed, even if you only reproduce three lines of text, your citation still could be found to violate the copyright owner's rights. Another reason to limit your verbatim citations is that, generally speaking, you want your voice to shine through the text, with external texts functioning in a supportive role. Extensive citations tend to take over the text, and they can be a sign of a novice writer.

In addition to reducing the amount of text quoted, you should consider the nature of what you quote. For example, methodology, while extremely important, is rarely worth quoting verbatim. Verbatim quotes should be reserved for citations that cannot be paraphrased without loss. This falls under two categories: extremely well-worded iconic expressions, and definitions you disagree with. In the latter case, of course, the reason for quoting verbatim is to pre-empt accusations that you are attacking a straw man.

11.2.2 Images

The best advice we can give is to avoid reproducing images unless you absolutely have to. If you can produce your own images, you are much better off. This may sound unduly negative, but hear us out. Let's assume you found a great image on the internet or in a book and you want to reproduce it, and let's even imagine that you have the budget to pay for it. First, you need to determine who owns the copyright. You might think that the publisher of the book or of the webpage where you found the image is the copyright owner. This can be true, but not always. Publishers disappear, are bought by larger publishers, or sell their intellectual property. For example, Academic Press was a publisher founded in the early 1940s. It was sold in 1969 to Harcourt Brace after the death of one of its founders. In 2001, Elsevier bought Harcourt Brace, so if you want to reproduce an image from an Academic Press book, you must talk to Elsevier. Once you've determined who the copyright owner is, you need to contact them. Some publishers respond quickly and efficiently, while others simply never answer you at all. Some publishers have automatic systems that charge you a standard fee, regardless of the size and nature of the image, which can be quite expensive.

Not all is darkness, however. If the author of the work is available and owns the copyright of the image, they are often willing to provide you with a letter stating that you are free to reproduce the image. We ourselves have experienced such heartening collegiality in several instances.

Let's assume that you have successfully addressed the copyright and budget issues we just discussed. You now need to prepare your images for the publisher. Be sure to read the publisher's instructions carefully and follow them to the letter. Usually publishers ask for 300 dpi (dots per inch) images, as lower resolution does not print well. Sometimes they will ask for a specific size, but most graphic software can quickly and easily convert size and resolution. For example, Preview, available on Macs, makes the whole process a breeze (it handles batch processes, meaning it can convert hundreds of images to a specific resolution in one shot).

Action item!

Publishers usually have their own guidelines and requirements for artwork (any figure, image, graph, etc.). Before submitting your manuscript, make sure to familiarize yourself with their artwork guidelines and consider the following points:

- Have you secured copyright authorization for all the artwork that is not copyright-free or created by you?
- Are the images you created the right resolution? If not, do you know how to edit them to increase their resolution?
- Are your images legible if printed in black and white? What should you change to increase legibility (use patterns instead of colors, add labels, etc.)?

The last hurdle is to send the images to the publisher. If you have a lot of them and they are high resolution, they may exceed the size that your email can handle. Using a document sharing program, such as Google Docs or Dropbox, is an easy workaround. Your publisher may have a preferred means of transfer, so ask them.

11.2.3 Other Products

Screenshots: Most screenshots or screen captures will be cases of fair use, since in most cases they are transformative, insofar as they add information that was not in the original, for example by focusing on a detail and discussing it. Generally, they don't function as a substitute of the original, so they cause no financial harm to the original image's copyright owner. For example, if I take a screenshot of a fragment of the Coca-Cola website to discuss the use of the color red in its design, my use is clearly transformative (Coca-Cola would have a hard time arguing that their website's purpose is to educate people about design), and it doesn't cause any loss of sales to the company (they are not selling access to their website). An example that violates the copyright owner's rights would be a screen capture of a photograph of capillaries in the retina, in the field of scientific photography.

Maps: Maps are tricky, in the sense that the information in a map cannot be copyrighted, but the artwork can. Fortunately, it is now possible to generate customized maps, using various types of software, some of which are free. Taking screenshots of Google maps or other resources is also becoming a go-to resource.

Music transcriptions: It should be noted that music transcriptions are considered derivative works and therefore fall under copyright. You will need permission to reproduce your transcription of John Cage's *4'33* or Taylor Swift's *Anti-Hero*.

11.3   Getting ahead of the Copyright Problem

Start by setting your budget. Your publisher will probably keep it very simple: Your budget is zero dollars. If you want to negotiate a budget for image reproduction in a book, you should do so before signing the contract for your book. Articles and other forms of publications generally do not allow for artwork budgets. Be prepared for the publisher to politely rebuff your request. However, depending on the nature of your book, it may be possible to negotiate a budget. One of us managed to negotiate a budget for illustrations for a textbook on eye tracking. Likewise, a book on art history, or on design, may be good candidates for a budget.

Whatever the size of your budget, you will likely exceed it. Some publishers charge high rates to reproduce their images ($300 per image is a common fee), and distributors of scientific images make a living doing so, so don't expect to find any deals here. Luckily, there are countless websites that are free or charge a small fee to download royalty-free images. There are also websites with royalty-free, public-domain high-quality images (such as NASA or Wikimedia commons). Many AI websites, such as Dall-e, can also generate images for a low cost. If what you need is illustrative, this may be a resource. Learning to manipulate and crop these images so as to be able to add legends, arrows, and other pointers will also make it easier to up-cycle stock images into images specifically meant for your audience. For example,

11.3 Getting ahead of the Copyright Problem

a stock image of the brain lobes can be annotated with the areas related to language or emotion processing, thus providing the crucial and specific information your readers need. Finally, if you are creative, you can resort to drawing your own images.

Planning is the key to dealing with copyright problems. When you outline your article, chapter, or report, you should decide at that time how much and what kind of visual support you will be using. Before writing your text, locate all visual aids (images, maps, etc.) that you plan to use, and start the copyright clearance process. This will make it easy to discard a planned image if you find that the copyright owner is asking for a sum that exceeds your budget. If you know that you have only one image available, you can build your discussion and description of experiments, locations, and circumstances on the basis of that knowledge. If you have a map of Europe and North Africa and are describing the Napoleonic wars, you can produce a legend that highlights exactly the battles and annexations that you have or will include in your map. If you have more than five or six images, we recommend that you set up a spreadsheet to keep track of your progress in negotiating the copyright fees, the availability of the images, all interactions with the publishers, and other issues that come up. If you input all the information in your spreadsheet as you find images and receive emails, you will save time by not having to hunt down the information months, if not years, after you collected it, and you will be able to easily email a copy of the spreadsheet to your publisher when they ask you for your copyright clearances. Be sure to number the images and give them a descriptive title. Be prepared to provide information about the size of the print run of your book, the size of the image as it will appear in the book (full page, half page, etc.), and whether you plan to use it for the cover of the book (which is generally more expensive). Note that publishers do not provide bulk discounts. If a publisher charges a $250 fee per image and you have ten images, the fee will be $2,500. Copyright clearance for text is simpler. You still need to determine who holds the copyright, but generally a simple request for the right to reproduce a chunk of text will get you a positive or negative answer.

Overall, the guiding principles for the use of copyrighted materials should be planning ahead and keeping your copyright use as small as possible. The use of copyrighted information (text and images) should be approached carefully and from a position of knowledge. Specific documents and visual supports (images, maps, and graphs) can be essential to the presentation of information and clarity of a text, although the process of securing copyright clearance can be complex and frustrating. We recommend clearing copyrighted material ahead of time to avoid frustrating rewrites or having to pay exorbitant fees.

Questions for Reflection

1. Try using AI to generate an image that could illustrate a concept in your work. What are the advantages and drawbacks of images created by AI?
2. Consider an example of text that is quoted in a paper of your choice. Did the author(s) really need to use the text? Could they have done without? Now turn the tables on yourself. Do you have any texts that you're quoting extensively or unnecessary images in your current project? Are there other ways in which you could effectively convey this information?

Questions for Discussion

1. What websites do your colleagues use for copyright-free images?
2. Do you and your colleagues publish in open access venues? If so, how does copyright work? Do you, the university, or the publisher retain copyright? Does your university support OA? Do they have resources you might use?

Questions for Your Mentor

1. If you fail to obtain copyright for an image that you absolutely need, what strategies and options can they suggest?
2. How did they deal with getting copyright clearance to republish articles in a larger work, like a book?

12 Creating an Index

This chapter is for readers who are completing a book project. First of all, congratulations on your colossal achievement. Don't forget to raise a glass (or two) to that almost complete manuscript. Second, you are now likely facing the daunting task of creating an index for your book. You know, the one that lists all the important names and terms at the end with the page numbers next to them? Yes, you get the lovely task of preparing it, but this chapter will make it easier. You may wonder, why bother to make an index in the age of digital documents and ctrl + F? An index is not just a tool that tells you where a given word occurs in a text (a concordance). Rather, a good index will tell you where a concept is discussed in a significant way and may omit any other random mentions of that concept that appear scattered through the book. In this chapter, we deal with the challenges involved in creating the index of a book. We present tools (software), as well as guidelines and examples, for you to create your index in a way that fits the content of your book, your tech skills, and your time availability.

12.1 Indexing Techniques

We are decades away from a usable index generated by a computer without human intervention, so you will always need to be involved in the process. This makes sense. You are the most knowledgeable person about your book. You literally wrote the book about the subject, so logically you are the best person to complete the index. However, you might have very little idea about what makes a good index, except for what you may have picked up from using indexes in your reading life. The good thing about putting in the time and effort to learn about indexing is that the process will force you to look at the writing in your book in ways you would never have dreamed of during the normal writing or reading process. Because of the detailed, microscopic attention required by the indexing process, you will notice things about your own work that will surprise you. When needed, you will be able to correct those aspects. For example, one of us had misspelled Quintilian's name as Quintillian and gleefully ignored the red underlining because they assumed the software simply was not up to date on their Latin rhetoricians. However, when the indexing software gave two entries side by side, they immediately saw the error and fixed it.

Academic books may have one or two indexes: an index of names, which lists the names of all scholars mentioned in the text, and an index of subjects, which lists all the important topics discussed. Often, the two are combined. Specialized indexes of other kinds (formulas, software commands, etc.) may also be produced as needed.

When faced with the task of indexing, your first decision will be whether you intend to do it by hand, with the help of software, or with the help of a professional indexer. Indexing by hand requires several glasses of wine and taking a copy of the book (usually the galleys or proofs – preliminary versions of the manuscript) and highlighting every word you want to index and then documenting the page numbers in which the word is found. This is a laborious, error-prone task, and you have to be careful not to obscure your page numbers with drops of red wine or tears. You then have to manually compile the index by creating the page ranges; for example, if the name Chomsky appears on pages three, four, five, and six, the properly formatted index will read "Chomsky, 3–6." Because errors can easily occur throughout this process, once you have a first draft of your index, you might want to print it out together with the proofs of your manuscript (if it's feasible), and with both documents side by side, revise every entry of your index, checking for spelling mistakes, missing elements, and page numbers.

A second technique is indexing via software, which can be accomplished by markup or extraction. If you are going to go the markup route, you will typically need to use a text editor that allows you to create a pure text file (one with no hidden characters). If you don't know what we are talking about, don't worry. Skip this part and continue reading about indexing by extraction.

Markup requires the writer to physically embed code in the text (as in HTML) to allow the software to retrieve the words to be included in the index. There are several software options to accomplish this; here, we include an example using LaTeX. Let's say that you are writing a book about linguistics and wrote a sentence that reads as follows: "Greimas's goal in Semantique Structurale is to formulate a deductive foundation of semantics on a Hjelmslevian basis." Now, there are three words in this sentence that are important and that you would like to add to the index: Greimas, Hjelmslevian, and semantics. In order to do that, you need to add a short piece of code to tell the software which word you want to index (\index) and under which reference entry to do it ({Greimas}). Your sentence with the added code will look like this: "\index{Greimas}Greimas's goal in Semantique Structurale is to formulate a deductive foundation of \index{semantics}semantics on a \index{Hjelmslev}Hjelmslevian basis." Using a simple search-and-replace function, you can then replace all instances of the

12.1 Indexing Techniques

terms that need to be indexed (such as authors' names and technical terms) with the code and then generate the index automatically.

Another route is using the indexing function in Microsoft Word, which also works via markup. If you select a word and would like it to become an index entry, you can do that by using the function ALT+SHIFT+X. This function will add up the word as an entry to the index. Once you have selected all words you would like to include in the index, you can generate it by using the function Insert Index or References, depending on the version you are using. The good thing is that your index is dynamic, meaning that you can update it to reflect new entries, and it will adjust the page numbers by itself. However, keep in mind that because it is dynamic, you cannot edit it directly (such as changes to font style), as any edits will be lost once you refresh it, so make sure to edit it at the very end, if needed, once all entries have been selected.

Indexing by extraction requires you, the author, to prepare a list of terms to be indexed. This can be done ahead of time and then fed to the software to generate the index or can be done within the software by setting some parameters (certain software can automatically extract all capitalized words, which can be a good starting point for an index of names, or have embedded features that recognize names). The software then takes the list and scans your manuscript file looking for any instance of the terms on the list, extracts the page number where the terms are found, and generates an index automatically.

You could also have your index created by a professional indexer. This may be someone who works with the publisher, and typically you won't pay for their work out of pocket, but the publisher will retain part of the royalties until the cost of the indexer is covered (check with your publisher before making a decision). You could also contract someone to do the work. A good place to start, if you don't know someone already, would be to ask colleagues who have recently published a book, or you can visit the webpage of an indexing association, such as The American Society for Indexing (http://www.asindexing.org/find-an-indexer/). Remember, though, that even if you or the publisher hire a professional indexer, *you will still need to work on your index*, revising it and fixing the inevitable errors that will be there.

Which method you choose depends on many factors, including your tech skills, budget, publisher support (sometimes they will give you access to an indexing software for free, but you will need to learn to use it), and time.

Action item!

Explore the characteristics of a few indexing software programs (see below or do a quick web search for "indexing software") to see if any of these matches your needs. Consider the following: cost and licensing options (Is there a free trial?), customer support (Where are they located? Can you call, email, chat?), learning materials and guides (instruction manuals, training videos, FAQs), and specs.

- TExtract, http://www.texyz.com/textract/
- CINDEX, http://www.scribendi.ai/cindex/
- Index Manager, https://index-manager.net/

12.2 Indexing Decisions

If you look closely at the LaTeX example we discussed before, you will notice that the word that appears in the text (Hjemlslevian) and the index entry under which we decided to index it (Hjemlslev) are not always the same, and that is because indexing is not an automatic process but requires some thinking and decision making. For example, Sal decided to index the adjective Hjemlslevian under the author's name, Hjemlslev, in the index, which means that he decided to tell his reader that this author is mentioned on the page where he uses the adjective Hjemlslevian. This was his decision, based on his knowledge of the topic and the book.

Something else you may notice in the same example is what words were selected to be included in the index. Semantics? Why is this word relevant, you may ask? Once again, that was the author's decision: semantics is an important concept in the field, so Sal wanted his readers to be able to locate where in the book he discusses it. Of course, this means that Sal will have to pay close attention to how this word is used in the text, because it should be included in the index only when it is used as a specialized term. Remember that you, the author, are the best person to choose what words to include in the index. Typically, you want to include author names, theories, and key or technical terms that are relevant in your area (similar to when you are choosing keywords for an abstract), so there is no one-size-fits-all approach here. Here are a few suggestions to help you decide which terms to include in your index:

- Look at headings and subheadings to find keywords.
- Consider important terms in the field/s of your book.
- Make sure to include new concepts you define or neologisms you introduced.
- Check for content words you are using frequently, because they are probably important.

There are several more decisions you will have to make regarding your index, and these will depend on your manuscript, field, and topic. Inevitably,

12.2 Indexing Decisions

you will have questions. We can anticipate some of these based on our own experience and struggles with creating an index, so we can offer you some answers and advice on how to go about it. Other questions will arise as you are working on your index. We encourage you to make a note of these questions and discuss them with a colleague or mentor.

> **Action item!**
>
> To find out how other authors have dealt with indexing decisions, pick a published book that will serve as a model (choose a book that you read, liked, thought was well written and – very important – was published by your publisher). If you have access to a PDF, even better, as you will be able to search through it quickly. Use the book to find the answer to these questions:
>
> 1. Did they index authors' names that are cited in the references? For example, let's say that "Attardo, S." appears on pages 4, 60, and 89 in the text, and then is also an entry in the list of references on page 103. Is page 103 included in the index?
> 2. Did they index authors' names that are only cited in the references but do not appear in the text? For example, if a reference appears in the text as "et al." but all authors' names are listed in the list of references, are their names also included in the index?
> 3. Did they create an index entry using the abbreviation or the spelled-out word for a concept? For example, is AU, Action Unit, or both used in the index?
> 4. If a given author is only mentioned once in the book (twice if we count the list of references), did they include their name in the index?
> 5. If they reference their own previously published work in the book, did they include their own last name as an entry in the index?
> 6. How did the indexer determine which authors' names should be included in the index?
>   a. Is it based on the number of occurrences (at least twice excluding references?)
>   b. Are only first authors included?
>   c. Are all authors mentioned in the references included (also second, third, etc. authors)?
>   d. Are all names included (also editors)?

As we approach the end of this exciting chapter, we offer you some further, very concrete recommendations for when you will be ready to begin revising your index. Yes, you will revise it more than once (more than twice for sure, actually). That's where the human intervention we mentioned comes in.

- Create the list of subjects and the list of names as two separate lists. You can always blend them and sort them afterwards if you decide to have only one index.
- Check that all names quoted in the bibliography or reference list are included. Tricky spot: editors may be indexed too, as we said.
- Check that all entries are in alphabetical order (things get moved around through each round of proofs).
- Check for consistency on full first names or first and middle name initials (depending on the style guide you are using, like APA, MLA, or Chicago).
- Check for changes in spelling of concepts (eye tracking vs eye-tracking, cue vs clue).
- Check for little things like commas after the initial of a name that may be missing or have become a period instead of a comma ("Attardo, S.," vs "Attardo, S," or "Attardo, S.").
- Check for spelling of names with accents or other diacritics and different alphabets. They often get messed up.
- Check initials for people with the same last name and corresponding references in the text ("Williams, M." vs "Williams, L. E.").
- Check for duplicate spellings of the same name (Boguslavskij vs. Boguslavsky).
- Disambiguate multiple names. For example, in a book Sal edited, he had the following:

    Johnson, Christopher R., 26–27, 36, 38–40, 55, 76, 223, 301, 303
    Johnson, Marcia K., 26–27, 36, 38–40, 55, 76, 223, 301, 303
    Johnson, Eric W., 26–27, 36, 38–40, 55, 76, 223, 301, 303
    Johnson, Mark, 26–27, 36, 38–40, 55, 76, 223, 301, 303
    Johnson, Stephen B., 26–27, 36, 38–40, 55, 76, 223, 301, 303
    Johnson, Trudy, 26–27, 36, 38–40, 55, 76, 223, 301, 303

    Note that all the Johnsons have the same page numbers, because the software does not know they are different people (it finds the key Johnson and attributes it to all the Johnsons). Sadly, disambiguation has to be done manually.
- Disambiguate authors whose name matches a common word. For example, in a book Sal indexed recently, he came across papers by Amanda Both, M. A. Just, D. L. Long, P.A. Low. Their names matched tens of false hits in the text of the book: both, just, long, and low. These are fairly common words in English that occur sometimes at the beginning of a sentence and are thus capitalized, making them unrecognizable even if the software is smart enough to not match lower case words. Current technology has no way to

12.2 Indexing Decisions

avoid these false hits, so they need to be sorted out manually by searching in the file for each instance of the word and checking which is which.
- Check page numbers to ensure these are adequate and correctly reflect where the content appears. You can do this with a quick *Find* search in the manuscript document to make sure the pages listed in the index are in fact where the term appears.

While some may find creating an index as exciting as watching paint dry, producing a good index is a surprisingly difficult and correspondingly rewarding process. A good index is a gateway to the content of your book, and you are the best person to index your book. Even professionals do not know as much about the content as you do.

Questions for Reflection

1. Have you ever used indexing software? Do you have the time and skills to learn how to use it for indexing your book? If the software offers a trial period, will you be able to learn how to use it AND create your index within that time frame?
2. Do you have some research funds you can request or use to purchase an indexing software license or to hire a professional indexer?

Questions for Discussion

1. Have a look at a couple of sample indexes and discuss their characteristics with your peers. Consider ease of use (Are they easy to consult? Does one of them stand out as particularly easy or difficult, and why?) and formatting (Are names and topics mixed in a single index? What do people prefer and why?).
2. With colleagues and peers, discuss how they use indexes. This might help you decide on the entries and convince you further that this is a task that matters.

Questions for Your Mentor

1. Almost everyone who has published an academic book has a story to tell about indexing it. Ask your mentor how they decided which way to go to index their books and if they can tell you about their indexing experiences. Were they satisfied with their choice? Would they do it again? What problems arose in the process? How did they fix those issues?
2. Pick a book written by your mentor and discuss the strategies they used to build the index.

13 Dealing with Reviewers' Comments (Including the Dreaded Reviewer #2)

In this chapter, we focus on dealing with revision requests, but first, we would like to start with a word to those who may have received a rejection from an academic peer-reviewed journal. Having your hard work rejected is no fun, and it may be a considerable blow to your academic confidence. If you received a desk rejection, do not despair; it is *not* the end of the world, or your career. Journal editors at Elsevier, for instance, desk-reject 30–50 percent of the articles submitted before they reach the peer review stage (Elsevier, 2015). That means that depending on the journal, as many as half of the papers never even get sent to reviewers. You just pick another outlet (see Chapter 15) and try again. Sal remembers getting one of his co-authored papers rejected eight or nine times before it got accepted into a reputable journal. Hilal submitted one of her papers to four or five different journals before getting a revise-and-resubmit. If, on the other hand, your paper first went to reviewers, and then got rejected, this is actually even better. Now you have something to work with, a chance to improve your paper before trying again. Do not disregard reviewer comments because they rejected you; if you can look beyond the rejection and work around the unpleasant feeling, you will find helpful comments in their reviews. Try, try again until you receive a revise-and-resubmit, and then come right back to this chapter.

Congratulations on the nonrejection of your manuscript! It may not feel like something to celebrate considering the work you now have in front of you, but not getting a desk rejection *is* worth celebrating. It's a step in the right direction. If you're wondering where to go from here now that you have received a round of revisions, this is the chapter for you. We will walk you through the process and try to make sure you are not reduced to a puddle of tears at the not-so-kind words of a ruthless scholar who tore your work to pieces, even though there clearly was merit in it (hence the nonrejection). This lovely person is known in academic circles as the dreaded reviewer number two, or Reviewer #2 for short. They may not always be the second reviewer, but it is their "delectable" style that earns them this title, not their number in the sequence of reviewers. The first thing to be accomplished, therefore, is to learn to overcome the emotional barrier of being criticized.

13.1 The Emotional Aspect of Rejection

As noted in Chapter 2, mental well-being is crucial to academic productivity. Having other experts in the field tell you that the work you have spent so much time and effort on is not good enough for publication as-is is a great threat to that. On top of that, you might get a Reviewer #2. Grad school taught so many of us that our entire self-worth was linked to our scholarship, which makes it impossible not to take rejections personally.

Throughout this process, just remember that a revise-and-resubmit is *not* a rejection. Your paper *was* good enough; it just needs to be revised. In an ideal world, you would receive reviewers' comments in the form of a list of issues to be addressed, starting and/or ending with the commendable aspects of your work, so as to build your confidence and acknowledge the parts that earned the manuscript a round of revisions instead of a desk rejection or a rejection based on reviews. The reality can be quite different, however. The wording in the reviews can be downright nasty: "a hodgepodge of ideas and notions" and "a waste of excellent data" are just some of the latest loveliness we have dealt with. Moreover, reviewer comments may not make sense because they did not read your work carefully enough or understand it well enough. They may even ask for things that would, once completed, amount to a whole different manuscript than what you have submitted. When things like that happen (or even when they do not), it is natural to go into self-preservation mode and be angry. While we are not qualified to tell you how to best process your emotions, we can tell you that you are entitled to those emotions, and you can definitely take some time (up to a week, perhaps) to come to terms with how you feel about what you have read. Heather sometimes has a trusted friend in her field or her partner read the comments, for instance, just to assure her that everyone does not hate her paper. It does not give her any practical advantage, but it makes her feel better. Hilal usually has Sal read the reviewers' comments. By the end of the conversation, the emotional aspects are effectively removed with surgical precision, and she is left with a cold, hard to-do list, which is much easier to tackle. (For more on how a mentor can help you, see Chapter 27.)

Action item!

To get started with the revision process ...

Select two or three items from the reviewers' comments that you feel confident about and could address fairly easily (e.g., without having to read a lot more, or without having to do more analyses). These can be partial items (such as parts of a comment in which the reviewer asks you to accomplish much more). Write these down and start jotting down your thoughts about each of these items.

> *To gain momentum* ...
> Go through the list of comments from the reviewers and set aside all those that do not require a lot of work on your end (praise, minor editing issues) but may simply be addressed with a quick "Thank you, I have done this" message.
>
> *To keep going* ...
> Make a plan and give yourself a deadline. Make a list of the actions you need to complete and add them to your calendar as if these were appointments or meetings. Make sure to have time set aside to address them. Do not underestimate the time you will need; if anything, it may be better to overestimate it.
>
> *Bonus!*
> Reward yourself (a coffee, a happy sticker on your calendar, a walk) after having accomplished any of these actions.

13.2 Whether or Not to Make Revisions

Know that you do not *have to* make the revisions. We are telling you this so you do not feel trapped or think that it is do or die. You have the option to refuse to make changes or to withdraw your submission, but you need to make an informed decision. Do you know for a fact that the changes you are being asked to make will not actually make the paper better? Are the reviewers really asking too much or missing the point? If you find that they are asking for things that you have already explained, or arguments you have already made, you may want to consider the fact that maybe you can do a better job of explaining/framing/organizing these things. We know exactly what we are doing and why we are doing it, but sometimes we do not explain our thought process well enough on paper. Sometimes we may explain a concept, a term, or a choice we made, but the reviewers miss it altogether. That should tell you that you did not explain it as well as you thought, or present it as well as you should have. If the reviewers did not understand you, chances are the readership will not, either. Your arguments and explanations are only effective if the readers can follow them.

If, however, you are positive your paper is better off without the changes requested by the reviewers, you can do a few things. You can follow the procedure we are describing below, but for those out-of-place change requests, you can respond with polite, rational, and fact- and scholarship-based explanations as to why you have not made those changes. For example, Elisa and her

13.2 Whether or Not to Make Revisions

> We agree with the reviewer that terminological issues are still relevant when discussing language teaching and learning. However, our task was also not to discuss what the labels Ll, L2, and HL mean in depth. Therefore, our definitions or explanations serve the purpose of clarifying, for the reader, what we mean when we use each term/label, and not to dig deeper into these terminological issues, as this is outside the scope of the chapter.
>
> We added a footnote in which we explain that discussing the differences between learning and acquiring is outside the scope of the chapter and added references in case the reader is interested in learning more about this topic.

Figure 13.1 Sample disagreement response to a reviewer comment

coauthors were once asked for an in-depth discussion of the terms first, second, and heritage language, but this was outside the scope of their paper. Figure 13.1 shows part of their response to the reviewer.

Notice how the response in Figure 13.1 still ends on a positive note and with a change, albeit not the one that was recommended. You may also write directly to the editor, armed with said scholarship that backs you up, and tell the editor that you decline to make the change. Explain clearly and succinctly why you will not change the text. As a last resort you might ask for the paper to be sent to different reviewers, but be prepared for the editor to simply decline your request. Always keep in mind that, unless the editor indicates that you may disregard some of the reviewers' comments, they agree with them. Remember that by refusing to make a requested change, you automatically become a "difficult" author. In other words, do not set foot on this path lightly. If, for some reason, you do not want to write to the editor or be associated with that journal anymore, you can also respectfully withdraw your paper. This, however, should be a last-resort option. After all, remember that they are asking you to revise – they have not rejected the paper. In any of these scenarios, you will have to resist the urge to criticize the reviewers and/or the editor, and express yourself in a calm, professional manner. Do not burn any bridges. During his time as a journal editor, Sal recalls a response from an author that started with "Your reviewers are [profanity]." That does not sit well with most academics. Academia is really, really small; you do not know when or where you might encounter these people again. Sure, the reviewers will not know who you are, but the editor(s) will; and once the paper gets published elsewhere, so might the reviewers. Your paper might also go to the same reviewers even if you submit it elsewhere. In principle, they should recuse themselves from reviewing the same paper twice, but you never know.

13.3 Working with the Actionable Parts of Reviewer Comments

When you feel ready to work on the revisions, ignore any unhelpful parts and go looking for actionable items. They might be hidden in a generally evaluative paragraph, or there may be more than one thing to address in a single comment, so to ensure you don't miss anything (and you don't want to miss anything), it is best to fish them out and list them separately. We find it helpful to create a document (a table, a spreadsheet, etc.) with the reviewers' comments on the left-hand-side column and your responses on the right. You will likely be asked to submit your responses to reviewers' comments when you turn in the revised manuscript, so form polite and professional responses, and state what changes were made where. Figure 13.2 includes an example from Hilal. Note that we have abbreviated it down to two comments from each reviewer, plus two of the very minor changes they asked for. We would also like to point out that in this case, there was no Reviewer #2, just a couple of extremely helpful reviewers.

Let us now discuss the choices Hilal made in forming her responses to the reviewers' comments, starting with the preface. You will notice that the tone exudes gratefulness, and that is no coincidence. You should always bear in mind that first, the reviewers are performing service to their discipline – they don't get paid to do this or receive any recognition beyond maybe a list of reviewers the journal might publish to acknowledge their contribution. Not all journals do this. As you will see in time, not all reviewers read everything carefully before they start commenting on your work. They don't always tell you what needs to change, just what they do not like, leaving you wondering how exactly to address their wishes (notice how Hilal thanked them for not doing that). These are the people who will largely decide the fate of your paper for this outlet, so you should be courteous and grateful in your responses. And here is a secret: Even if your reviewers are not as well informed, polite, and helpful as Hilal's, you still need to respond as if they were. Think of it as being the bigger person, or taking the high road. If this is a journal you really want to publish in (and we established previously that it is), you have to go through the reviewers first, and you can catch more flies with honey than with vinegar.

We should also look specifically at why Hilal chose to start with a preface at all. It is like what we try to teach our students to do. You know how sometimes they write an email to you as if you are in the middle of a conversation and it is their turn, but you have no idea what they are talking about, or even what class or section they are in? We ask them to start emails with who they are, what class they are in, what assignment they are talking about, and so on. Try to put yourself in the reviewers' shoes and write accordingly. Wouldn't you like to see some pleasantries before diving back into work? In the preface, Hilal also reminds the reviewers that this was a paper they liked. By the time the reviewers read your letter, it will have been weeks (at least) since they have

13.3 Working with the Actionable Parts of Reviewer Comments

I would like to thank the reviewers for their positive feedback on my manuscript, especially regarding the originality of the study and the interest it can garner from the readership of the journal. I am also grateful to the reviewers for not only indicating the areas of improvement, but for also giving me very helpful pointers to address these shortcomings. I have highlighted each item that suggested a change and kept the cotext to help make sense of the suggestion. My responses are in corresponding shells. Thank you, and I hope I have been able to sufficiently address each point.

Reviewer 1 comments	Author responses
A significant part of the qualitative analysis (pp. 10–18) is dedicated to providing examples of different kinds of mitigators attested in the data under scrutiny. As already mentioned, this definitely helps readers grasp the relevant concepts/terms, but it seems rather unexpected and unjustified. In the preceding sections (as well as in the title of the paper), the author has placed particular emphasis on the role of smiling and does not clearly announce that part of the study is to demonstrate the wide range of mitigators identified in his/her data (on the contrary, the abstract appeals to be more informative concerning the content of the paper). My suggestion would therefore be that the author revises the introductory sections and the title so as to better prepare the readers for what is to follow. It is important to state from the beginning that the study is not exclusively about smiling.	Introductory section revised to better set up reader expectations, including explicitly stating that the paper is more than just smiling. Title of the paper also changed.
When the author discusses smiling as a mitigation strategy (pp. 18-27), s/he includes all the examples in a single, quite long section. The author could divide this analysis into smaller subsections so as to highlight the similarities or differences between different cases.	"Smiling as sole mitigator" subsection has been grouped into "enforcing the L2 only policy," "saying no," and "other"
Reviewer 2 comments	
On the whole, the ms. presents an original and very stimulating topic that is of great potential interest for [journal] readers. The data are taken from a corpus of 16 horns of recordings in three adult language classrooms in Turkey (some additional lines on the context of data gathering would be useful).	Additional information on the context of data gathering now added under the section entitled "The Current Study"
p.3, 1.44 "all smiles were positive.. ": clarify!	Clarified with a parenthetical and in the following paragraph
p. 2, 1.34 to lessen the face threat→to weaken	Changed.

Figure 13.2 Sample response to reviewer comments with a preface

seen your manuscript, so it is a smart idea to set up their expectations for what they are about to read, a paper they had previously praised. This is assuming that the revised manuscript goes to the same reviewers, but it is possible that it will go to different ones if the first reviewers did not agree to review it again or are not available. Then it is still a smart idea to tell the new reviewers right off the bat that this was a manuscript that the previous reviewers had really liked.

We now turn to the contents of the comments and the responses. The first thing to know here is that you have to address everything to the best of your ability; there is no picking and choosing what you want to work on and ignoring the rest. Hilal boldfaced the actionable parts of the comments to make sure she didn't miss any. If, for some reason, you are unable to make changes based on a comment, it is perfectly acceptable to say that, as long as you explain what that reason is, and it is a valid one. Maybe they are asking for demographic information on your participants and you have not collected that information; you can say so. Mostly, though, you will want to make all the changes and address all the comments thoroughly. Secondly, you will notice that not all comments ask for major changes, so don't let the sheer length of the list of reviewers' comments intimidate you. While some may require you to go back to the literature, others will be as simple as changing a single word. If you would like to read more on that, Rojon and Saunders (2015) compiled an anonymized list of reviewer comments ranked by how easy they are to address.

13.4 A Thematic Approach to Your Response to Reviewer Comments

While creating a table or spreadsheet is often the most straightforward approach to revisions, we would like to show an alternative method that Heather uses to structure responses to reviewers thematically. This method will not always be appropriate, but in those happy instances where the reviewers' comments are similar, this approach can be useful. Alternatively, this method can work well in instances where you receive contradictory feedback from your reviewers. For example, say that Reviewer #1 wants you to expand on one of your points, while Reviewer #2 wants you to cut that point altogether. By placing the reviewers' comments side-by-side, you send the not-so-subtle message that your work was probably fine as is, or at the very least, it would be impossible to completely satisfy both reviewers in this case.

Figure 13.3 shows an example of an introductory paragraph from a co-authored article on online community building, as well as the comments and responses related to the theme of cultures.

As you can see in Figure 13.3, this theme (number three out of five shared themes in the reviewers' comments, identified by the coauthors) includes one comment from Reviewer #1 and two comments from Reviewer #2. All comments relate to the term "cultures" as it is defined in the paper, so the coauthors

> **3. Cultures**
> *Comment from Reviewer 1:*
> "Cultures" needs to be further defined so it is not as vague. The authors seem to be confusing their definition of cultures with Cultures from the Standards. This may be why their results were not as definitive as they would have liked.
> *Comment from Reviewer 2:*
> Does "cultures" mean The American Council on the Teaching of Foreign Languages "Cultures" standard? This should be clarified.
> *Comment from Reviewer 2:*
> When authors first mention the second "C" in the section "Cultures and Online Spaces" on page 6, the definition is unclear and the term seems to come out of nowhere. Two pages later, on page 8, authors mention the second "C" again. Authors need to be more intentional with their use of quotes to make sure that they actually help establish the definitions and arguments that you are trying to create. At times, it seems like there are contradictory definitions for the same terms.
> *Revision:*
> Reviewers were correct in that our writing had at times conflated our definition of cultures with ACTFL's "Cultures" standard. We completed a major revision to define our study's relationship to both terms. In the Cultures and Online Spaces section of the Review of Literature, starting on page 5, we included several additional sources to help clarify our definition of cultures and how it relates to ACTFL's second C. With this revision, we also made the initial quote about ACTFL's 2nd C clearer. We clarified the research question in the Methods section to more clearly distinguish and define what we intended by cultures.

Figure 13.3 Thematically arranged responses to reviewer comments

found it appropriate to address all three comments together to avoid repetition and save time for the reviewers. In the response to the reviewers, the coauthors admit that their use of the term cultures was not clearly enough defined. They then go on to explain in detail exactly how and where they revised the paper to clarify the term. No matter what method you choose for responding to reviewer comments, your goal should be clarity and ease of understanding for the reviewers. You want them to be able to verify, as quickly as possible and with minimal effort on their part, that you have addressed all their concerns.

As you become more familiar with the process of submitting your work and receiving comments from reviewers, you will begin to notice common suggestions as part of the review experience. For instance, reviewers often recommend additional scholarship for your article or chapter. In best-case scenarios, the scholarship they suggest is relevant to your research and adds a valuable new perspective to your work. In worst-case scenarios, you may encounter reviewers who are trying to promote their own scholarship (which may or may not be relevant to your article) or who see the field through their own particular theoretical lens and believe that you should be using that same lens. In cases

110   13 Dealing with Reviewers' Comments

like this, if you can mention the work briefly to appease the reviewer, this might be the path of least resistance. If the publication they ask you to add simply does not make sense for your article, you may need to (very respectfully) craft a response demonstrating that you understand the work and have considered it but cannot include it because it is out of the scope of your argument.

13.5 Staying within the Word Limit While Revising

Even reviewers who truly want to be helpful may suggest an overwhelming amount of additional research. In this case, we suggest reading the reviewers' comment carefully to understand which sources are deal-breakers for them and which are truly suggestions. Check out the reviewer comment and response in Figure 13.4 for an example, similar to feedback Heather received for a chapter on a different topic.

The reviewer from Figure 13.4 asked Heather to expand the theoretical framework, noting that there are many other sources. They did not demand that she use one specific source or all of the sources they mentioned, so she felt comfortable choosing the theories that seemed most applicable to the chapter. Reviewers frequently ask for an expansion of ideas or concepts, even if you are already at the word limit. It then becomes your job to keep the reviewer happy by expanding your ideas while also staying within the word limit set by the journal. You can see an example of this in the comment reproduced in Figure 13.5.

In the case illustrated in Figure 13.5, Heather had to eliminate some examples in order to fully develop her ideas about other examples. She used her best judgment here, as she did not want to eliminate too many examples, not knowing which ones the reviewers found most convincing. While the revised document was 800 words over the limit, she felt comfortable submitting it with the highlighted paragraph that she had marked for elimination. The reviewer

---

Reviewer Comment: Although you argue that feminism is not the same around the world, your critical framework still focuses on western feminist studies, particularly [Theorist 1]. In order to create a more balanced, less Eurocentric approach, consider expanding your framework to include non-western scholarship. There are other sources, such as [Theorists 2, 3, and 4].

Response: I expanded my critical framework to be less Eurocentric. As you suggested, I incorporated [Theorist 1] with scholarship by [Theorists 2 and 4], You will find references to this framework throughout the chapter, with a particular introduction to [Theorist 1] on page 3, as well as a detailed explanation of [Theorist 2] on pages 7–8 and [Theorist 4]'s work on page 10.

Figure 13.4 Partial disagreement response to a reviewer comment

13.5 Staying within the Word Limit While Revising

> **Reviewer Comment**: This chapter covers an ambitious amount of material, but the central argument needs to be clarified to offer a more consistent argument about the texts under analysis throughout the chapter. The various literary texts need more contextualization in order to understand their value as literary artefacts.
>
> **Response**: Throughout the chapter, I tried to be more explicit in stating my arguments about the central topic of the essay, as seen through the literature and film. I eliminated some of the less convincing examples from the texts and films in order to expand slightly on other, more captivating examples. Even so, the revised chapter ended up at approximately 6,800 words. In the chapter, you will find the paragraph about the short story "Botella" highlighted, as well as two citations in the References section that pertain to that paragraph. I believe this paragraph could be eliminated without losing too much from the chapter. I would be happy to eliminate this paragraph and its references if you would like me to do so.

Figure 13.5 Response to a reviewer comment about expansion of content

agreed with Heather's assessment, the paragraph was eliminated, and everyone was happy.

Getting yourself to start working on revisions is a tricky business. Most of us resist it, and understandably so: it is work we had previously compartmentalized as "done and dusted," and it is difficult to drag it out and put it on the to-do list again. So how can you get yourself back into the process again? One thing we find useful is tricking our brains by initially focusing on the mechanical and simple stuff. First, you convince your brain to start working on this unwanted task by telling it that you are not actually working; you are just organizing to be ready for the moment when you will really start working. You sit down in front of the computer, and you pull up the review document. At this point, you just move the actionable items to the table/spreadsheet we covered above. You do not have to do a single thing more. Next, you tell yourself that you will *only* work on the really simple changes the reviewers wanted. You pull up the latest draft of the submission and rename the file to include "revised." You look through the list and pick the easiest changes to work on. You add or delete a word here, change a pronoun there. If you have taken just these two initial steps, what you have done is prepare all the files you need, and, while reading through the comments trying to find the simplest ones, really familiarize yourself with all the comments. Hopefully, at this point the remaining comments will not look as daunting. You will keep picking the next simplest task on the list, and before you know it, there will only be a few things left. No matter how major, you will be motivated to just finish the task. After all, the promise of a published paper is dangling right in front of you the whole time!

Questions for Reflection

1. Due to evolutionary reasons, the human mind dwells on the negative a lot more than the positive. Time to fight that tendency! What positive feedback have you received on your manuscript? Copy and paste the reviewer comments to a new document and highlight all the good things the reviewers said about your manuscript. Don't skip anything.
2. Self-preservation mode can sometimes color our judgment, and in the case of reviewer comments, we may feel inclined to think all the comments are garbage. If you find yourself angrily dismissing all of the comments, try to work through the anger and approach the comments objectively. To start, what three reviewer requests can you convince yourself to work on?

Questions for Discussion

1. If your relationship allows, ask your colleagues to share memories of dealing with reviewer comments that hopefully led to eventual publications. How was the process for them?
2. Are there any requests for changes from the reviewers you are thinking about declining? Discuss with your colleagues how to best counter them, and what change(s) you can make instead that you are happy with (ending the refusal on a positive note).

Questions for Your Mentor

1. What particular comments from the reviewers in your current round of revisions are proving difficult for you? These comments could be unclear, ask too much, have multiple ways in which they could be addressed, and so on. What insights can your mentor provide for you?
2. The first time you prepare a response to reviewer comments can be tricky. Would your mentor be willing to look it over for content and style?

Part III

The Genres

14   Writing for Different Audiences

All writing has a component of rhetoric. Part of it is persuasion, especially when it comes to academic writing. When you write academic texts, you are trying to convince readers (editors, reviewers, colleagues, committees, journal readers, book readers, etc.) that you have something important to say and something worthwhile to contribute to the field. You need them to understand you in order to be able to convince them of anything. For that reason, you need to start from where they are and build the text up from there, while keeping the conventions and requirements of the specific medium in mind. In other words, you need to show audience awareness. Who is your audience? What do they know? Why are they reading your piece? As active academics, we all participate in conferences and conventions to present our research. The focus of the conference is our first consideration when preparing our presentations. If it is a pragmatics conference, for instance, we do not bother going into detail about well-known concepts in that field. We assume everyone knows and is interested in these things, hence their attendance at a pragmatics conference. If the presentation at this same conference ties pragmatics into second language acquisition, however, then we need to more carefully define and describe our terms, so the audience isn't lost listening to us. They are experts of pragmatics, not second language acquisition. Academic writing should be like that as well; the main questions are, who is your audience and what do they need in order to understand you? In this introductory chapter to the different academic genres of writing, we discuss writing for different audiences with examples from common conversions (such as from conference presentation to article manuscript) and practical tips.

14.1   Publishing Your Dissertation

Many early career researchers find it difficult to differentiate between writing for a dissertation committee and writing with academic authority. You do not want your papers or book screaming, "I was a dissertation" (see Elsevier, 2018, for useful lists of the differences). While writing a dissertation, you were mostly concerned about making the process transparent. If you made a claim, you talked about who else made that claim – at length. If you conducted a statistical analysis, you shared not only the results, but all the steps and relevant details of your analysis. You wanted your chair and the committee to see that you had done your homework, as you should have. You also needed to provide all that in case there were any errors in interpretation and reporting. In sum, you did not speak from a place of authority (because you did not hold that authority yet). The rules of the game have now changed. You are an initiated member of the scholarly community, and you need to speak (and write) as such.

That is not to say you no longer have to show a basis for your claims or make your process transparent, of course, but the output will look different. Instead of going into detail about every little concept or classification or idea, you can (and will have to, due to space constraints) briefly summarize them or pay your dues to them with parenthetical citations. Some of them will need to be skipped altogether. Your data, instead of going in the manuscript, can be shared as separate files if your chosen journal has a database for it or directs you to one. Therefore, pages and pages of texts and visuals from your dissertation will have to remain in your dissertation. For instance, in her dissertation, Hilal spent upwards of 500 words defining the term oral corrective feedback, citing numerous sources and examining the term itself along with terms that it partially and fully overlaps with. She had to do this because the committee needed to see that she knew what the term meant, where it came from, what other terms it overlapped with, and so on. She had to show that she had done the work, because that's what her audience expected. In her first published paper, she took about forty words to define the same term. She knew that the paper was not a dissertation, and she didn't have to prove her deep knowledge of something (publishing in a peer-reviewed, internationally indexed scholarly journal is already proof of that), and that the reader needed only a statement to define her use of the term. That was it, and that is what we mean by writing for a committee versus writing with academic authority.

The confusion between the two happens so often that publishers and other experts keep warning writers against it; for instance, take this advice from De Gruyter, a reputable European publisher: "Remember, a book is not a dissertation. You do not need to convince anyone anymore that you are the expert and that you have done your reading. The reader of your book trusts that you are, and that is why they bought it" (Rittgerodt & Wagenhofer, 2021, para. 14). Similar warnings are also available from Elsevier (Mesquita, 2018) and Taylor & Francis (*Extracting a Journal Article from Your Thesis: Top Tips from Award-Winning Author*, n.d.), among others.

14.2   Turning Class Papers into Publications

As a student, you produced many, many papers as part of your coursework during your tenure in an academic program. Some of these papers are for the professor's eyes only and meant to stay that way. Not every class paper should be turned into a publication. However, some are good. To identify a "good" class paper, one that has potential for publication, see if it contributes something to the field. Go beyond the limited research you likely did at the time and really dive into the research; perhaps you have something novel. Another way to identify a promising paper could be through your professor's feedback. When we run into an impressive piece of scholarship as professors, we make sure to let students know, so go back and look for feedback from your professors on papers you were especially proud of. If you are still a student, you can consider borrowing a page from Heather's book. As a graduate student, she would always save papers that got really good comments into a special folder on her computer for potential future publications and similar expansions. When she started her tenure-track job, she already had quite a few potential papers that she could choose to work on.

Class papers that fit the bill can be improved to submit to a journal. The keyword here is "improved"; what you write as a course assignment will almost never be enough for publication as is. The most important reason is the difference in the overall goal of the two texts. For a class paper, you are trying to convince your professor that you have understood course content, done the readings, and can now summarize or synthesize information. For a journal article, you have full authority on the subject, and your goal is to disseminate information to other scholars who are now your peers. Let's look at an example. When writing a paper for her Language and Culture in the Classroom course as a graduate student, Hilal used the very important concept of *pragmatic failure*, which was central to her argument (of explicitly teaching second language learners about pragmatics). However, she only cited it from the coursebook. She probably only read about it in the coursebook, as well. Now if she were to change that paper for publication, she would have to really look into the concept. Who coined the term? Why is it significant? What classifications of it are out there? Who else used it in research relevant to Hilal's? These are but a few of the questions that need to be answered before that class paper can be ready for submission to a scientific journal.

As you change your narrative and the quality of your work for publication, consider the following: The professor may have expected only a small number of references, required course readings to be cited (or not be cited), asked for a smaller word count than you would need for a publication, and so on. Also, if some time has passed, you may need to update your references. You may have analyzed a small number of data, not explained all of your methodological choices, or forgotten to cite important works in your literature review. These aspects of your work will need to be improved for your paper to be good enough for submission to a scholarly journal. Always remember who will be reading your paper and why.

14.3 Turning Conference Papers into Publications

Contrary to class papers, conference papers are, in most cases, already halfway to publication. You have already established a research question (or five) that the organizers and/or reviewers thought was noteworthy, done at least some of the work, shared it with the conference participants, and hopefully received some feedback on your work. Now it's time to use that feedback and get ready to submit.

The traditional conference presentation model where there is time for a Q&A at the end is the best opportunity to get useful feedback, though you may run into members of your audience after the presentation and talk about it, or they may even seek you out to ask more questions or give you their appraisal. People's questions will prompt you to approach your study from different angles, possibly reinterpret your results, and overall indicate whether or not your presentation was received well (if the questions build on what you presented, participants likely saw no issues with anything; if they question your choices or ask for more-than-simple clarifications on slides, then that's different feedback you definitely need to take into account). There may also be questions that are barely relevant or interesting; use your expertise to filter those out. In any case, do not view the Q&A as something to get over with. We understand that it's nerve-racking to present to other experts. You just finished this ordeal and are still riding the adrenaline, making it difficult to focus on the questions. Still, make an effort to reground yourself and pay attention so you can not only answer them to the best of your ability, but also write them down afterwards, so that you are likely to have something useful for the betterment of your paper. It's best to write the questions down immediately after the presentation lest you forget. At Hilal's last conference presentation, the audience members practically wrote the discussion section of the pending manuscript for her.

After presenting a paper at a conference, the natural next step is to write it up and submit it to a peer-reviewed scientific journal. You will need to make some changes and possibly expand the coverage first. A conference paper may be reporting on a limited number of data points or an ongoing study, but journals, editors, reviewers, and readers will expect more. Due to time restrictions at conferences, your literature review probably is not exhaustive, either. Conference papers usually only cite works of immediate relevance to the study. A paper needs to place the study in the larger context of the field. Again, it comes down to who you are writing for and why. At a conference, you are simply informing people of what you are doing and what you have found so far, asking (even if implicitly) for feedback. In a peer-reviewed article, you are doing all of that, *plus* situating your contribution in the larger field with more extensive connections and overt significance.

Audience awareness becomes a focal point in this process, as well. First of all, the tone and audience of different journals will vary. As always with your outlet choices, pay close attention to the scope and readership of the journal of your choice as presented on their website. How do they define their readership? Look at the papers in the sample issue that's available free of charge. What is the tone of the papers? Sometimes they are more research-oriented, sometimes geared more toward practitioners, for instance. You will emphasize different aspects of your research accordingly, knowing that researchers are less likely to be interested in practical tips, as practitioners are less interested in the details of, say, study design.

Second, the mode of delivery between a conference paper and a manuscript is different. Even if you wrote your paper down and read it out loud as a presentation (e.g., in literature, scholars often write their paper down and read it out loud at the conference, whereas in applied linguistics, scholars present their work primarily in spontaneous speech, using visual aids and moving around), it will need to change. Even though conference presentations involve highly academic language, spoken and written language will invariably differ, and adjustments will need to be made.

Third, the participants of the conference and readers of your journal may be different in terms of the scope of their expertise; things that did not need explaining at the conference may need to be laid out more clearly for the journal audiences, and vice versa. Speaking of clarity, a presentation can always be further clarified during the Q&A, but for published papers, what you put on the page is what the audience gets, which makes a clear line of argumentation a lot more important. Besides, once you have made your presentation, your audience cannot return your work to you if you did a subpar job. It's done. Journal editors can, though, and they will.

Action item!

Choose a course paper you are working on right now or plan to work on in the near future. Select a paragraph in which you are crafting your main argument or discussing an important concept.

Now, think about the following different audiences and rewrite that same paragraph to convey the same argument or discuss the same concept. Examples could be an advanced undergraduate course for students with little to no prior experience in this area, a specialized academic conference with experts who are well versed on this subject, or an academic paper in a specialized journal.

Consider the following issues: How much time or space (words) will you have? Will you speak or write? What is your goal (making sure the concept/argument is understood, employing the concept to then build on it in your research, convincing colleagues of your novel argument)? Do you need additional examples or other materials?

Overall, writing for different audiences involves putting yourself in others' shoes and anticipating and fulfilling their expectations, while also abiding by the conventions necessitated by the medium. There are questions to constantly ask yourself, such as "What is my role as the author?"; "What voice is appropriate?"; "Who will read this?"; "Why will they read this?"; and "What are they likely to already know, and what needs more explanation?" This rhetorical awareness that we constantly employ in our day-to-day lives without even realizing is relatively easy to apply to our writing once it is brought to the forefront of the mind.

Questions for Reflection

1. Think back to your coursework. Do you have any papers that you received particularly stellar feedback on from your professor? Or one that you invested a lot of time and effort into? Consider how you might start adapting this paper into a version of itself that could be sent out for review and potential publication.
2. Look through your past conference presentations. If the subject is still relevant and the contribution timely, is any of them worth turning into a paper?

Questions for Discussion

1. With colleagues or friends, discuss your current research projects so they can help you identify which papers you should focus on preparing for submission for publication. If you haven't considered preparing any of these projects for publication, could it be that impostor syndrome is telling you your work is not good enough for publication (see Chapter 2 for more on impostor syndrome)?
2. Bring some of your work that you think may be worth trying to publish. Share and give each other feedback on what changes need to be made, considering the different audiences involved.

Questions for Your Mentor

1. After finding a promising paper to edit for submission into a scholarly journal, with your mentor, discuss the differences in your old and new audience and what changes you should make to transform the class paper into the first draft of a publishable article.
2. If your mentor previously taught you, ask them whether they remember anything they read from you that impressed them. It could be the basis of your next paper!

15 Choosing the Right Outlet

Many early career researchers struggle with finding the right journal to publish in. Whether you already have a manuscript or you're just starting, we've got you. In what follows, we will focus on journal articles, because they tend to be one of the most common and cross-disciplinary genres, but this information can be adapted to any genre (book reviews, reports, white papers, encyclopedia entries, etc.).

15.1 Journal Rankings

Within any given discipline, there are many journals to choose from. For example, there are 106 journals in "Cognitive neuroscience." Many of them are more specific, perhaps dedicated to autism or aging disorders, but a few journals are general, meaning they cover topics of interest to all scholars in that field. Depending on the nature of your paper, you will choose the most relevant journal.

However, this is only the first step. Journals are ranked, either informally or formally. Formal rankings are published by various organizations, using various methodologies. For example, the impact factor measures how often the average paper in a journal is quoted over a three-year window (it is published by Clarivate, which owns the Web of Science). Scimago publishes rankings for Scopus publications (Scopus is owned by Elsevier). Google publishes the h-index and ranks journals on its basis. Most of these rankings use bibliometrics data, meaning data on publications and their citations. For example, the h-index is the number of articles having at least h citations (if you have five papers with at least five citations, your h-index is five). If you add up all the h-indexes of a journal, you get an overall h-index. Essentially, these metrics measure, in one way or another, how many citations the articles get, on the assumption that more influential papers get cited more. Other metrics are based on interviewing experts, on how often papers are quoted in social media, and even the number of web links to the articles (another Google metric). Informal rankings are the word-of-mouth assessment of your peers, colleagues, and respected elders in the field. "That's a hard journal to get into" is the best review you can get, whereas "They take anything" is as bad as it gets. Believe it or not, informal rankings may be quite important, because it is rare for a tenure committee or a colleague to actually look up rankings. Most academics trust their opinions, which can be a good or a bad thing, depending on how reliable they are. Neither is infallible. Moreover, in the humanities, metrics are considered less significant while the general prestige of the journal is more important. If you want to get a sense of how valued certain journals are in your field, one strategy is to check the CVs of other academics whose work you have read and admired, especially those who are working on similar topics to yours. This is a good way to find potential venues to publish your work, and you might even learn about new journals.

Obviously, you want to publish in the highest-ranked, most prestigious journals, all other things being equal. What we mean is that there may be good reasons to choose a lower-ranked journal if the fit is better content-wise. You want the specialists in your field to read (and possibly quote) your work. For this reason, it may be better to publish in a topic-specific lower-ranked journal.

Action item!

One way to select a range of journals for which your work would be a good fit is to look at the references you cite in your paper. Go through the list of references of your paper and focus on the journals where those works were published. Make a list of the three to five most popular ones among your references. These are all potential publication avenues for your work.

15.2 Tiers and Expectations

Academics sometimes speak of top- and bottom-tier journals, or of Q1-Q2-Q3-Q4 journals. There are no agreed upon definitions, except that the Q1 notation refers to the top quartile (top 25 percent) of journals, according to a given metric, Q2 to the second quartile, and so on. Top tier may refer to Q1 journals, but also more generally to the top 33 percent (if you assume a top, mid, and bottom tier), or possibly to the top 50 percent as opposed to the bottom half. Regardless of the specifics of how you or your supervisor, tenure committee, funding agency, or other entity that pays your salary define top and bottom tiers, the reality is that there are different expectations for the tiers.

These expectations can be hard to define generally, because, in part, they are discipline- and field-specific. However, we can attempt to draw some generalizations. Top-tier journals are leaders in their fields, so they expect to publish articles that advance and possibly shape the field itself, and they look for articles of considerable significance (high impact). If you replicate a study and you find that the study was essentially correct, your chances of publishing this in a top-tier journal are very low. If your replication fails, unless the study is considered a cornerstone of the field, it will not be general enough to warrant publication in a top-tier journal, either. Conversely, if your replication fails, but you present a different theoretical interpretation that accounts for the original data and those from your study, then suddenly your chances of getting into a top-tier journal increase. It is crucial that you select a journal of the appropriate tier for your paper. It can be hard to be objective about your work, so as always, seek the advice of your mentors or peers.

Some disciplines have academic wikis (https://humanitiesjournals.fandom.com/wiki/Humanities_Journals_Wiki) or websites dedicated to journals within the field, where individuals can learn more about others' interactions with a particular journal. While these are not official sites, individuals can anonymously post about their experiences with different journals (quick or unreasonable wait times, types of feedback received from reviewers, tips for submitting a manuscript, etc.). You will need to be a critical reader of these comments, of course; one disgruntled author's rant may not be extremely helpful, but a pattern of negative or positive comments is revealing.

Action item!

When choosing between two or three possible outlets for your work, assuming these are all aligned with the scope of your work, consider what is important to you at this particular time of your career or in relation to the topic of your paper.

Is prestige relevant (maybe because your tenure review is getting closer)?

Does the language of publication align with your work (if you are planning to write about the acquisition of Spanish, should you write your article in Spanish and find a journal that publishes in Spanish)?

Do you have a specific journal readership in mind (language practitioners, scholars who work on race, etc.)?

Is accessibility an issue you care about? Do you want to publish in an open access venue?

Pick the two most relevant criteria and then, using the journals' webpages, compare and rank them.

15.3 Predatory Publishing

So far we have assumed that all the journals in a field are bona fide journals, dedicated to furthering science and knowledge. However, this is not always the case. Predatory publishing is a relatively novel phenomenon that has had a serious negative impact on scientific and academic writing. You know how you sometimes get emails from "scientific" journals that act like you're the God of the field, and your contribution to their journal is going to essentially save humanity, even though you may be in actuary science and the journal in question is in dentistry? Those are the easiest to label as predatory publishers. They aren't always that obvious, though, so here is the nitty gritty. In a nutshell, predatory publishing is any form of publishing (books, journals, conferences, etc.) that, under the pretense of offering a venue for scholars to disseminate their work, seeks to extract payments from the scholars. The crucial word here is the "pretense" aspect. It is normal for conferences, for example, to charge an attendance fee: How would they pay for using the rooms, the AV equipment, printing the programs, and so on? The same goes for publishing books and journals. Many respectable university presses and scholarly publishers cannot generate enough revenue to justify publishing books that sell only a few hundred copies. So, they survive on state funding and other forms of support, including asking authors or their institutions to help defray the costs of publishing.

This all changed with the advent of digital typesetting and distribution and on-demand printing. In the 1990s, the publishing industry switched to digital production (books are printed off digital files, such as pdfs). It is far cheaper to email a pdf than to print it out on paper, bind it, and ship the physical object. The digital revolution allowed the distribution of digital files essentially for free. The other revolutionary technology is the print-on-demand machine: While fairly expensive (it can cost a quarter of a million dollars), they can produce one copy of a book or hundreds at the same cost. This allows publishers to avoid having to print a run of a book (which is an expensive proposition, as the books must be then stored and shipped, returns must be handled, etc.) and instead print when a would-be reader orders it from an online bookstore.

Suddenly the traditional constraints on the production of academic works, printing journals and books in hard copy and in one print run, were gone: This opened up two predatory markets, predatory book publishing and predatory journals. While the mechanics are different, the underlying idea is the same: a gullible academic is lured by the siren song of publication into paying money to publish their work by a publisher with no standards. Predatory publishers accept and publish anything they receive. As we discuss in Chapter 29 (Open access science), their goal is to publish as many papers or books as possible, because they collect more from every submission. Now, you might object saying that this is true for journals, but what about those publishers that will publish your book and do not charge you upfront fees? How can they make money? This objection is misguided: In the old (hard copy) publishing model, indeed, they would lose their shirts, so that is why publishers were very careful about what they chose to publish and made sure it was reviewed by some well-established scholars. They needed to ensure

15.3 Predatory Publishing

that they would recoup their expenses and make money on top of that, in addition to wanting to advance knowledge. However, in the print-on-demand model, aside from the cost of the print-on-demand machine, which is a one-time expense, they can literally print a single copy of your book. Then if your mother buys a copy (or you buy one to send to her), or you purchase a couple of copies for your promotion committee, or someone randomly comes across your book and is intrigued enough to buy it, it is almost pure profit. Print-on-demand has virtually no expenses, as they typically don't advertise your book; that's up to you. You may object that they can't make a lot of money that way. That is absolutely correct, but the model works extremely well at volume: if you have a thousand books that generate $100 profit each, suddenly you are in the six figures revenue.

While the details of predatory journals vary (we discuss them in Chapter 29), the principle is the same: accept anything and make money in volume. Getting caught in a predatory publishing scheme is a very bad deal for the naive writer. Not only does the publication not "count" toward tenure or any annual report of your activities (since there is no merit in publishing a piece in a venue that accepts anything) but it nonetheless counts as having been published. Most serious journals will not accept it if you try to resubmit it after finding out you were tricked. This is true for articles in journals and books.

If you work for an organization that self-publishes reports or white papers (which are, essentially, informative reports about a topic or project), such as the National Endowment for the Humanities, you don't run the risk of submitting to a predatory journal or publisher. However, you still have the problem of recognizing sources that have been published in predatory venues, in order to avoid them, as they have not been properly reviewed. Let's be clear that being published in a predatory venue is not definitive evidence that a source is useless. Anyone could end up having a chapter in a book published by a predatory press. Sal submitted a paper to the proceedings of a conference which, he was told, was going to be published by Cambridge UP. When he received a copy of the book, it was published by Cambridge Scholars – not quite the same. Authors of chapters in books often have little control over what the editors do. The same goes for articles in journals. Writers may end up publishing articles that might have made the cut in a proper journal in a predatory venue, just because they received a solicitation and figured, why not? Having said this, having multiple publications in a predatory journal affects your credibility as a scholar.

15.3.1 Avoiding Predatory Publishers

So, how do you keep your work away from all things predatory? Let's start with predatory presses. First, talk to your colleagues, mentors, and other experienced writers who have published books in your field and look at the presses they used. Presumably they went with good presses. Second, do your homework. Research the publisher before submitting anything or even contacting them. Obviously if the publisher is famous or one of the top publishers in your field, you may skip this step (Cambridge University Press, anyone?). If you are not familiar with the publisher, check what else they have published. Do you recognize any names? Are they good scholars? Completely ignore any promises of help, financial returns, facilitations, ease of processing, or marketing that the publisher may make. They are most likely empty verbiage. If you can, check their product. For example, is it professionally typeset and proofread? Any flaws should be a red flag. Third, if the press approaches you, especially using flattering language like we mentioned above, consider that a very bad sign, especially if you are early in your career. While a press may contact you for a project, this only happens when your name has become a selling point, which won't be right out of graduate school for most of us. Predatory presses target freshly minted PhDs and authors who submit papers to conferences, so be extra vigilant and always ask your advisor if you have any doubt. Fourth, look up Beall's list of predatory publishers. It was removed from the University of Colorado's website because of the threats of lawsuits, but it was archived and is now available in various places on the internet, such as https://beallslist.net/. Another resource is Cabell's list, which is behind a paywall, but your organization may have access to it. To sum it up, don't commit to publishing your precious book with any publisher you have not thoroughly vetted.

Avoiding predatory journals and articles is harder. Some predatory journals go as far as impersonating prestigious journals, by replicating their websites (while changing the contact information) or by providing fake mailing addresses and phone numbers to make it appear as if they are located in the United States or Europe. If you receive an email soliciting publication in a journal, assume it is predatory. If you want to check it out, don't click on links they provide, but search for the journal and go to their webpage independently. This way you can be sure you are not being spoofed.

Unlike outright mendacious operations, most predatory journals are fairly open about what they do. They advertise the speed of their refereeing (it's fake, of course; they accept anything), some going as far as promising acceptance within a few days. Obviously you should steer as far away from these as possible. You know what they say: if it looks too good to be true, it probably is. Other journals muddy the waters by claiming that they do not require Article Processing Charges (APCs), but they charge "typesetting" or "proofing" fees that can add up. You should again not have to pay for services that journals provide as a matter of course, nor should you pay for "editing" or "language checking" if you are a non-native speaker of English. Any journal that promises to accept your paper in days, or weeks, is predatory. A good journal will take at least a couple of months to do reviews, and often much longer. Another dead

15.3 Predatory Publishing

giveaway of a problematic journal are spelling or grammar mistakes in the copy on the journal webpage or amateurish typesetting.

To make things more complicated, there are legitimate journals, some well-known, that charge exorbitant APCs, offer language-checking services for a fee, take a normal time to review, and provide legitimate reviews. However, their publishing model pushes editors to accept as many papers as possible and thus increase their revenue. Ultimately, the alignment of incentives is negative and the quality of the journals is bound to drop, so in our opinion you should avoid any journal that charges APCs, unless they are the normal practice in your field. Your advisor or mentor will be able to tell you about that.

Finally, with plenty of excellent diamond (free) open access journals available (see Chapter 29, Open Access Science), why would you waste your hard-earned cash to pay for APCs? In our opinion, it's best to resist the lure of special issues to which you are invited, if participating will cost you three thousand dollars. Rather, suggest that the special issue be moved to a diamond journal or, better yet, edit your own special issue in a diamond journal. The best way to avoid falling for predatory journals is to never pay for publication, unless of course this is the norm in your field.

Questions for Reflection

1. Do you have an aspirational list of journals? What journals are "too good" for you to submit to? What would it take for you to submit to one of those?
2. Do you regret submitting to any journal or proceedings? Why? What made it a mistake? How can you avoid this in the future?

Questions for Discussion

1. With colleagues, discuss what you consider to be the top five journals in your field? What criteria did you and your colleagues consider in the creation of this list?
2. What strategies do your colleagues use to avoid predatory journals and make sure a publishing invitation they receive is legitimate?

Questions for Your Mentor

1. What are the best matches between your research and journals in your field? You can discuss this in general or with regards to a specific paper you are working on.
2. What are the best journals to submit to, in terms of overall experience?

16 From Dissertation to Publication

You have successfully written and defended a dissertation. Congratulations! Some dissertations remain unpublished, but we hope that yours does not meet that end. Some turn into books, and some turn into several papers, as is our focus in this chapter. The advantage of starting your publishing journey with your dissertation is twofold. First, you have already done the work. You have saturated yourself in the relevant research, collected the data, done the analyses, and drawn the conclusions. Now you need to repackage your work into one or more smaller, yet impactful, pieces. The other advantage is the vote of confidence. At the beginning of the tenure process, or when you are still in the job market, impostor syndrome (see Chapter 2) usually runs rampant in our minds. Coupled with the fear of the unknown that is the publishing process, you can constantly doubt your ideas and competence. With your dissertation, however, even if you do not (yet) trust your own judgment, you can trust your committee's. Multiple scholars from your department, and one from outside your department or institution, thought your dissertation was a good idea. You have received a lot of feedback on it and have already perfected it. They gave you a doctorate for it! Armed with this confidence, you are bound to feel more secure in the quality of your work, which should hopefully help you through the process. Now it's time to publish your hard work.

16.1 Reasons to Publish Your Dissertation

An academic quip goes as follows: a good dissertation is a done dissertation. A great dissertation is a published dissertation. A perfect dissertation is neither. You should publish your dissertation, and do so expeditiously (within a few years of your graduation). There are three reasons to publish your dissertation work. We review them in this chapter and then address how to do so.

Before we get into that, however, we would like to acknowledge the possibility that you are very tired, and you might think your dissertation is unworthy of seeing the light of day ever again. Writing a dissertation involves years of hard work like you've never experienced before. It is mentally taxing and academically rigorous, and it wreaks havoc on your previously well-established self-confidence. You got

16.1 Reasons to Publish Your Dissertation

into a doctorate program because you most likely excelled at everything academic. After passing through the wringer of grad school, you probably feel like you almost didn't make it, like you barely passed, or like your work is not worth much. If this is not your experience, that's wonderful. However, these thoughts and feelings are very common, so if it is your experience, please know that you are not alone (and take a look at Chapter 2 on impostor syndrome). If you are unable to convince yourself that your dissertation is worth publishing, perhaps you can appeal to your analytic side: What is the worst that can happen? If your dissertation is indeed not worth publishing, then the editors and reviewers can let you know (though you really should try multiple times before you believe them). They can also accept it. Moreover, your dissertation director and your committee members assessed your dissertation positively, so much so that they were willing to sign off on it. How likely is it that they did so just to get rid of you? Their reputations in the field would not last long if they did that routinely.

The first reason for publishing your dissertation is that you have already done the bulk of the work. Your dissertation established significant expertise in a certain corner of the discipline, so letting it sit in the cloud or in your drawer would be a waste. Switching to a different topic will require retraining yourself and reading widely in a new area. You are far better off exploiting your expertise in the topic of your dissertation. If you try to rationalize your reluctance to publish by arguing that your research is already available to scholars through such services as ProQuest, you should remember that many scholars refrain from quoting unpublished dissertations and that most meta-analyses do not include dissertations. Dissertations are part of what is known as "gray" literature, not quite officially published, such as white papers, reports, and working papers.

The second reason is that a published dissertation has been found to be the best predictor of academic success in various disciplines, such as social work (Green et al., 1992). Among postdoctoral factors predicting success, having served as a peer-reviewer and having a stable academic position were the first and second most important factors, far ahead of time dedicated to research. Given this result alone, publishing your dissertation sounds like a good idea. However, there is an even more powerful reason to do so. In order to discuss it, we first need to review some startling evidence about publication patterns amongst PhD graduates.

Only 25 percent of psychology dissertations are published (Evans et al., 2018) and the figure is quite similar for social work dissertations: 28.8 percent (Maynard et al., 2014). Pediatric medical dissertations in France show the same pattern (27.9 percent). The delay is 2.2 years (Fabre, 2015). There is significant variation, however, as Santos et al. (1998) report that 96.6 percent of doctoral and masters' theses at one research-based program resulted in at least one publication and 24 percent resulted in five or more. Lee (2000) found significant differences between chemistry, psychology, and literature: chemistry

PhDs publish more than PhDs in psychology, and they both publish more than literature PhDs in the period of 1965–1995, although the literature PhDs narrow the gap in the later years. Dinham and Scott (2001) found that 43 percent of PhDs "disseminated" their research, either via conference presentation or through a paper. They also found a notable difference caused by supervisor's support/encouragement (for more on mentoring, see Chapter 27). Anwar (2004, p. 152) argues that these results are program-specific. Fabre (2015) reviews seven studies from various countries worldwide and shows that the percentage of medical dissertations that are published ranges between 5.8 percent and 30 percent. Anwar (2004) studied a group of fifty-four library science graduates for a ten-year window (the five years to complete the degree and five years after that). Fifty percent of the graduates did not publish at all. The other 50 percent overall published less than two papers per dissertation, not counting publications unrelated to the dissertation.

The time frame of publication is also significant. Anwar notes that about 60 percent of publications took place within two years of completion of the dissertation, which would suggest these scholars started the process as soon as they graduated. There is a general consensus that a five-year window is sufficient to document the productivity of a graduate. The exception here is Lee (2000), who considers only one year after graduation. In other words, it is unlikely that a dissertation will lead to a publication after more than five years. Green et al. (1992) find a negative correlation between years since graduation and publication.

Given the surprisingly low number of publications that come out of dissertations, publishing your results is a great idea, because it signals that you are an outstanding researcher (literally, you stand out from the rest who do not publish).

16.2   Turning Your Dissertation into Several Papers

A dissertation can be split into several papers in different ways (based on research questions, data, methodology, etc.). First, though, a word to the wise: don't separate what needs to be a single paper into multiple papers. This is referred to as salami slicing or salami publication, and it is considered a form of self-plagiarism (see Chapter 5). Your dissertation is a good candidate to be published in several papers, for instance, if you worked with several research questions that are inevitably connected but also distinct from each other. A distinct research question would have led you to collect separate data from the other questions, take a different outlook, implement a different method of analysis, utilize different statistical tests, and so on. Let's say you conducted an ethnography of a workplace. Your analyses for the dissertation may have focused on the employees' perspective and the employers' perspective separately, which can now be reported in two separate papers. The division into several papers could also be methodological. Perhaps your dissertation focused on teacher immediacy behaviors in the classroom in which those behaviors have been described using the accepted parameters in the field and then analyzed for effectiveness based on student success as operationalized by the retention of specific target items. Provided that your description of the immediacy behaviors has revealed information that would contribute to the theoretical discussion in the field, that could be a separate qualitative paper. Then, the effectiveness of those behaviors for the students would be a separate quantitative paper where you run statistical tests on the data points. Take a look back at your research questions and subquestions. How many of them can warrant separate papers?

Action item!

To get started, scan through the results section of your dissertation, where you present all the data you have, or go back and have a look at the raw data files. Can some of these data be analyzed from a different perspective (different statistical analyses or theoretical lens)? Are there data you did not analyze or include in your dissertation? If yes, write it down. You may have found an idea for a new paper.

Another approach is to scan through the discussion and conclusions from your dissertation. Make a short list with the main findings from your work (no more than one sentence per result). Can some of these results be presented independently, without omitting anything crucial and without too much overlap with your previous work? If the answer is yes, you may have found your next paper.

You could also take a slightly different approach, depending on what your dissertation can contribute to your field and on whether you are willing to add to it a little. As journal editors Halpern and Phelan (2020) put it, "[y]our dissertation is not a display case for a single fully formed diamond. It's a storeroom of gems in various stages of processing, and you are the lapidary" (para. 27). For example, perhaps you have a strong literature review that you might turn into a state-of-the-art article or synthesis paper. Maybe you created a detailed spreadsheet on your sources as you were writing your literature review for the dissertation, and it can now help you create a literature synthesis or a meta-analysis. Alternatively, your dissertation may have had a teaching-oriented focus. It would have invariably had a theoretical component, but now you can separate the theoretical part from the teaching-oriented part. While submitting the former in a more research-oriented journal, you can add materials and guidelines for teachers to the latter and publish it in a practitioner-oriented outlet. Another possibility is to analyze your existing data in new ways, with new questions.

For instance, Hilal had conducted an entire replication study as part of her dissertation, but the results never found their way into the dissertation because the replication was a side product of the framework she was using and not the focus of her research questions. She later published that study separately. It was work that had mostly been completed anyway; she just had to run some different tests. Heather's dissertation consisted of several chapters, each of which functioned as a comparative literary analysis of two texts. She ultimately decided to publish her dissertation as a book, but there was one chapter that didn't fit as nicely with the rest of the chapters. Heather removed this chapter from the book project, divided it into two articles (one on each literary text), and published two journal articles from that chapter. The list of approaches to splitting your dissertation could go on, but we are hoping these give you an idea as to your options. It may be worth consulting your dissertation chair and/or committee members on this, too, since they know the work well and may not mind offering you some guidance as to the best route for your specific situation. Remember, if it seems utterly unsplittable, then maybe it is meant to become a book (more on this in the next section).

> **Action item!**
> Typically, in the conclusion section, you mention future avenues for research and limitations of your dissertation. Pick one of these tasks from your dissertation conclusion to expand upon in your next paper. This will be easier than starting from scratch, because you most likely will be able to reuse some of what you already wrote (like parts of your literature review).

Once you have identified what the first paper from your dissertation will be focused on, your first instinct may be to start copy-and-pasting text and tables and figures from the dissertation to a new document. Resist that urge, because you need to start the writing process from scratch, for two reasons. First, your new papers cannot read like a dissertation (see Chapter 14 for strategies on avoiding this). Second, copying and pasting information isn't very helpful when you're trying to split the dissertation into multiple papers instead of producing a single paper.

There is only a certain degree of overlap between different papers based on the same dissertation that is allowable, and you will need to make sure you are not repeating the same things over and over. The first overlap that is allowed is mostly thematic. It is not only OK but expected for a researcher to have a niche and to organize their research efforts around it. It is also perfectly acceptable for them to subscribe to a specific methodology or theoretical framework. And finally, it is acceptable to analyze the same data as long as the research questions and contributions to the field are new and noteworthy. These three things are a pretty exhaustive list of components that can be similar across papers. And "similar" does not mean "the same." You still need to explain these things in original ways for all your papers (in fact, many journals ask you to address this issue explicitly in the cover letter; see Appendix H for a sample cover letter). You need to decide in advance what goes into one paper, what goes into another, and another, as needed. For example, you may initially think that the methodology and analyses may be easily divisible, but the review of literature is going to be the same for all the papers (leading you to think you will have to rewrite the same thing multiple times), but you may be pleasantly surprised. The literature review is dependent on the research questions; once you separate the research questions, they will take the relevant review of literature with them. If it is a theory-versus-practice divide you are striving toward, then the practitioner-oriented piece will require a lot less theory and much less scientific jargon.

To avoid both of these pitfalls, then, your first order of business should be to create outlines of each paper you now have in mind (see Chapter 6 for more on outlines). Having these outlines initially will help you delineate the scopes of each paper and allow you to see how everything fits together. It will also ensure that you do not have any unfortunate overlaps among papers. Once you have created the initial outline, it is time to go back to the literature. Chances are, it has been a few months to a few years since you conducted that part of your dissertation. New scholarship will have come out in that time. As you do your search for all your key terms, download the papers, put in the interlibrary loan requests, and so forth; don't forget to go through the top-tier journals and publishers in your field. This will allow you to conduct keyword and database searches to catch any important works that may have escaped you. If you are currently affiliated with a university, you can also talk to your research librarians. As you resaturate yourself in the literature and catch up on the past few months' or years' worth of research, add any relevant pieces of information in the outline. Better yet, start a new document and start summarizing, quoting, and paraphrasing the relevant aspects of the work as it relates to your paper. Did you catch that? You have a paper now! At this point, you can peruse the other chapters in this book as needed on topics like journal articles, finding the right outlet, and whatever else you need to know.

16.3 Turning Your Dissertation into a Book

Because dissertations are long like books, and they're bound like books, it may seem as though a dissertation can just be sent to a publisher as a book. As nice as this would be, it is unfortunately not the case. Dissertations and books have different purposes and different audiences. A dissertation is written to prove your newly acquired expertise in the field to your committee, and let's be honest, to cater to some extent to your committee's preferences when it comes to the contents. When you publish a book, you will still have a small readership due to the narrow scope that is your niche, but it will be a different audience with a different purpose.

For a book, you need a good publisher. While dissertating, you are writing for essentially a few people: your committee. Though your committee is gone from your life as decision makers, they are now replaced with the publisher, whose editors and reviewers will also have some strong suggestions. If you pick a good publisher, when they ask for changes, you can trust that it is for the good of the manuscript and its marketing. To choose the right publisher, check their websites for the kinds of books they publish (also, read Chapter 15). Check out the book exhibits at the academic conferences you attend and talk to their representatives. You can also get in touch with editors for more information.

What is a must in a dissertation may have no place in a book, and vice versa. It may help to make peace with the fact that parts of your dissertation will have to be left behind, and that's OK. You needed those parts then; you don't need them now. Create an outline (see Chapter 6 for more on outlines) for your new book, and don't be afraid to divert from the dissertation's table of contents. Just as you will cut out some parts, you will also need to write new parts that better suit your new voice; for example, the introduction will probably look much different, in our experience. Remember the book needs to tell a coherent story, so don't be afraid to take a critical look at what's already in the dissertation and what needs to be eliminated or added. Once you have a publisher in mind and a solid outline, you can start working on the book proposal (see Chapter 20 on how to write book proposals). Bear in mind that you will most likely need to complete one or two of the chapters to submit with the book proposal. Details can be found in the book proposal template from your chosen publisher.

Whether you are turning your dissertation into a book, a paper, or several papers, remember the change in your voice and your audience. You are no longer trying to have an advanced degree conferred upon you. You are now imparting unique knowledge on the world, and that requires a different voice, and a different approach. Also, congratulations on setting yourself apart from the majority that don't publish their dissertations.

Questions for Reflection

1. Everything else being equal, would it be easier for you to turn the dissertation into a book or a set of articles? Why? What aspects of the processes we described in this chapter do you find more challenging?

2. After having created the outline(s) of articles or a book based on your dissertation, is there any work that you ended up not including? This could become a separate paper. Are there any relatively easy additions you can think of that would warrant a separate study?

Questions for Discussion

1. Talk to your colleagues who turned their dissertation into a book and ask them how long it took them, which parts they had to eliminate, and which ones they had to write from scratch.
2. Deciding if your dissertation should become a book, a set of articles, or both can also depend on your career goals and timeline. Discuss with colleagues what decisions they made and the factors that contributed to those decisions.

Questions for Your Mentor

1. Discuss with your mentor (or a senior colleague who knows your work well) the pros and cons of turning your dissertation into a book or a set of articles.
2. If you decide to go the book route, discuss with your mentor what presses and/or book series could be a good fit. What are the advantages and disadvantages of publishing in a book series?

17 Book or Media Reviews

Writing a book or media review is often a recommended and relevant project for early career writers who would like to gain more name recognition while getting writing experience and exposure to recent research. Plus, you get a copy of the book you are reviewing for free (as long as you make sure to ask for one). In this chapter, we discuss the mechanics common to good reviews, including having a summary followed by an evaluation (or vice versa), and taking a constructively critical approach. We begin by discussing the most traditional form of reviews, book reviews published in academic journals, and then discuss some alternative types, such as reviews of media content (software, webpages, etc.) or reviews that can appear online in alternative formats (blogs, podcasts, videos, etc.).

17.1 Book Reviews in Academic Journals

Book reviews have a much longer history than one could imagine, going back to 140 BC (Orteza y Miranda, 1996), although their key features have not changed much and tend to apply across disciplines. Orteza y Miranda (1996) identified the following as the characteristics of successful reviews: an evaluation of the contribution of the text, a discussion of the text within the broader context, a discussion of the strengths and weaknesses of the arguments in the text, and some involvement by the reader.

Book reviews published in academic journals are often by invitation, which means that if you are a graduate student or a junior scholar, it may be difficult for you to get invited to do a review, as review editors tend to invite established scholars or past reviewers (people who have collaborated with the journal before and so are already in the system) for this type of task. However, there are options for you to become part of this inner circle. First, get the word out to your colleagues and mentors. They may know someone who is looking for reviewers for a book in your field or may have been invited to do one and can suggest your name to the editor. Alternatively, look for journals that accept unsolicited reviews. Either you can ask the journal for a copy of the book you want to review or send in the review if you already have the book. If the journal does accept unsolicited reviews, their webpage will say so. You may also be able to

17.1 Book Reviews in Academic Journals

contact the review editor and ask them (see a sample email in the Appendix G). Either way, we do recommend that you ask the review editor. If you go this route, keep in mind that book reviews traditionally deal with recent books. This means that you should try to review books the year they come out. You can also look for other platforms (distribution lists, wikis, specialized webpages, newsletters, association webpages, etc.) that list books available for review or that will consider unsolicited reviews. Not all journals publish reviews, and those who do may have very different policies about what gets published and how. For example, despite being called "second class citizens of scientific literature" (Riley & Spreitzer, 1970), nowadays book reviews often go through a standard or modified peer-review process (checked in-house by the review editor).

Once you have found your venue and have access to the book you will review, what's next? Our suggestion is that you familiarize yourself with the review guidelines of the journal (these will be available on the journal's website, often in the author's portal or section; if you can't find them, ask the review editor) and have a look at a couple of past reviews that were published recently. They will serve as your models. Depending on your field and the journal, you may find that reviews are structured in fixed, clearly labeled sections (in medicine journals these often include Field, Format, Audience, Purpose, Content, Highlights, Limitations, and Context; see Hartley, 2006) or follow a more flexible structure. Some are as short as 75 words or as long as over 2,000 words (Peate, 2008). Some require that you include references while others forbid it.

Action item!

Reviews typically include two main sections: one in which you present, describe, and summarize the book (let's call this the summary), and another in which you evaluate the book from a critical perspective (let's call it the evaluation). These sections can appear one after the other, with either of these as the first one (summary first is more common in applied linguistics, but other fields can do things differently), or they can appear integrated throughout the review.

Choose a couple of recently published reviews in the journal you plan to submit to, and consider these questions as a way to familiarize yourself with this genre:

- What is the structure of the review?
  - Summary first, then evaluation
  - Evaluation first, then summary
  - Summary and evaluation integrated throughout
  - Other:

- How long is the review?
  - How long is the summary section?
  - How long is the evaluation section?
  - Are references included?
  - Other:

- What elements are included in the summary?
  - Length in pages/chapters
  - Overall structure of the volume
  - Overall internal structure of the chapters
  - Table of contents and index
  - Editors' and authors' background or expertise
  - Other:

- What elements are mentioned in the evaluation?
  - Selection of topics/authors
  - Methodological aspects (research methods, data analysis)
  - Contribution to the field
  - Relationship with previous research
  - Other:

As you have probably noticed while analyzing and comparing published reviews in the previous Action item, these tend to share a set of four rhetorical moves across disciplines (Motta-Roth, 1998; Nicolaisen, 2002), the first two corresponding to what we call summary. The last two correspond to the evaluation part of the book review: introducing the book (topic, readership, author, field), outlining the book (organization, chapter/section, additional material), highlighting parts of the book (evaluation), and providing general evaluation of the book (recommendation, positive and negative aspects).

With a better understanding of what is expected from a book review, as you begin reading the book, have a notepad, Word document, sticky note, or anything you can write your notes on available next to you. Write down all the ideas you have while you are reading. Are chapters or sections organized in a particularly useful way? Write it down. Is there something missing (an image that would have been helpful to explain a concept, an introduction, a table of contents)? Write it down. Is a chapter you just read particularly strong and well-written? Write it down. Are certain methodological choices standing out as particularly original, novel, or insightful? Write it down. You get the gist. Write down anything you read that could end up being part of your review, and don't forget to note page numbers, authors, chapters, and other relevant information.

17.1 Book Reviews in Academic Journals

Next, with your notes and some general ideas about the structure of book reviews and their parts fresh in your mind, you are now ready to start writing. You know what you need to talk about (thanks to your notes) and how to organize the information, but we have yet to discuss some linguistic features of this type of academic genre that will help you decide how to write your book review. One of the most challenging but most valued aspects of book reviews across disciplines (Hartley, 2006) is the critique and evaluation: Readers are looking for a critique of the argument of the book and an evaluation of its academic credibility. Writing these parts of the review may be challenging for students or junior scholars, who may feel like they are lacking the expertise, trajectory, and authority to do so (Impostor syndrome, anyone? You are not alone. Read Chapter 2). Not everyone is like Noam Chomsky, who famously wrote a highly influential and very critical book review that had a deep impact on the entire fields of psychology and linguistics (Chomsky, 1959). Nonetheless, readers will be interested in your opinion about the book, so how can you write an evaluative critique that conveys criticism in a constructive way? Based on our experience and findings from previous studies, we suggest that you aim for an informative but also entertaining style (Wessely, 2000), such as a mix of journalistic and academic style (Crown et al., 2000). Keep the amount of praise and criticism in check. While Hartley (2006) found reviews to be more positive than negative, we also know there are differences in writing style and reception of book reviews by gender, seniority of the author of the book and of the reviewer, and by field. Your critique or evaluation should be well argued, as you want to avoid veiled allusions and any comment that could be perceived as a personal attack, as it's much easier to make powerful enemies in academia than it is to train a murder of crows to bring you shiny gifts. Below are some more specific recommendations based on Hill (1997), Boring (1951), Johnson (1995), Squires C. (2020), Squires P. B. (1989), and Burd (2009), with examples (Figures 17.1 to 17.4, with relevant parts highlighted with gray background) to illustrate each suggestion extracted from published reviews:

- Use descriptive comments to present the problems you found in the book and let readers arrive at their own conclusions (see Figure 17.1).
- Use examples or explanations to back up and clarify any criticism. This will avoid any misunderstanding of your arguments (see Figure 17.2).
- Be constructive and, if you can, provide suggestions for improvement. Keep in mind that these may end up being included in a future edition of the book (see Figure 17.3).
- Frame any criticism within the context of this particular book and its scope and goals. Remember that no book can include everything, and omissions are normal (see Figure 17.4).

> Although the editors have made a commendable effort to provide comprehensive topical coverage on [field], there are a few areas that could have received more attention. For example, two areas that remain underrepresented in this volume and that are deserving more attention are [area 1] and [area 2]. Given their current relevance in [field], a more extensive discussion on these topics would be valuable to a large number of readers.

Figure 17.1 Descriptive comments in book reviews

> The volume would have benefited by a greater precision in the definition and use of some concepts across chapters, namely: [list of concepts]. As an example, it is not clear what criteria were mobilized to differentiate between [concept 1] and [concept 2] in [chapter] and how this distinction fits in with the definition of [concept 3].

Figure 17.2 Examples to clarify criticism in book reviews

> There are two elements missing from this volume that would facilitate its reading and consultation. An introduction by the editors, so that the reader, before delving into each chapter, could better understand the goals of a project of such broad scope and perspective, and an index of subjects and authors to facilitate the search and consultation on specific topics that, otherwise, in a volume of more than 800 pages, can be difficult to locate.

Figure 17.3 Suggestions for improvement in book reviews

> Although the editors have made a commendable effort to provide comprehensive topical coverage on [field], there are a few areas that could have received more attention. For example, two areas that remain underrepresented in this volume and that are deserving more attention are [area 1] and [area 2]. Given their current relevance in [field], a more extensive discussion on these topics would be valuable to a large number of readers.

Figure 17.4 Examples to frame criticism within context in book reviews

17.2 Media Reviews in Academic Journals

Up until this point, we have discussed the most prototypical type of reviews, book reviews that are published in a scholarly journal. However, books are not the only type of scholarship you can review. In recent years, we have seen more published reviews of alternative scholarship material, such as websites, software, online digital resources, learning platforms, and so on. Almost everything we said about book reviews applies here as well, because the venue in which you will get published is still an academic journal (but see the next section about other options). However, the product you are reviewing is different, and you will likely be focusing on and including a few new elements, such as:

- The date on which the media was accessed. This is crucial if you are reviewing dynamic content that gets regularly updated, such as a website, a video series, software, etc.
- The type of media you are reviewing and how it was accessed, which is particularly important in case there are multiple versions of the same media (such as a browser and an app version of the same software).
- A thorough description and informed summary of the media and its parts. While you should include this part in any review, it becomes more relevant for nonbook reviews because the content can be organized in many different ways. The reader needs to be able to get a sense of it without having even used or seen the media.
- Additional details that may be relevant to situate the media in the field, which may include number of subscribers, access model and cost (free, registration, etc.), date of creation, distribution (local versus international), number of media resources included (number of videos, audio clips, units), features (search box, glossary, newsletter, helpdesk).

17.3 Alternative Types of Reviews

In the first two sections of the chapter, we considered traditional reviews of books or media that appear in written format in academic journals. We now turn to nontraditional reviews. For example, you may be asked to review a book on a podcast, in a blog or vlog, or for the press. The old-fashioned term for these kinds of writing was "vulgarization." Nowadays, we prefer "popularization," but the meaning is the same: taking a complex text and making it available to the people (the vulgus). Good popularization is an extremely important part of the process of scientific diffusion, and reviews of books and articles for a general audience are part and parcel of the process. The main difference of these reviews is that they will generally be less formal and demanding than regular academic reviews.

You should strive to start with a "hook," a catchy anecdote or statement that will grab the attention of the casual reader. This is different from other academic writing, which does not always require this sort of device. You should also try to end the review with a memorable or "punchy" conclusion. This organization is typical of journalism and is known as the "inverted pyramid." Essentially you start with the most important information (what even the most casual reader should know) and then provide more detail. This is still relevant – but not crucial – information, as you assume that the reader may quit at any point. The conclusion (the tip of the inverted pyramid; see Chapter 8) is where the writer's opinion would usually be placed.

An important aspect of making your writing more accessible is to avoid jargon, which is easier said than done. Typically, you will be asked to write a review of a book or some other work because you are an expert in a given field. That expertise that you worked so hard to achieve can now get in your way. Technical terms, acronyms, allusions, and references to information everyone knows (everyone, that is, in the very restricted circle of experts about the topic) are so ingrained in the way experts express themselves that they become completely "natural," and hence invisible to the expert. Defining a novel as a "postmodern picaresque," referring to the "aspects model" of syntax, or alluding to the "end of history" are all rhetorical moves that would come naturally to those in the know but that will fall flat among the noninitiated. A good strategy is to ask a friend or relative who is emphatically not in your field to read your text and flag anything they don't understand. Eliminate or explain any of the things they flag. More generally, shorter, simpler sentences will make your writing easier to process. Along the same lines, the passive should be avoided, as should unnecessary nominalizations. For example, "Unlike for men, the expression of feelings is stereotypically associated with femininity in Western Culture" is much harder to read than "In Western Culture, the stereotype is that women express their feelings and men do not."

If you are writing for an oral medium (a podcast, for example), remember that it is very hard to write natural-sounding speech. It is far easier to write up notes and lists of points to make and then speak naturally about them. If you prefer or need to have a written script to work from, you will need to simplify your syntax even more, avoid constructions that are complex or require a heavy processing load, such as long subjects, and use left and right dislocations to express emphasis and focus. "The chatbots, they are coming for our jobs" sounds like spoken language. "Serious challenges to full employment of academics will come from chatbots" does not.

Finally, here are two strategies we have found useful in popular writing. First, present one idea at a time. It's hard enough to make one point clearly, let alone two. Second, repeat your point at least three times. General readers don't necessarily pay attention and they definitely do not take notes, as you might expect an academic reader to do.

Questions for Reflection

1. Do some research and find a couple of recent books or media products that you find interesting and would like to review. What would be your two biggest challenges? What would be the two biggest advantages or positive aspects of writing the review?

2. What journals in your field accept and publish reviews? Find a few by browsing their webpages, and familiarize yourself with the type and style of reviews they publish.

Questions for Discussion

1. If some of your colleagues have published a book (a research monograph, a textbook, or an edited volume) chances are that their book has been reviewed. Ask them about the reviews of their work. What did they appreciate? What parts stood out? What parts were the most useful or interesting to them? Was there anything they disagreed with or felt could have been improved?
2. Reviewing someone else's work can be intimidating if you are a junior scholar or a graduate student at the beginning of your career. Discuss with some more senior colleagues the challenges they faced and the strategies they employed to overcome them.

Questions for Your Mentor

1. Let your mentor know that you would like the opportunity to write your first book review. Ask them about journals that could publish the review, as well as review-worthy books that have recently come out.
2. Maybe your mentor is willing to co-author a review with you in a major journal. This may be more or less common depending on your field (and depending on how much Belgian chocolate you've gifted to your mentor). If not, they can still guide you through the process.

18 Journal Articles

Journal articles are, in many ways, the backbone of academic writing. With 2.9 million science and engineering articles worldwide in 2020 alone, a National Science Foundation report (White, 2021a) indicates they remain the primary outlet for research findings. Many universities and academic positions require journal articles for promotions and sometimes even as a requirement for initial employment. Holding a tenure-track faculty position in many fields, for instance, depends on publishing journal articles (among other things). Some doctoral programs require journal article publications with reputable publishers before candidates can earn their title. In specialized fields like medicine and pharmacology, companies spend millions of dollars on research that eventually gets published in journals. Regardless of circumstances, journal articles stem from scientific research and form a genre of their own. While we provide an overview of key types and considerations here, note that there are entire books available on the subject for a closer look (such as Yan, 2020).

Finding what to write a journal article about can be a struggle for academic writers. We would love to give you a secret ingredient that makes the whole process a breeze, but unfortunately there is no writing in academia without lots and lots of reading first. Sorry, not sorry, as our friend Demi Lovato says. The less you know what you want to write, the more freedom you have on what to read. At the very initial stages (if you are a graduate student, a researcher looking for a new subfield to explore, etc.), you can read anything in your area. Feel free to jump from subject to subject and paper to paper until something sticks out to you. Scan titles, abstracts, and blurbs and see what interests you. You don't want to be stuck with a topic that you don't enjoy, so look for something that you don't mind spending the next few months (or years) on. At least for tenure-track people, there is a certain level of flexibility with research topics, but committees will want to see a research trajectory that shows both continuity and growth, just as long as the new research still makes sense and is connected to what you've previously done. It is important, though, that you choose a subject that's not only interesting but also has something left to say. And technically this shouldn't matter (but it does), but you need to pick something with at least a little buzz around it. A lack of interest from the field in what you do is a surefire way to get lots of rejection letters from journals. That may not always be the case; you could get published and even become a trailblazer. It all depends on how confident you feel that your field needs what you study. If you find it difficult to gauge new, open, potentially fruitful research lines, state-of-the-art articles and recent reviews in books, edited volumes, and handbooks from reputable publishers can be helpful. They usually make a point to include where research is still needed and why it is important. Once you know what your topic of interest is, you can start looking for publications specifically on your chosen subject and methodology. Eventually you are likely to decide to write a research article or a review article (with subtypes). These are not the only types of articles out there, but they are the most frequent and important ones for the scope of our book. We now turn to each of these article types.

18.1 Types of Journal Articles

18.1.1 Research Articles

In research articles, scholars report findings derived from qualitative, quantitative, and mixed methods studies. The purpose is to contribute to the scholarly conversation in your field by establishing a warrant or reason for the study at hand and then reporting the findings of a study in an objective manner. Writing a research article involves many stages prior to writing, including but not limited to designing the study, an Institutional Review Board application, finding participants, carrying out the experiments, observations, recordings, transcribing and annotating data, running statistical tests, and so on.

While there may be some discipline-specific differences, research articles usually comprise sections on the statement of the problem, literature review, methods, findings, and conclusions (see Part II of the book for details on these sections). Talking of discipline-specific formats, experimental studies (which are the bread and butter of such disciplines as psychology or the medical sciences) are rigidly organized as five parts:

1. A generally short overview or introduction, which establishes the general problem
2. The literature review, which surveys the previous research on the subject
3. The methodology, which describes how the experiment was organized, the data collected, and so on.
4. The results (how your experiment turned out)
5. The discussion of the results

For humanities scholars, keeping the results apart from their significance is the hardest thing to do, but if you read a lot of lab reports, experimental research, or medical research, it becomes second nature.

> **Action item!**
>
> Detailed information on the required and desired contents of a research article can be found on publishers' websites, in discipline-specific publications (editorials, special issues, invited articles on best practices in publishing in the specific field), and in academic style guides (the 7th edition of the American Psychological Association's [APA] manual provides a detailed account of reporting standards for fields that use APA).
>
> To familiarize yourself with the structure, organization, and contents of a research article, follow these steps:
>
> 1. Select a published research article in your field.
> 2. Using the five-part structure explained above (or the equivalent from your discipline-specific guidelines), identify each part of the article. Are there more or less than what you expected? Is the order the same as what we discussed above?

Prior to writing their studies up, many academics prefer to share their study designs, initial findings, and research trajectories at academic conferences to receive invaluable feedback from colleagues in the same field. Preprint repositories are also an option (see Chapter 29 for more on those). Presenting a study at a conference first can help you smooth out any rough edges due to the different process involved in preparing for a presentation instead of working on a written draft.

18.1.2 Review Articles

Sometimes a topic is so thoroughly researched that the literature review can be the entire article, which brings us to review articles. In a review article, the purpose is to provide readers with the big picture when it comes to your topic: Where it started, where it is now, and where it is going. Writing review articles is not for the faint-hearted. You should know the literature really well and be able to synthesize it and show what it means for the field at large. This is true of every type of article, but here you have the space to actually show it. A review article, like a research article, should also answer a research question. The article should not just be a chronological summary but should take an angle. What trends are evident in the research? What has not been established on this subject yet? What still needs attention? Why does it matter? What are the implications of the extant research on the subject, and where does it lead for future research? Individual papers need to focus on very specific aspects of a phenomenon, and good research yields new questions, which yield new studies and papers. It is very easy to lose sight of the whole as we focus on our minute corners. A good literature review puts everything in perspective (see Chapter 9 on literature reviews) and can even give new direction to the field (or to a few researchers, at least).

Within what we call review articles, we can also identify specific types based on the methodology employed for the review: meta-analysis, meta-synthesis, scoping review, and systematic review. A meta-analysis is a quantitative method employed to statistically examine data and findings from previously published works in order to reach broader conclusions or to determine trends in a field. The idea is that this method allows researchers to consolidate findings and data in order to reach generalizable conclusions. A meta-synthesis is similar to meta analyses in that this is also a method to analyze and combine data from multiple studies, but of a qualitative nature. So, we are not testing a hypothesis as in the case of a meta-analysis, but rather bringing together qualitative data to build new theories (you could also opt for a mixed method review, including data from qualitative and quantitative studies). A scoping review is essentially a method to identify a gap in the literature by providing an overview of the available research based on a set of criteria. A systematic review, on the other hand, seeks to answer a specific question regarding, for example, the effectiveness of a certain process or tool and summarizes all available research on that topic to be able to offer an answer.

Action item!

Familiarize yourself with the Preferred Reporting Items for Systematic Reviews and Meta-Analyses (PRISMA) paradigm and protocols to conduct these types of reviews: http://www.prisma-statement.org/PRISMAStatement/ Checklist for systematic reviews and http://www.prisma-statement.org/Extensions/ScopingReviews for scoping reviews.

18.2 Submitting Your Article

Once you know what you are writing, the next step is to decide on a journal (see Chapter 15), which we'll talk about here in connection with your journal article contents. Choosing where to submit your paper may seem a daunting task at first, but there are a few ways you can go about it. The most sensible one is to go to journal homepages and read about their scopes to decide on a good fit. An easy way to make this decision is by looking at the list of references for your paper. What journal in your field are you citing the most frequently? You might have your answer right there. It is possible that the journals you cite the most are top tier and therefore might seem out of reach to you, so we would like to take a small detour and talk about submitting to top-tier journals.

How do you get into a top-tier journal? You can start by making a list of two or three top-tier journals in your field. Those will be your targets. The next step is to thoroughly familiarize yourself with these journals by reading the last five or six years of their issues, cover-to-cover. Take notes as to what topics, methodologies, and types of research they publish. If a journal publishes empirical research, you'd waste your time submitting a theoretical paper. You need to produce a paper that fits the journal you are submitting to. Next, research the editor-in-chief and the editorial board, including the managing editors (who are most likely to handle your paper). If their work is related to yours, you should thoroughly familiarize yourself with it. This is the lens through which they will assess your work. Then, start planning your paper; for example, if you are doing an experimental study, make sure that the work you are reporting matches the type of experiments they usually publish. If you are analyzing a literary work, make sure it's the kind of work they usually discuss. If you are doing a qualitative study, make sure the type of population and questions match what they usually publish. You may need to collect new data, meet stringent criteria that your original data do not support, look at some new work you did not analyze previously, or go back to your data and re-examine them under a different light. Yes, it's lots of work, but it's worth doing.

Top-tier journals are not for everyone, and that's OK. If you have a supervisor or mentor, they are likely to know exactly where your paper would fit due to their extended experience in the field, so you should ask them. They are also more likely to know the impact level of your paper (you may have a ground-breaking gem in your hands and not quite be aware) and can advise you as to what tier journal(s) you should aim for. Then again, some people would like to start small, and go bigger for subsequent papers as they gain experience, while others want to start at the top, fully expecting not to get in, but to learn from the feedback they receive. You may be pleasantly surprised by an acceptance or revise and resubmit. If your paper is rejected by a top-tier journal, you can submit it to a lower-impact factor journal or try again at another higher-impact factor journal and get accepted (Teixeira da Silva et al., 2018). In any case, you need to have a list of journals to which you can submit the paper. Yes, a list; you should not expect your paper to be accepted by the first journal you submit it to. A paper can be rejected an average of three to six times before being accepted (Azar, 2004;

18.2 Submitting Your Article

Huisman & Smits, 2017). If your paper is rejected, don't get discouraged. There are a multitude of reasons a well-written piece of scholarship can get rejected (see Dwivedi et al., 2022 for nine editors' perspectives on this).

After you have decided on the first journal to submit your paper to, you need to read their author guidelines. Note their word or character limit for the abstract and the paper and make sure not to go over the limit. Then there is the question of formatting. While some journals will accept any consistent formatting for the initial submission, others will want certain things; they may even tell you what headings your manuscript has to have. Here you have a choice to make. Do you write the paper following the accepted style in your field (APA, MLA, etc.) using your own formatting preferences? You definitely can, since that first journal may not even send your paper out to reviewers, meaning you would have to start anew with the author guidelines of another paper, which would likely differ. You could also choose to write the manuscript following the guidelines of your first-choice journal, which would save you time if they accepted the paper. This may be a moot question if you are using modern bibliographic software, which will format references for you (see Section 9.1). The choice is yours to make. Be sure to check out Appendix H for a sample cover letter to send in with your submission. Once you get your first round of revisions, see Chapter 13 for how to deal with reviewers' comments. Happy writing!

Questions for Reflection

1. Are you considering submission to a top-tier journal? Think about the pros and cons, for example how long the peer review takes (it may be longer in top-tier journals) and if you have any deadlines for promotion coming up (by when you need to have the paper published).
2. Are you working on a niche topic? Consider publishing in a more specific journal, even if it may not be as well known. Which other scholars do you know who publish on this topic (or related topics)? Check out their CVs to see which journals they have been publishing in, as this may give you ideas about new venues for your research.

Questions for Discussion

1. Share the pros and cons about publishing in top-tier journals with your colleagues. Do they agree? What other factors would they consider?
2. Talk about publishing in open access but lower-impact journals. What are the benefits and pitfalls? For example, you may be able to reach a wider or more specific audience while losing some of the prestige associated with higher-impact journals.

Questions for Your Mentor

1. What are the top journals in your field, and how did your mentor manage to get published in them?
2. Are there any journals in the field that you should avoid and why? For example, some journals may look fine on paper but be in some sort of crisis or on the decline in terms of quality.

19 Chapters in Edited Volumes

Let's say you're thinking about writing a book chapter for an edited volume. Unlike Snuggies (a writing essential, in our opinion), book chapters are far from a one-size-fits-all situation. In this chapter, we will discuss the positive aspects of writing a book chapter, mention things to consider when choosing whether to write a chapter for an edited volume, and, finally, note some important differences between writing book chapters for handbooks, research volumes, and conference proceedings.

A book chapter for an edited volume differs from an article in a peer-reviewed journal in several ways. In regard to content, an edited volume centers on a theme or cohesive set of arguments, which is not the case in journal issues (unless the journal is publishing a special issue). By contributing a book chapter for an edited volume, you have the opportunity to participate more deeply in a specific academic conversation closely related to your research. Your chapter will be read within the context of the larger conversation of the edited volume, in which (hopefully) big thinkers in the field are participating. If a well-known researcher is contributing to the volume, scholars may be drawn to the book by their name but stick around to read your chapter as well. Being part of an edited volume means that your name becomes associated with the names of others doing similar research, establishing a community of sorts and potentially leading to future collaborations. Book chapters also differ from journal articles in that, while the editor of the volume may send out a call for papers, chapters are often invited. If you are invited to submit a chapter to a volume, you can feel fairly confident that the editor will accept your work, unless you let your cat write the chapter by rolling around on your keyboard. Participating in an edited volume can be an appealing alternative to submitting an article to a journal, where your piece will wait in a queue to contend with hundreds of other papers. In fact, depending on your field, it may be good to have a balance of articles and chapters in the pipeline so you can keep publishing and advancing in your career.

While it can be reassuring and flattering to be invited to write a book chapter, because of the process we just described, many fields within academia rank book chapters lower on the publishing hierarchy than journal articles, as the peer-review process can be less rigorous. While it is true that editors may be pre-inclined to accept chapter submissions, as they need content in order to publish their volumes, many editors engage in a substantial review process. Contributing to a volume with an editor who is thorough and serious about the process can be a fantastic learning experience. Another consideration to keep in mind when deciding whether to write a chapter is that an edited volume will likely not be as wide-reaching of a venue for your research as a journal would be. While most university libraries have electronic access to a range of journals, they may not purchase an edited volume, meaning that your work would not have the same access to citations by other scholars that the visibility of a journal article would provide (Bourke & Butler, 1996).

19.1 When to Contribute to an Edited Volume

Despite these concerns, you should not discount the idea of writing a book chapter. Rather, you should consider book chapters as a valuable type of writing within your diverse research agenda. Think about it a little like eating deviled eggs at a barbeque. Two or three are delicious, and an excellent addition to your plate, but your stomach wouldn't thank you if your entire meal (or CV) consisted of deviled eggs. Before deciding whether to invest in that bulk, jumbo-size tub of mayonnaise ... er, we mean, before deciding to write a book chapter, we suggest you reflect on the following considerations to determine whether this specific book chapter is the right opportunity for you.

Define the key players related to the edited volume. Who is the editor, and where will the volume be published? Is the editor well-published and well-respected in your field? A top-notch editor can bring needed visibility to an edited collection. Is the publisher reputable, or is the editor's brother-in-law publishing the collection out of his basement? If possible, ask the editor for a list of confirmed contributors and their chapter titles. This will give you a much better sense of the scope of the project and its potential impact. A mix of scholars at different tiers of institutions, ranks, and research profiles is perfectly acceptable. If all the contributors are beginning scholars, however, this could mean less visibility for your work, as their names won't attract as much attention as more established researchers.

Learn as much as you can about plans for the book's release and marketing. If the volume is initially coming out only in hardcover and there is no book tour or promotion plan in place, you might understandably be skeptical about the dissemination of the project. Academic books are often printed in hardcover first and later in paperback if they do well, but hardcover books are more expensive and won't sell as many copies. If the book is simultaneously being published online and in print, this is a huge benefit, as it will be instantaneously available to a wider audience at a more affordable price. You may also be wondering about royalties. If that's the case, stop wondering. You aren't getting any. That's the harsh reality of academic publishing. Usually all you will get is a copy of the book and the gratitude of all those involved in the project.

Get a sense of how your department or institution views book chapters. If you are in a tenure-track position, it may be wise to talk to a mentor in your program or other tenured members of the department to understand the department's perception of book chapters. Right or wrong, if they don't place much value in book chapters, you may want to seriously consider whether it's worth the investment of your time (and it could well still be, especially if the book has an amazing editor or publisher).

All this being said, we don't want to discourage you from writing a book chapter. Participating in this type of scholarship can be particularly rewarding, as it allows you to delve deeply into a topic that interests you, and it's a great form of networking (with the editor and other authors), something that may pay off in the future in ways you would never expect. For example, Heather was asked to write a chapter for a handbook, which allowed her to learn more about the editor's research and establish a professional relationship with her, and now she is co-editing a volume with her former editor. Other contributors to a volume or your editor can easily become collaborators on future projects and conference presentations, or even external reviewers of your work when it comes time for promotion.

19.2   Invitation to Contribute to an Edited Volume

While each edited volume is unique, when you are invited to contribute a chapter, the editor should provide you with a variation of the following information:

The publisher: Knowing where the editor intends to publish the volume will allow you to assess their reputability, as well as how much visibility a particular publisher will provide for your work. The editor may also let you know whether they have a contract with this publisher, have submitted a proposal, or are still in the early stages of the process. It is common for editors to solicit book chapters before having a signed contract, which is no cause for alarm. If the editor doesn't have a clear idea of where they hope to publish, this could be a red flag; at the very least, it indicates that you won't see your chapter in print for a while. A chapter Sal once submitted was published seven years after the fact. That's probably extreme, but these things do happen.

Organization of the volume: If your editor can provide a table of contents for the volume or an overview for the section your chapter will be part of, this will help you get a sense of how your chapter fits into the bigger picture. Don't be afraid to ask clarifying questions about your editor's vision for the chapter before accepting the invitation, as this will guide your writing and possibly save you from researching and writing material out of the scope of the chapter. Figure 19.1 includes an example of what the organization portion of the invitation might look like.

Word count and deadlines: The invitation should include a word count and deadline for chapter submissions. If it doesn't, ask your editor for the maximum

> The Companion will provide an introduction to the interdisciplinary connections between Animal Studies and Literature and Film. It will have two sections. The first section will trace the theoretical connections between the two fields, and the second section will include chapters that address particular themes related to Animal Studies in specific literature and films. We invite you to contribute to the second section by writing a chapter on posthumanism in a literary text or film of your choice.

Figure 19.1 Portion of an invitation email to contribute to an edited volume

word count (and remember, that includes citations for your references) before you start writing. As you write, save any notes, sources, and text from your chapter that the editor cuts, as you can use this research for subsequent publications.

Sources: Don't be surprised or offended if the editor sends you a list of possible secondary sources with their invitation. This is a fairly common way for the editors to ensure that important research in the field is included in the volume. Even if you choose not to cite the sources the editor shares with you, you should read them and peruse the bibliographies of those sources to center yourself within the conversation and get a sense of the topics your editor considers relevant. If your research leads you to aspects of the topic that you're not familiar with, spend some time investigating buzzwords, central concepts, and current debates related to your chapter. This will help guarantee that you're using the most up-to-date terms for your field.

Style guide: Some editors will send a style guide along with the invitation, especially if they already have a contract with a publisher. Others may not share a style guide initially, or they might send one from the publisher they hope to work with, but this could change if they don't receive a contact from that publisher. When you're working on a chapter for a research volume, be prepared for several rounds of edits, including style changes. In most cases, your chapter will be revised first by the editor and second by readers solicited by the publisher.

19.3 Types of Edited Volumes

Now that the invitation email has provided you with information about the chapter and you have decided to contribute to the edited volume, let's discuss three of the most common types of book chapters: handbooks, research volumes, and conference proceedings.

19.3.1 Handbooks

Handbooks serve a variety of purposes, but they generally fall into one of two categories: those aimed at undergraduate and graduate classroom audiences (either as a useful secondary resource or as a text to be assigned as primary

19.3 Types of Edited Volumes

reading) and those for researchers (designed to capture the "state of the art" of a field or discipline). As much as possible, it's smart to know the editor's intended audience for the handbook, keeping this in mind as you write a clear, succinct chapter that is accessible to your audience. Handbooks tend to include a larger number of chapters (sometimes shorter than usual), and the editor will often define the scope of your chapter for you. Despite their length, handbook chapters include substantial research and can greatly benefit the academic community.

One unique aspect of handbook chapters is that their aim is generally to offer an overview of a certain theme or topic rather than presenting new research, experiments, or data. Here are some tips for writing a handbook chapter (see Figure 21.3 for a detailed breakdown of a sample handbook chapter outline).

1. Establish the scope of your chapter. You likely don't have a large word count, so which themes or topics are absolutely crucial to include? Create subheaders for the different sections in the body of your chapter, and focus your research on sources that are relevant to these subheadings.
2. Be selective when choosing the content for each section. Depending on the aims of your chapter, the content of the sections will vary, but your sections might discuss the history of the topic, give a current overview of the topic, present issues related to the topic, and look toward the future of the topic. You should synthesize the existing research, pointing out connections and patterns rather than providing an in-depth analysis of the sources.
3. Keep your introduction and conclusion brief (see Chapter 8 for advice on writing introductions and conclusions).

19.3.2 Research Volumes

In contrast to handbooks, research volumes tend to include fewer chapters, which provides authors with the space to expand on their topics of interest. Research volumes generally allow for more creativity, as they don't have the same strict or uniform structure as handbooks.

Writing a chapter for a research volume is very similar to writing a journal article (see Chapter 18 on journal articles). We suggest that you start with an outline (see Chapter 6), where you establish your research question(s) or thesis statement. Break your chapter down into sections, which may include a literature review, methodology, analysis, and discussion. Follow the strategies you would for a journal article, while adhering to the specifications of your editor and addressing any theories, debates, or topics they have asked you to cover.

19.3.3 Conference Proceedings

Conference proceedings differ from handbook and research volume chapters because they stem from papers written for and presented at specific conferences. Depending on the field, conference proceedings can be published before or after the conference, often accessible through the conference website – which allows the research to reach a wider audience more quickly – and/or published by a university press. The value of conference proceedings varies greatly among academic disciplines. Because conference proceedings take less time to publish, this is a way to present new insights and ongoing research in a timely manner. For fields like computer science, mathematics, and the sciences, conference proceedings hold great value and can be ranked higher than a book by evaluation and promotion committees. In other fields, like literature or history, where the data is not changing at such a fast rate, conference proceedings are lower in the research hierarchy. Again, we recommend that you talk with others at your institution to get a sense of the extent to which conference proceedings will benefit you. In some cases, you may decide to contribute to conference proceedings as a favor to the conference organizer or because there is a big name in the field associated with the conference proceedings. One positive aspect about conference proceedings is that you have essentially written the chapter for your presentation at the conference. Once you've been invited to contribute to a published conference proceedings, you will make any style changes and revisions suggested by the editors.

Now that you know more about the different types of book chapters, you will be equipped to make decisions about when to commit to writing a book chapter, as well as knowing what to include in the chapter when you do.

Questions for Reflection

1. A good strategy for building your CV is to have a side project that is not taking up a lot of your time and that could fit well in an edited volume (e.g., a literature review can become part of a handbook, or a side research project can find its way into a research-oriented edited volume). Think about your research agenda. Are there smaller projects you could start or maintain with this goal in mind?
2. Think about your research trajectory for the next five years. How do book chapters fit into your plan? Make a list of your publications so far, divided into categories (book chapters, journal articles, books, etc.). Think about the article-to-chapter ratio you would like to achieve in the next five years and plan accordingly.

Questions for Discussion

1. What were the experiences and outcomes for peers and colleagues who have published a chapter in an edited volume? How long did it take for their work to get published (from the invitation to the actual publication)? Were these works well-cited or well-read? Did the chapter lead to conference invitations or any other networking activity?
2. Ask your peers who have experience with edited volumes what they see as the major difference between publications in handbooks, research volumes, and conference proceedings. Do they have specific advice for each type of publication?

Questions for Your Mentor

1. We have identified some discipline-specific aspects of writing in edited chapters, such as the prestige and acceptability for promotion. Ask your mentor to clarify these aspects for your specific area.
2. Ask your mentor to tell you about their experience with conference proceedings. Under what circumstances have they contributed to conference proceedings? What do they see as the benefits and drawbacks of this type of publication?

20 Writing and Submitting Book Proposals

Once you have an idea for a book, which may be based on your dissertation or several papers that you published, the first step toward making this idea into reality is to prepare a book proposal, also called a prospectus. While each publisher will use their own template for it, most book proposals are between five and ten pages and include the same sections, and we will discuss each of these in detail below. In any case, you should check the publisher or book series webpage first and follow their specific guidelines. If you cannot find the guidelines online or are not sure if the guidelines apply to the specific book series where you would like to submit your work, don't worry. You can contact the editor to inquire about it (see Chapter 31 and Appendix B). Most likely, they will reply and email you the document with the information you requested.

How do you know when you are ready to write and submit a book proposal? The very academic answer is: it depends. Some people wait until their book is fully drafted, while others prefer to submit a proposal at the early stages to be able to integrate the reviewers' comments as they write. Probably, the best strategy is somewhere in the middle. If this is your first book, most likely it will be based on your dissertation. In that case, most publishers will want you to submit a few chapters together with the proposal; in some cases, they may even ask you to share your full dissertation with them. Our advice is that you should have at least a couple of chapters drafted before you submit your book proposal, to be able to show the publisher what the book will look like, how you write for your target audience, and how the book differs from your dissertation (see Chapter 16 for more on this last topic).

The most important decision you need to make is whether the book will be a scholarly monograph, a textbook, a book to support a course, or a general audience book. Don't try to argue that your research monograph on the poetry of sister Juana Inés de la Cruz can also be used as a textbook and is of interest to the general public. Although you want to prove that there's an audience for your book, claiming that it will be everything for everyone will just make you lose credibility. Editors have a good sense of the field they work in, and the reviewers are sure to catch any overoptimistic assessment.

The goal of the book proposal is for you to sign a contract and set a date for turning in the full manuscript to the publisher. Having a contract and a set date can be useful for your promotion (e.g., a tenure-track scholar at an R1 institution may be *strongly encouraged* to have both in hand by their third-year review, but this is not the case at regional institutions). For the publisher, the proposal serves to determine whether your book will be a good fit for their collection and something they will be likely to sell. If you identify a series that is a perfect fit for your book, you should submit to it (they sell better) and explicitly mention how your project fits with the series in your proposal. Before submitting the proposal, you may want to contact the series editor to ask whether they think your proposed manuscript would be a good fit. You don't have to give a lot of details at this stage, just the intended title and a brief description of the topics and goals of your book (not a fully developed book proposal).

Much like submitting papers, you may be rejected, but don't take it personally. Just submit it elsewhere right away. If the editor does see some potential in your proposal, it will be sent to external reviewers (depending on the publisher, we have seen up to five different reviews at each stage of revision). Each reviewer and the editor of the book series will comment on the value, fit, and impact of your proposal to determine whether to accept it or not. Reviewers are typically asked to comment on the following (based on our experience):

- the market and subject area, commenting on whether the book will make an important contribution to the field, who will likely read it (the audience of your book), whether the field is growing and attracting more interest, and whether it could be used to teach certain courses (this has an impact on how many copies will be sold).
- the quality of the proposal, including methodological issues, assumptions on which it is based, controversial points, shelf-life of the book, content (which chapters are particularly strong or weak), and writing style.
- your reputation, which boils down to whether the reviewers think you'll be able to accomplish this project (they typically consider your publication record, your dissertation, but also where you graduated and who your advisor was).

20.1 Parts of a Book Proposal

20.1.1 Title and Summary

Typically, a book proposal includes some basic information about yourself and your book. You will be asked to provide a tentative title and a short summary of the whole book. The title should be catchy but not too wordy. One good strategy is to think about the keywords that best represent your work and use those in the title. Beware of including new terms that you've coined in the title or keywords that are too specific and will not be understood immediately by a wider audience. A good title should be representative but also easily searchable, while piquing the interest of the reader. If the book is based on your dissertation, it's common for a publisher to ask you to include both titles, as one key goal of the book proposal is to see how it was changed from a dissertation into a research monograph (see an example in Figure 20.1).

The summary should not be too long (normally around 300 to 500 words, but again, check with the publisher as this may vary) and offer an overview of the book, focusing on its novel contribution and, if applicable, original results. This summary will be sent to reviewers who will be asked to comment on your book proposal. Two criteria that are always considered are the originality and novelty of the manuscript. Make sure the abstract clearly *shows* how your work is novel and what you contribute to the field. We say *shows* and not *tells* because you do not want to vaguely hint at your original work, as in the example in Figure 20.2. Instead, you want to make sure reviewers can see the novelty.

In the paragraph reproduced in Figure 20.2, the author was telling without showing and failed to mention several key aspects that made their proposed book unique and novel: We do not know what the theoretical foundations that they mentioned are and how these are applicable to syntax. We also know nothing about the methodological orientations or activities for the L2 classroom and how what the author is proposing represents an advance in their field. Figure 20.3 shows the same paragraph, reworked after two rounds of comments from the editors, who insisted on having more details and a clear explanation of how the book makes an original and impactful contribution to the field.

Original dissertation title: Multimodal and Eye-Tracking Evidence in the Negotiation of Pragmatic Intentions in Dyadic Conversations: The Case of Humorous Discourse.
Modified book title: The Multimodal Performance of Conversational Humor.

Figure 20.1 Original and modified book title

This book includes the presentation of a set of theoretical foundations of [discipline] applicable to the analysis of syntax. [...] Specifically, a broad set of methodological orientations are presented that guide the teaching of these units and a series of [discipline]-based activities are proposed to learn the units of syntax which constitutes a clear advance in this area.

Figure 20.2 Abstract that tells without showing

20.1 Parts of a Book Proposal

> This book constitutes an original contribution to the teaching of syntax from three perspectives: theoretical, applied, and experimental. First, it offers a complete overview of syntactical units and their main characteristics. [Paragraph with specific examples]. Second, it provides a set of basic keys for the teaching of syntax, focusing on its characteristics and applying [discipline]-inspired teaching strategies. [Paragraph with specific examples]. Third, it includes an empirical study that shows the advantages of integrating the [discipline] approach for teaching a specific class of syntactical units, such as [examples], in English as a second language. This last contribution is particularly significant if we consider that empirical research is still incipient in [main field] and it needs to be reinforced by studies, such as this, that expand the findings and applicability of empirical studies conducted in [other field].

Figure 20.3 Abstract that shows and tells

The revised paragraph is rich with details and examples, and clearly guides the reader through the three main methodological contributions of the proposed book. Some publishers will ask for a specific goals section, while others will simply ask for a book summary, in which you should include all this information.

> **Action item!**
> Make a list of all the novel things your book does. For example, are you the first to connect two specific areas of inquiry? Do you have original empirical data or materials (teaching materials, but also data collection protocol, a glossary, etc.)? After making the list, build it into a coherent paragraph by elaborating a little on each point. For example, how or why did you connect these two areas of inquiry, and what are the benefits of doing so? How are your data or materials original? Why would people benefit from having access to these? Which group(s) of people in particular would benefit from your book?

In your summary, or in a dedicated section of the proposal, you should also address how your work is relevant, timely, and impactful. Again, these are important criteria that will be considered by reviewers and editors. When discussing relevance, you can underscore the novel theoretical perspectives that you are bringing together and show how your book is in conversation with current research in your field. When discussing timeliness, you can refer to aspects of your specific field that are growing because more people are interested in it, new methods or instruments are being used, or new applications are being discovered. When discussing the impact that your work will have, you can mention how your methods, findings, or novel perspective are likely to change the field. Think big, but also be realistic. Are you offering specific materials, ideas, perspectives, or results that your audience will likely adopt? If so, you are changing the field. Make sure you say so.

20.1.2 Outline and Chapter Summary

After the title and the summary, it is likely you will be asked to present an outline (see Chapter 6 for more on outlines) and a short description of each chapter in your book, with an approximate word count. Let's first look at the outline (see Figure 20.4). As we discussed for the title, keep all headings short, clear, and interesting. Avoid being so creative that your headings become obscure and include all chapter titles and headings in the outline (again, check with the publisher, as they may ask you to include headings up to a certain level). For each chapter, you may be asked to indicate an estimated word count. If you do include a word count, make sure you are following the publisher's guidelines (if they ask for 80,000 words, budget each chapter to reach 80,000 words in total).

---

1. **Approaching the multimodal study of conversational humor (approx. 8,000 words/16 pages)**
    1.1. Introduction
    1.2. The field of humor studies
    1.3. Conversational humor
    1.4. Humor markers
        1.4.1. Terminological issues in the study of humor markers
        1.4.2. Prosodic markers of humor
            1.4.2.1. Empirical studies of prosodic humor markers
        1.4.3. Laughter as a marker of humor
        1.4.4. Markers of irony
    1.5. Organization of the volume

2. **Performing humor multimodally: An overview (approx. 8,000 words/16 pages)**
    2.1. Introduction
    2.2. Individual smiling behavior
    2.3. Joint negotiation
    2.4. Smiling synchronicity
    2.5. Gaze
        2.5.1. Gaze aversion and conversational humor
        2.5.2. Gaze to the mouth and conversational irony

Figure 20.4 Sample book outline and chapter sections

> **Chapter 1 (approx. 8,000 words/16 pages)**
> - Introduction (approx. 1,000 words/2 pages)
> - The field of humor studies (approx. 100 words/2 pages)
> - Conversational humor (approx. 100 words/2 pages)
> - Humor markers (approx. 4,000 words/8 pages)
> - Organization of the volume (approx. 100 words/2 pages)

Figure 20.5 Word count allocation for chapters and sections

As shown in Figure 20.4, something that worked well for Elisa was to first allot a certain word count to each chapter, and then do the same for each major heading within a chapter, as illustrated in Figure 20.5.

The strategy exemplified in Figures 20.4 and 20.5 can be useful for the outline that you will include in the book proposal, although this may be field-specific. We recommend you check with the publisher as to how much detail you are expected to include. Adding a word count to your outline will also help you when you are ready to start writing, as it allows you to break down the writing task into smaller units, making the overall project more bearable and easier to accomplish. It is also helpful to imagine how the chapter will be shaped, and how much information you will be able to include in each section. Needless to say, these numbers will change, but having smaller, more manageable tasks to accomplish will help you get started and maintain a good writing pace.

Next, for each heading or subheading in your outline, write down a list of all the major points, ideas, and authors that you plan to discuss there. This will help you not only with getting started (again, one step at a time), but also with checking for repetitions or omissions and making sure chapters and sections within chapters are logically connected and your arguments flow nicely.

After the outline, you will likely be asked to include a short abstract for each chapter. These should focus on the original and novel contributions of your work, explaining how you will address the main topic(s) of the chapter, what issues will be discussed and how, and how everything you are doing is contributing to the field. You should basically follow the same guidelines we discussed for the book summary.

When the book proposal is based on a dissertation, the publisher may also ask you to show how the book differs from the dissertation. This is very important because, first of all, the dissertation and the monograph are two distinct genres (see Chapter 16), and second, this is another important criterion that reviewers will employ to judge your work and decide if it should be approved or not. When addressing the dissertation-to-book changes, one good strategy can be to include a two-column table in which you show, side by side, how the two products are different structurally and content-wise and how each dissertation chapter (in the left column) contributes to one or more book chapters (in the right column). The same can be done for each chapter, showing how the goal of the same chapter in the dissertation differs from its goal in the book manuscript. You can also easily show what has been deleted or added, making the reviewers' job much easier. Anything you include in this table should still be discussed in one or more paragraphs, as you will need to explain the rationale behind these changes.

Action item!

Choose one or two scholarly books that you recently read and liked. Have a look at their table of contents, and pay attention to how the chapters are organized. Is there an introductory chapter or a data chapter? Does each chapter work as an independent short story? Are the chapters organized chronologically or thematically? Whatever it is that these books are doing, you can do it too. Make a note of these aspects, and use this information to plan your table of contents.

20.1.3 Market and Readership

The next part of the proposal typically includes a brief but on-target market analysis and potential readership. The market analysis should mention journals that might publish a review of your book and associations that could give your project visibility after publication, by providing opportunities for conference or book presentations. The market analysis should include a list of competitors, that is, books that overlap in part with yours. Competing books might overlap with your proposed project due to similarities in methods, perspectives, or overall topic, but there shouldn't be a total overlap between your book and a competitor's. If that's the case, you may have a problem, because the publisher is unlikely to publish your book unless you offer something new that is not already available. If you are publishing in a second language field, however, things may differ. For example, you may be proposing a book in Spanish on a specific aspect of Spanish L2 teaching that has only been discussed in English, so your proposed volume may have the advantage of being used by Spanish teachers worldwide, as they will all read Spanish but not necessarily English.

To prepare your market analysis, think about volumes that have been published on your topic. These are books that you should have already read and cited, so this information should be easily available to you. Next, consider what these books do

20.1 Parts of a Book Proposal

> Some of the chapters from [competing book] overlap with the proposed book in terms of topic (chapters 2, 3, and 4), but none offers a comparable, in-depth analysis, touches on the multimodal aspects of humor performance, nor adopts an interdisciplinary perspective.

Figure 20.6 Discussing competing books

and do not do. For example, they may be excellent but a bit outdated, they may employ similar methods to yours but on a different topic, or they may be written for a different audience than your book. The idea is that, in this section of the proposal, you show that you know your competitors, you offer an accurate assessment of their strong and weak points, and you demonstrate how your book is different (possibly because you address some of those weak points or do things differently). Be mindful when writing the market analysis, because some of the authors of these books may end up being the reviewers of your book proposal. Remember that your goal is not to be overly critical of anyone else's work, but to show how your book addresses a gap in the research. In Figure 20.6, from Elisa's book proposal, after describing a competing book in positive terms, she notes a gap and how her proposed volume contributes to filling it.

Last, you will need to include a section in which you discuss your book's audience. This is extremely important, because the audience sets the tone for your book. Typically, your audience will be students (either undergraduate or graduate), practitioners (such as second language teachers), or scholars. It is unlikely that your book will appeal to all of these people at once, as they have different needs, interests, and levels of expertise. So think hard about your target audience and be honest. When doing this, also consider geographical areas (will people in Europe be equally interested as people in the United States? What about Asia? Latin America?). Language may be one barrier, but also remember that what would work for students, practitioners, and scholars in your contexts may not work for them in another country. If your book has an international appeal, say so and explain how and why. If the audience will likely be limited to people in the United States, you should say so and explain why. If the book can be used as a textbook, you should include the name of relevant courses, their level (undergraduate or graduate), and the names of some universities where these courses are taught.

20.1.4 Timeline and Reviewers

The proposal usually concludes with a proposed timeline for completing the manuscript and a list of potential reviewers. The timeline should be realistic, and you can see an example in Figure 20.7. To calculate more or less how long

	Jan	Feb	Mar	Apr	May	Jun	Jul	Sep	Oct
Writing	Table of contents Outline chapters	Ch1	Ch2	Ch3	Ch3 Ch4	Ch5 Ch6	Ch6	Table of contents Introduction	Index Figures Tables
Revision					Ch1	Ch2	Ch3 Ch4	Ch5	Ch6	Introduction
Others	Integrate feedback References							Formatting References	References

Figure 20.7 Sample book-writing timeline

it will take you to finish the manuscript (and by finishing it, we mean the whole thing, including any figures or tables, all revisions, all references, formatting, etc.), start by making a list of chapters. Based on the amount of changes needed to write new chapters or move from dissertation to book, calculate how many weeks you will need to either write the chapter from scratch (this could range from two to six months, depending on your other obligations), expand or substantially revise it (one month could be enough), or complete final revisions (one month or less should be enough). Give yourself another month to prepare all documents before the final submission. Once you arrive at a number, double that figure, as we are all awful at estimating how long a project will take.

The list of reviewers should include names and contact information of people who are experts in your field and could offer relevant and constructive criticism that you will then use to improve your manuscript. Publishers tend to ask authors for a list of suggested reviewers to evaluate their proposal and full manuscript, but there is no guarantee that these are the people they will ask or, if they do, they may not be available to review your book. It can be a good idea to have a mix of people from different contexts (domestic and international scholars) and at different stages of their career (while both perspectives are useful, junior scholars may be more up to date with the latest developments in the field, while senior scholars will have a broader view of the discipline). When selecting potential reviewers, you should keep in mind that, often, you are not allowed to include people with whom you have collaborated recently. What an editor means by this can vary slightly, but in general a reviewer should not be a coauthor or copresenter on a paper, someone you have taught with, or one of your supervisors. As one acquisitions editor explained, potential reviewers should be people you know "at arm's length, at best." If you must choose between two reviewers, pick the one with better academic credentials. Their opinion will carry more weight with the publisher.

20.2 Submitting Your Proposal

Once your proposal is finished and all sections are completed, you are ready to submit it. However, before you do so, be sure to check it thoroughly; small typos or errors in the references may discourage the editor. Not to make you paranoid, but the editor literally has nothing to base their decision on besides your proposal and possibly a couple of sample chapters (aside from your reputation, as established through your CV). If this isn't your first book, that is reassuring to the editor who is assessing your proposal, since if you did it before, you can do it again. However, if this is your first book, they are taking a leap of faith, and they will scrutinize your proposal accordingly. Once you have checked the proposal on screen and on paper and received feedback from at least a couple of people (colleagues, mentors, and others in your field), you can submit it to the editor. You may already be in contact with the editor, either because you have met at a conference (see Chapter 31) or because you emailed them to request the last version of their publishing guidelines. If you have never submitted a book proposal before and are unsure of what exactly you should include in your email, have a look at Appendix B for some recommendations and sample language.

After you submit the proposal, you will most likely receive a response from the editor to acknowledge they have received it, and, if you are lucky, they may even tell you what comes next (maybe it's ready to be sent out to reviewers, or the editor will ask you to make some adjustments). It's also possible that you will not hear anything for a while. If you need to follow up with them (if a month has passed and you have heard nothing, then it is OK to follow up with the editor) and ask about the status of your proposal, in Appendix C you will find a sample email that can help you get started. Our recommendation is that you attach a copy of the proposal to your follow-up email to refresh the editor's memory of your project.

Questions for Reflection

1. When developing an idea into a book proposal (and later a book), it is important to consider your audience and the purpose of your book. What would you like your book to do? Who will it speak to? Remember, you cannot try to accomplish too many things at once, so be specific.
2. If you teach college courses and would like to publish a textbook, think about your courses. What are some important things that books on the market fail to address, meaning you have to complement the textbook with your own materials when you teach the topic? If you are teaching that course, you can take notes after each class and start from there. They may come together in your next book (but may or may not count toward tenure, if that's the path you're on).

Questions for Discussion

1. Ask colleagues to share their experience as proposal reviewers. What are they looking for in a proposal? What mistakes do they see junior scholars making? Are there any red flags that would make them more inclined to reject a proposal?
2. Conduct a small, informal survey among colleagues in your field. What books does the field need? What topics would they like to read more about? Those ideas could inform your next book project.

Questions for Your Mentor

1. Ask your mentor about their first book proposal. Was it their dissertation? How did they decide to publish it? If it wasn't, how did the idea for the book come about?
2. If your mentor has published several books with different publishers, ask them about their experience. Their stories can help you select or avoid a publisher.

21 Edited Volumes

Edited books may not be the most common type of publication for a junior scholar, since some of these (like handbooks) are edited by more senior scholars who have a longer trajectory in the field; a broader knowledge of its themes, topics, trends; and, importantly, a network of academic contacts who could contribute to the project. But if you have a good idea for an edited book or have been invited by a publisher or a colleague to work on an edited volume, then by all means, go for it. In this chapter, we guide you through all the steps and decisions involved in such a large collaborative process, from the initial steps, such as choosing coeditors and authors and writing guidelines and templates for authors, to mid-project actions, such as staying in touch with authors to monitor their progress, and postproject initiatives, including promoting the volume. We will also discuss the process of choosing and working with the publisher.

First things first, we now assume you have a good idea for an edited volume, either because it came to you in a dream (we told you not to eat that third helping of lasagna) or the publisher suggested you work on a proposal (see Chapter 20) or a colleague has invited you to join them as a coeditor. How do you decide if this is the right time to begin such a big project? Editing a volume is a very big project that will keep you busy for years (two or three on average). Moreover, some may regard an edited book as less prestigious than a monograph. So, how do you decide if it's the right time to pursue such a project? Our suggestion, before saying yes, is to consider a few factors:

- How invested are you in the topic of the volume? If this is your main research area, then an edited volume is probably a good opportunity for you to dig deeper into it, develop new contacts, and establish yourself as an important voice in this particular field. At the same time, you need to know enough about this topic to be able to choose the right subtopics to be addressed in each chapter and the right authors to do so.
- How much time do you have? Of course, there is never enough time. If you don't have other major projects ongoing or planned for the next few years,

then you may be able to pull this off without much delay. This edited volume will become your major project in the months to come.
- How many people do you know who work in this area? This is an important question to consider. While it is true that editing a volume will expand your network of contacts, if you are starting with just three people in mind who could potentially write a chapter, it will be hard to find contributors.

> **Action item!**
> There's nothing better than a good old pros and cons list to help you make a decision. Consider the points we mentioned above and jot down a few ideas. We recommend discussing your list with a mentor or trusted colleague.

As usual, if you are not sure, talk to a mentor or colleague and brainstorm with them, using the questions in the bulleted list above to get started. If, after reading up to this point, you've made up your mind and decided to edit a volume, keep reading for more advice.

21.1 Coeditors

At this point, you will have to juggle three big decisions that are all related: choosing a coeditor or not, choosing authors for each chapter, and developing a proposal. Let's begin discussing the choice of coeditors, if any, as there are advantages and disadvantages to each scenario. If you decide to go solo, all the burden of the work will be on you but, on the other hand, you will have control over the whole process. You may still seek advice and suggestions from colleagues you respect, for example to make a final decision regarding the authorship of a certain chapter, but it would be unreasonable to ask them to do more than that. If you decide to work with someone else, then who you choose will join you at every step of the process and will impact the progress of the project. Based on our experience, before choosing a coeditor, you should consider the following aspects:

- Have you worked with this person before, or do you know someone you trust who has worked with them? You will be a team, so it is important you can work well together, get along, share views and goals, and so on. The quality of their scholarly work is surely important, but so are their personality and work style.
- Do they have prior experience editing volumes? This would be a big plus if it is your first time, as they may have suggestions but also sample documents or strategies that will come in handy.
- Are they interested and available? This may seem strange to consider BEFORE inviting someone, as you may assume they will let you know if

they are. However, you should do a bit of research to make sure that the project is interesting enough to them (it fits well in their research agenda) so they will be more inclined to accept and ready to invest the necessary time and effort. You should also make sure that they are not already busy with other major projects, since they may accept based on their initial interest, but then slow you down due to other commitments (academics are notoriously bad at saying no).

If you have someone in mind who could be your coeditor, make sure that when you invite them to join you, you share detailed information regarding the scope of the project, your intended timeline, and your roles and expectations with them. If you already have a draft of the proposal, you may want to share that as well, so that your potential coeditor can get a clear sense of the project. Remember that each project is different, so you want to avoid any miscommunication.

21.2 Proposal

While you are busy choosing a coeditor, you should also be thinking about the proposal and potential authors for each of your chapters. This process is exciting but will require that you leverage your research skills and your network of colleagues. Before thinking about the authors, you should have a good idea about the scope of your project, its intended audience, and a possible draft for a timeline. Put all this in writing, as it will be part of the book proposal you submit to the publisher. Figure 21.1 offers a sample timeline developed for

2020		
	May 2020:	Prepare proposal, chapter structure, handbook structure.
		Preliminary list of chapters and authors.
	September 2020:	Contact authors.
	October 2020:	Authors submit abstract.
	November 2020:	Abstract revised and modified if necessary.
2021		
	April 2021:	Authors submit outline of chapters.
	June 2021:	Outlines go back to authors with our comments (min. 2 reports per outline).
	November 2021:	Authors submit first draft.
2022		
	January 2022:	Authors receive back chapters with comments.
	March 2022:	Final chapters.
	April – ?:	Editing, Index, etc.
	September 2022:	Publication.

Figure 21.1 Sample timeline for an edited volume

a handbook with thirty chapters and over sixty authors (and keep in mind these numbers will likely change). Needless to say, with this many chapters and authors, the actual publication date ended up being more than a year later than the intended one. In fact, the editors intended to submit the whole manuscript to the publisher for a final review in September 2023, but submission did not happen until January 2024. Don't be surprised if the same happens to you.

At this stage, we recommend you keep track of all your ideas for authors and the proposal on two separate documents. An Excel document can help you keep track of chapter titles and possible authors, including their affiliation and email address, link to their profile, and co-authors (more on this later), and a Word document can help you build the draft for the proposal. If you are working on a research volume, it will likely have a more manageable number of chapters and authors, and it is not uncommon to contact authors *before* submitting a proposal to the publisher. On the other hand, if you are working on a larger volume such as a handbook, you will likely be dealing with a large number of chapters and authors and, typically, you will submit your proposal to the publisher before having contacted potential authors. Keep this in mind as you continue reading, because it affects the order of some of the steps. Typically, in a proposal for an edited volume you will be asked to include the following:

1. *Title and collection/series*
2. *Rationale* (up to 500 words). Contextualize the field in which the volume will make a contribution, say why this volume is needed (the famous "research gap" it will help fill), and explain the goals of the volume and its intended audience.
3. *Intended completion date and length of the volume* (an estimated number of pages and words). To give you an example, the handbook discussed before had an estimated length of up to 600 pages and 260,000 words.
4. *Content overview.* Here you should give the publisher and reviewers a clear sense of how the volume will be organized. If you are dealing with a research volume, give a detailed overview of each topic covered, highlighting its timeliness and originality, as you would, for example, in an abstract for a research article. If you already have confirmation from some authors, you may ask them to write an abstract and include it in the proposal. If not, as for a handbook, you want to include a short paragraph about each topic and how it will be treated (see Figure 21.2), an explanation of the internal organization of the chapters (see Figure 21.3, this is an important piece of information that you will also send to authors to help them stay on track and understand expectations), an explanation of the sections of the volume and the chapters these contain, and an explanation of how the authors will be selected (promoting co-authorships, targeting certain geographical regions, including established as well as junior scholars, etc.). For this last point,

21.2 Proposal

> This chapter bridges the pedagogical tradition of SLT and L2 teaching with the multiliteracies approach. It offers an historical overview of the concept of literacy (its origins and meaning, from a historical and pedagogical perspective) as it evolved into multiliteracies. The chapter then addresses current definitions, applications, and approaches to multiliteracies for SLT.

Figure 21.2 Sample chapter description for a handbook

A. **Introduction (Introduction)**
   (approximately 400–500 words)
   (200-word abstract in Spanish, 5 keywords; 200-word abstract in English, 5 keywords)
B. **Aspectos históricos y teóricos (Historical and Theoretical Aspects)**
   (*know* – declarative knowledge) (approximately 1500 words)
   1. What is (topic)/State of the Art historical overview, state of the art.
   2. Issues related to (topic): explanation of the theoretical issues related to the subject of the chapter; terminology (considering the interdisciplinarity of the volume)
C. **Aspectos metodológicos (Methodological Aspects)**
   (*know & know how* – declarative and procedural knowledge) (approximately 1500 words)
   1. How (topic) has been researched methods, populations, instruments, etc.
   2. Main contributions of applied research for L2 teaching and learning, including action research and the teacher as researcher
   3. Open debate: outline possible future lines of research (areas in which there is not enough research, new areas and trends)
D. **Aspectos pedagógjeos (Pedagogical Aspects)**
   (*know how* – procedural knowledge) (approximately 2500 words)
   1. How to integrate (topic) in the Spanish classroom and/or curriculum/General Perspective: (dealing with a specific subtopic or a concrete aspect of the main topic)
   2. Guidelines: general guidelines to integrate (topic) and methodological aspects
   3. Practical applicability in the classroom (with examples of what has been/can be done)
E. **References bibliograficas (References)**
   (approximately 1500 words)
   1. Cited references for sections A, B, and C of the chapter.
   2. Annotated key reference (theory, textbooks, and other resources; max. 3 items). This part will allow SLT researchers and practitioners to gain access to relevant publications originally written in English or languages other than Spanish

Figure 21.3 Sample internal organization of chapters for a handbook

think about whether you will be inviting authors or will publish a call for papers. As usual, there are advantages and disadvantages to each option, but we recommend that, if your plan is to edit a large volume, you opt for

inviting authors. The project will already be challenging to manage as is without the added complexity and uncertainty of a call for papers.
5. *Credentials of the editors.* Here you need to make a case for why you (and your coeditor) are the right people for the job. It's a sort of short biographical note.
6. *Readership and market.* See Chapter 20 about book proposals, as this is virtually the same.
7. *Comparison with competing books.* Again, see Chapter 20.

Once your proposal is ready (i.e., circulated among trusted colleagues and read and revised multiple times), you can go ahead and submit it while you continue working on the list of potential authors and a set of documents that will come in handy once the proposal gets accepted. If the publisher is interested in the project, the proposal will be sent to reviewers (we have had between three and five reviewers for this type of volume), which gives you plenty of time to work on what follows.

21.3 Authors

Now, let's get back to the list of authors. There is an art to it, as you need to find people who are competent, of course, but there may be additional criteria to consider, such as those listed below. Don't be afraid to ask your trusted colleagues for names of people who could write specific chapters, sharing with them what you are looking for. We recommend having more than one person listed for each chapter, not only because you may want to promote co-authorships, but because if your top choice is too busy to accept the invitation, you are ready to move on to your second or third choice without wasting any time.

- *Seniority.* You may or may not want to include younger voices in your volume, or you may choose to stick with the big names in your field, if they accept your invitation. A call for papers is a possibility for an edited volume, but it is unlikely that you will receive submissions from any of the big names. It will add a lot of work to your plate as you sort through a lot of subpar submissions. Make sure you have a rationale for your choice. You may also want to strive for a good mix of established and young voices.
- *Co-authorship.* Are you willingly promoting certain types of co-authorship (e.g., pairing young and senior scholars or people who work on the same topic but from different geographical or disciplinary perspectives)? While this could be enriching and a selling point for your volume, it will require more work on your end, and may turn off potential authors.

21.3 Authors

- *Affiliation, geographical location, and other factors.* Unless you have a very good explanation for it, it is not a good idea to include all authors from the same institution, country, and so on. An edited volume will typically offer a wide perspective on a specific topic, and if every author shares the same views, then how can you do that? Make sure you keep track of who your authors are to diversify and include a wide range of points of views. An Excel document with a column for each of the criteria that matter to you is a good strategy to manage the list of authors.

Once you have your list of authors, and before you contact them, we recommend you draft a set of documents that will make your life easier in the future. Start by drafting the first few emails you will send to each one of them: the initial invitation email (which will be fairly long and include scope of the volume, list of sections and chapters, brief blurb of the corresponding chapter, general structure of the chapter with sample length of sections, and main deadlines of the project); the email proposing a co-authorship (if needed); the email with some additional information in case they accept (such as the style guide, the publisher contract, and any additional documents that can help them develop the chapter you are looking for); and a follow-up email you will send when the first deadline approaches. We recommend that you share the same information with everyone, even if you already have a personal relationship with some of the authors (in that case, you may just add a line at the beginning to personalize the invitation, and then copy the official email below). You can have a look at some sample emails in Appendix I.

As you get more involved with the project and the authors start to send in their contributions, remember to keep track of E.V.E.R.Y.T.H.I.N.G. We cannot stress this enough, as it is easy to misplace a file, forget who sent you what, delete an email by mistake, and so on. You will be dealing with many people and many documents, and we guarantee that they will each have a nice excuse for being late and messing up your nicely planned timeline, so just keep track of everything. Again, an Excel document will be useful to list, in each column after a chapter, at what stage they are (see Figure 21.4 for an example), and you will need multiple numbered folders to save all the versions of the documents you will receive.

In Figure 21.4 you can see that for each chapter (on a separate line) we listed the major deadlines and milestones and used those columns to keep track of the status and any additional comments needed, such as who reviewed what and when (as there were two coeditors, Ed 1 and Ed 2 in Figure 21.4). We also used colors to mark the urgency or readiness of each document.

Chapter	Invitation sent	Bilingual abstract received	Abstract feedback sent	Outline received	Outline feedback sent	Chapter draft received	Chapter feedback sent	Revised chapter received	Bio received
1 (Ed 1)	31/1/2021, 2nd author Feb 1	12 Feb	20 Mar	31 May	25 July - Issues	Reminder 18 Feb 2022	2 Mar	Yes	Yes
2 (Ed 1)	31/1/2021	15 Feb	29 Mar	29 May	25 July	17 Dec	2 Mar 2022	Reminder 3 June	Yes
3 (Ed 2)	31/1/2021	15 Feb	28 Mar	27 May	22 July	10 Jan 2022	20 Feb	Yes	Yes

Figure 21.4 Sample tracking document for edited volumes

Action item!

Because edited volumes are big projects with many steps and people involved, you may consider using a project management software (these are useful to manage any type of project). Have a look at some options below to see if you find something that fits your needs and skills (we include only those with a free plan below, but there are many others available):

- Monday https://monday.com/lang/es (free up to two users)
- Trello https://trello.com/ (free plan with some restrictions)
- OpenProject www.openproject.org/ (free and with interesting features for research)
- Asana https://asana.com/ (free plan with some restrictions)

Last but not least, you will need to decide how to handle the revision process and what documents will be reviewed by whom. You can opt for in-house revisions, which means that you and your coeditor will take care of that, or a process similar to a standard peer review in which reviewers may be external to the project or internal (i.e., the authors review each other's chapters). You know the drill: There will be ups and downs no matter what you choose. In-house revision is faster, because you don't have to invite anyone, but time-consuming, because you will have to read and comment on each chapter. It gives you control over the whole project, which is why it is a good option for a large project such as a handbook, but you may also be facing some difficulties because you may not have the required expertise to judge every contribution. Internal peer review is the second fastest option. It's a good option if you are working with a research edited volume, because everyone you invited is an expert, and they will not only be qualified to review but will probably also be interested in other chapters in the volume. Last, external peer review will require more time and effort, but could be a good idea if you opted for a call-for-paper model rather than inviting authors.

21.3 Authors

Your publisher may have a strong preference about the review process, and their decision goes, needless to say. While working on an edited volume can be a lot of work, it can also be a fantastic opportunity to build professional networks and gain valuable experience.

> **Questions for Reflection**
>
> 1. Editing a book requires considerable time and effort, which means that you will not be able to take on other major projects. Will this affect other areas of your job in a negative way? Do you have a heavy teaching load? Does your department expect you to publish a monograph instead? Consider your current commitments and goals to see how an edited volume would fit into your schedule.
> 2. Look back at the sample timeline in Figure 21.1 (which one of us actually produced). Would a timeline like this make sense given where you are in your career right now? Could you shorten it to make it fit your current situation (maybe by including fewer than thirty chapters, etc.)?
>
> **Questions for Discussion**
>
> 1. Ask colleagues how they perceive edited volumes in terms of prestige and academic reputation. What do they consider to be the pros and cons of editing a volume?
> 2. If any of your colleagues have already had the opportunity to edit a book, ask them if and how that has advanced their career.
>
> **Questions for Your Mentor**
>
> 1. Ask your mentor when, if ever, they edited their first volume and how they approached this project (was it by invitation or submission, how did they keep on track, etc.?).
> 2. Editing a book requires a serious time commitment. At the stage of your career you are at, would it be a good idea to invest time and energy in editing a book?

22 Grant Proposals

In this chapter, we address a specific type of academic writing: grant writing. We begin by briefly discussing how to find a funding source that is a good fit for your project and then move on to discuss three key parts of most grant applications: the narrative, the work plan and timeline, and the budget. Throughout the chapter, we discuss how grant writing is different from other forms of scholarly writing and help you understand the multiple components of a grant, their purposes, and the different steps and offices that are involved in the process of submitting a grant proposal.

Being able to secure external funding for your research agenda or to support your program may or may not be a requirement of your current position; either way, grant writing is a desirable skill that will not only give you access to additional funds but can also gain you the respect of the administration (or even a "seat at the table") and open up possibilities for alternative, non-academic careers. However, grant writing is a skill that is not often taught in graduate programs, and many scholars find it particularly challenging because it is quite different from the type of writing that we normally do for research articles or books. Grant writing is essentially writing about a research project you have not completed yet in a convincing, specialized but accessible way, while also making sure that your goals, methodology, and expected results align with the funding agency's mission and will make an important contribution to society at large beyond your specific discipline. If you can outline your plan for world peace in the proposal, that's always a bonus, too. It's a lot, but we will break down the process and its parts for you.

22.1 Finding the Right Funding Program

First things first, if you have an idea for a project that needs funding, you need to do some research and identify some options that could be a good fit. These vary a lot based on the country in which you work or in which the project will be conducted, your current title (doctoral student, junior faculty, etc.), your field or the main area to which the project contributes, the scope of the project (organizing a conference, writing a manuscript, consulting archives, etc.), the stage of the project for which you are seeking funding (planning stage, proof of concept, or consolidation), and what can be funded (travel, stipends, materials, etc.), among others. A good place to get started would be talking to a grant specialist at your institution or college, someone who knows internal and external funding opportunities and can help you find one that matches your needs. If you don't know if there is one, ask a colleague who has been around longer than you or do a quick Google search. Another option is to consult one of the many grant databases that currently exist. These may vary by country, but some options include www.profellow.com/ (for fellowships), www.Grants.gov (mainly, but not exclusively, if you are based in the United States), https://euraxess.ec.europa.eu/funding/search (mainly, but not exclusively, if you are based in Europe), https://convocatorias.conicet.gov.ar/ (in Argentina), or https://us.fulbrightonline.org/types-of-grants (with different options based on the country). Additional subscription-based options may be available via your institution, such as https://pivot.proquest.com/funding_main or https://spin.infoedglobal.com/Home/SOLRSearch. Walker and Unruh (2018) offer many recommendations for grant writing and fellowships in the humanities and social sciences, including a detailed comparison of different funding agencies (p. 18 and following) and an index of funding agencies (p. 197 and following) that can orient your initial search.

22.2 Crafting the Narrative

Once you have identified one or more funding agencies for your project, it's time to start thinking about your narrative. In general, a grant proposal will include at least these key parts: a narrative, a work plan and timeline, and a budget. The narrative is probably the most complex and important document of the application, as it is where you explain why your project is relevant for the world and for this funding agency, demonstrate your knowledge of the field and your suitability to successfully complete the project, and convincingly show the impact that this work will have on the scholarly community and, more importantly, beyond it. Essentially, the goal of the narrative and of the whole set of documents you will submit is *to sell your idea and yourself as a researcher* (Connor & Mauranen, 1999). This is why the style of a grant narrative shows some key differences when compared to other forms of academic writing. Connon and Upton (2004) describe these as "strongly informational, closely edited texts that use an explicit, precise and non-narrative structure to appeal to potential donors" (p. 253). These tend to use less hedges (words like *may* and *would* that do not show a strong commitment on the part of the author) and more boosters (words like *significant, relevant, contribute*) (Feng, 2002), but remember that you should also clearly say why or how it is significant or relevant. The writing style is more energetic, direct, and concise; to achieve this, you should use active voice, strong phrasing, and direct references to yourself and your work in the first person, while avoiding jargon and lengthy sentences with complex syntax (Porter, 2007).

Within the narrative, the initial paragraph is probably the most important one, the place where you engage your reader by asking a relevant and meaningful question and then explaining in a compelling and feasible way how you will answer it. Every word you decide to include in your narrative must be worth its weight in gold, or, as Porter (2007) wrote, as you read one of these texts, "[e]ach time you learn something about a subject entirely new to you" (p. 38). Because the stakes are so high and the word count is limited, there is no space for empty phrasing. Figure 22.1, taken from a successful grant application that Elisa wrote, illustrates the different

We are applying to the Level I DHAG to support the initial stages of a large innovative project with the end goal of creating the first annotated, bilingual, multimodal corpus of written and oral discourse produced by heritage speakers of Spanish in the United States in English and Spanish.	**Main goal of the project (what do you plan to accomplish with these funds?)**
The corpus will purposefully include speakers from different socio linguistic generations of the understudied and underrepresented varieties spoken in the DMV (the DC-Maryland-Virginia area).	**Strength 1 (why this project is worth funding)**
The project will engage scholars, educators, and students in the field of Spanish as a heritage language (SHL) as well as members of the Latinx community…	**Strength 2 (why this project is worth funding)**
…to create an open-access online resource that will facilitate the study of SHL discourse and support research in languages in contact, bilingualism, and heritage language discourse, which will not only serve to enhance current research areas in the SHL field…	**Strength 3 (why this project is worth funding)**
…but also impact SHL teaching at all levels, from teacher preparation programs to curriculum design and SHL assessment.	**Strength 4 (why this project is worth funding)**
The corpus will also serve as a digital repository representing the voices and experiences of the diverse population of Latinx Spanish heritage speakers from the DMV area.	**Strength 5 (why this project is worth funding)**

Figure 22.1 Breakdown of the first paragraph of a grant narrative

22.2 Crafting the Narrative

parts of this first paragraph, which tend to be organized around a subset of moves that structure the overall document: territory, gap, goal, means, competence claim, importance claim, and benefits (Connor & Upton, 2004, p. 239; but see also Connor & Mauranen, 1999, who identified thirty-four moves). If you think about it, these are similar to the moves you will find in a research article (minus the competence claim), with some important differences. First, in a grant narrative, you should justify the research need based on real-world, nonacademic issues, while in a research article you can do that while staying in the academic, research territory. That is, in a grant application your goal should not be to study, explore, or analyze a theme or issue as you would in a classic research project (Porter, 2007); rather, in your application you should clarify that your goal is to solve a real-life problem. Second, in a grant narrative, you can only claim potential contributions, since the research has not been done yet, while in a research article you already have your data and results. However, it is worth remembering that every grant is different, and your narrative must meet the specific criteria of the grant you are applying to.

Before you start writing, make sure to have a look at some past awarded projects, which are typically available via the funding agency website. Another source of help is the grant officer at your institution, who can review your documents and offer feedback before you submit, or a colleague with some grant-writing experience. Additionally, some agencies will indicate a sort of early submission date for those potential applicants who would like to receive feedback ahead of the official deadline. Last, remember that very few people get funded on their first attempt. You should not get discouraged if that happens. It's extremely common, and you will receive some feedback even when your project is rejected so you will be able to improve it and try again. Persistence is key.

Action item!

Go through previously funded projects and find a couple that are close to what you would like to do (either based on the field, general topic, or level of funding). Now, select the award criteria for the grant you are applying to. Make sure to have both documents available side by side. Go through the narrative document and identify the parts that speak directly to each of the award criteria. Notice the overall organization (does it include the moves we presented before?), the degree of explicitness, and the use of certain formulas and expressions (can you identify some of the linguistic features we discussed?). Use these as your guide to get started on your own narrative document.

22.3 The Work Plan and Timeline

The work plan is the document that shows how and when you plan to achieve everything you proposed to do in your narrative. A good work plan is specific and includes all tasks and subtasks you will need to accomplish, and therefore it will go into more detail than the narrative. A good work plan is also realistic, feasible, and, thus, credible. You will not get funded if your plan sounds too ambitious, but your proposal also won't be attractive if your plan is underachieving or not well thought out. If the goal of the narrative is to convince the committee you have a good, impactful idea, the goal of the work plan is to convince them you know what it takes to get there and how to do it.

> **Action item!**
> A good strategy for writing your plan is to use a backwards design. First, make a list of the main goals you plan to accomplish. Then, using a calendar, mark the end of the funding period (this is typically given by the funding agency and marks the end of your project) and plan to accomplish your main or last goal a bit before that date to give yourself some wiggle room. Then, insert all the intermediate goals or steps in the calendar, going backwards. On a third pass, add any minor steps or tasks that will be necessary to accomplish each goal.

You can structure your work plan in phases or goals, and you should develop each of these into a coherent paragraph in which you tell the committee who will work on it and when, keeping in mind a realistic timeline and including some buffer weeks (or months) in case things go wrong. When preparing this document, make sure to include meetings, training sessions, recruiting, archival work, trips, and so on, and consider each collaborator's workload, the percentage of time and effort they will dedicate to the project, and an estimate of how much time each task will require. For example, if a collaborator is already teaching four courses per semester, it may be unrealistic to expect they will spend ten hours per week on this project.

A few additional recommendations when writing your work plan include adding a risk assessment and potential solutions section and a concluding evaluation phase. When assessing potential risks you will face, try to think about what could go wrong with your data collection, your participants, or your collaborators. What if the archive you plan to use is temporarily closed? What if a global pandemic disrupts your travel plans? What if your collaborators quit the project to follow Taylor Swift around the world on her next tour? You should be able to anticipate at least some of these risks and have solutions in place. For example, the archive may offer some remote access to a limited

22.3 The Work Plan and Timeline

section of their materials, you may be able to interview participants remotely instead of in person, or you may identify some additional collaborators or have recruiting plans in place.

Last, it is good practice to include a final evaluation phase in your project, in which you look back at what you said you would do and how, and then consider what was actually done. It is normal for a multiyear project to change a bit over time, so don't be too worried if things didn't go exactly as planned. However, every agency has certain requirements and restrictions regarding what can change with no consequences, what can change but must be approved, and what cannot change. When writing the section of your work plan about evaluation, consider how you will do that: you could meet to discuss challenges and improvements, as well as plan the next steps of the project; you could distribute a survey; you could have been collecting data throughout the project that allow you to assess how things went.

As part of your work plan, it is not uncommon to include a Gantt chart. At times, it is required and even if it's not, we recommend you do include it as it is a good way to show, in a snapshot, how your project will unfold. A Gantt chart is essentially a color-coded calendar that highlights the phases, tasks, and subtasks of your project, as well as who will work on each of them and for how long. If you have never made one, don't be afraid. There are plenty of templates online that you can download and then edit to fit your needs. You can use the backwards calendar that you created before to set up your Gantt chart. Figure 22.2 shows a portion (yes, Gantt charts can be long) of the Gantt chart submitted with the narrative in Figure 22.1.

Even though Gantt charts can be long, we recommend fitting it in one page, since you want the committee to be able to get a quick and efficient view of all the

TASK DESCRIPTION	PLAN START	PLAN END	ASSIGNED TO	2021 J F M A M J J A S O N D
Phase 1 - Planning and preliminary steps	9/1/2021	12/7/2021		
Schedule first team + collaborators meeting	9/1/2021	9/16/2021	EG	
Meeting with UMD librarians RE platform requirements to host corpus	9/16/2021	10/1/2021	EG (ML, ECT)	
Meeting 1 - planning	10/1/2021	10/16/2021	EG (ALL)	
Identify features of SHL discourse	10/16/2021	11/15/2021	ML (FB)	
Secure external collaborators in the DMV	10/16/2021	11/15/2021	ECT	
Data collection protocol draft	11/16/2021	11/30/2021	EG (ECT)	
Draft and submit IRB application	11/16/2021	11/30/2021	EG (ML, ECT)	
RAs job descriptions draft, dissemination list	11/17/2021	11/27/2021	EG, ML	
Meeting 2 - revise materials & next steps	11/27/2021	12/7/2021	EG (ALL)	

Figure 22.2 Sample Gantt chart

work you plan to accomplish. Another option can be to create different, separated Gantt charts for each main phase of the project, accompanied by brief descriptions.

22.4 The Budget

Rule number one of creating a budget is: *Do not do it yourself.* You need to work together with someone in the financial office of your unit, college, or institution. You should have a budget in mind, meaning, you should know more or less how much each item in your work plan will cost, but there are so many hidden costs and rules that you are probably not aware of that whatever initial budget idea you have in mind will surely change. Be prepared to be flexible and adjust your plan once you figure out your real budget. As an example, universities typically retain part of the money you will be awarded to cover certain costs (space, for example), so even if you are awarded one million dollars, you will not have a million to spend. Another example is fringe benefits for people working on the project, which vary based on their role, salary, and time commitment. Additionally, the funding agency may have some specific rules regarding the budget (what can or should be included, how it should be presented, etc.), and the person in the financial office should be familiar with these rules or, if not, should be able to decipher what those requirements mean. Because of all this, do not, we repeat, do not leave the budget for the end, but start talking with your financial office person early on. This way, you will be able to tailor your project, its goals, and the work commitments of all collaborators to the funds you will actually receive.

Action item!

Who is the administrative assistant who will be working with you on your application? This person plays a key role. If you don't know who this is, you must figure it out as soon as possible. Ask colleagues, talk to your chair, or email the college. Let them know that you are planning to apply for a grant (tell them which one and what is the deadline), and ask who will help with the budget and the financial aspect of it.

22.5 Additional Items

As we mentioned at the beginning of this chapter, a grant application will surely include a narrative document, a work plan and timeline, and a budget. However, there are several other documents that you may be required to submit, so it's a good idea to carefully read the funding notice and any appendix or attachment

22.5 Additional Items

available (yes, sometimes these additional documents are explained in an attachment). Other typical documents you may be asked to submit are:

- a curriculum vitae for each collaborator (check the requirements, as your fifty-page-long academic curriculum will probably not be accepted, and you will have to edit it);
- biographies of all collaborators (you should emphasize anything relevant and related to the project, as the goal of these is to show that your team can do the job);
- list of references in your narrative (keep in mind that self-citations are much more common and expected in grants proposals compared to research articles, because they contribute to building your reputation as an expert in that particular area with the necessary skills and expertise to successfully complete the project); and
- data management plan (if you are based in the United States, think IRB: you are explaining how you will handle the data you will collect to ensure personal information is protected, data are securely stored, and no one will be hurt in any way during the process).

Besides these additional documents, you should also factor in some time to register as a user in the grant platform website. This process is usually not straightforward and requires approval from different people at your university, which can take days or weeks. You may have to ask for initial approval to register, request that the university assign you a username, then log in and actually register. Before you even start working on your application, you may be required to grant access to your application package (empty, but still) to any financial officer at your institution, as they will play a key role in crafting, submitting, and monitoring the budget and other financial elements of the application. Make sure to have a look at the website and read the instructions early in the process.

Submitting a grant may be a great idea to foster your career, and it can earn you some serious kudos from your superiors (who will likely benefit from indirect costs and the likes). However, when deciding to apply for a grant, remember that relatively few are funded and, unless your institution is particularly enlightened, unfunded grants usually don't count toward tenure and promotion. We encourage you to discuss the possibility with your mentor *after* you have read this chapter. One of the best ways to get started in grant writing is to come in as a co-investigator with your mentor or a close colleague.

Questions for Reflection

1. Similar to large edited volumes, grants take time and effort to write and even more to manage, which may prevent you from pursuing other relevant academic activities. Imagine you do get the grant. How does it

fit in your current schedule and workload? What should you change, if anything, for the project to progress smoothly?
2. There are most likely a few things that you will need to learn to be able to write a grant (Gantt charts?), manage it, or develop the whole project you are proposing. Are you ready and interested in learning those skills? Do you know who to go to for support?

Questions for Discussion

1. Time management for grants is a crucial skill, and the bigger the grant, the more difficult this will be. Discuss with your colleagues how they handle big projects and what strategies they prefer to use (see Chapter 21 for some project management options).
2. What types of grants have your colleagues been successful in securing? What funding programs are more popular or fit best with your field, area, or research program?

Questions for Your Mentor

1. Depending on your field, you may get credit toward promotion for just writing a grant or, sometimes, only if you get the grant. Ask your mentor what is more common in your field.
2. Depending on the type of grant and your institution, there may be a few hidden steps to applying and receiving funding (internal deadlines and pre-selection processes, fees and benefits to account for, etc.). Ask your mentor to share what they know and guide you as you learn to navigate this process.

23 Nontraditional Academic Writing

We live in a world of influencers and web celebrities. Entire new genres have appeared, seemingly out of the blue. While there may not be much of an audience for reaction videos to Reviewer #2's comments on your latest article (then again, maybe there would be; we've seen parents record reaction videos to their kids' report cards, after all, and someone must be watching those videos), the potential for engaging in valuable academic discussions online is expanding all the time. For example, while few scholars would have dreamed of appearing on a podcast or doing a book trailer twenty years ago, most of us probably follow an academic podcast nowadays. All the nontraditional media we will briefly mention can offer wonderful opportunities to spread the word about your research and findings. In the next section of the book, we will discuss joining relevant conversations and communities within your discipline, as well as self-promotion. Both these important activities take place largely online and on social media.

But first, a word of warning. Before you get started with any endeavor in the genres that we will discuss in this chapter, check that your employer (department, foundation, etc.) is comfortable with you engaging in these activities and will value them when the time comes. There is a real risk that you might spend precious time on something that your employer won't see the value in. For example, we have a colleague who self-published a book, which is a common practice (according to Wordsrated, 30 percent of e-books are self-published), and many authors generate some sales doing so. However, when our colleague tried to claim the book as a publication for the annual faculty report, the book was not accepted because it was self-published and hence not peer-reviewed. So, while the genres we will discuss may be an excellent medium to get your ideas out there, create "buzz," and ultimately build a strong reputation, you need to make sure that you know what you are doing *before* you start. Of course, if you plan to do this as a parallel but independent venue, then this caveat does not apply.

23.1 Types of Nontraditional Academic Writing

23.1.1 Blogging

Blogging started in the late 1990s, so for some of our readers, it's always been around. For those of us more chronologically challenged, the idea of writing stuff online for other people to read, and then uploading video and sound files for the people to see, has been novel and liberating. Blogging in all its forms has enjoyed enormous popularity, largely because it can range from almost any domain and cover any topic, from personal disclosure (like an online diary) to hard-core political or scientific discussion. There are an estimated 600 million blogs out there. The upside of having an academic presence online is that it attracts attention and can result in readers or other scholars and researchers finding out about your work. The possible downsides are tied to revealing personal, corporate, or organizational details that might embarrass or, worse, expose yourself or your employer to liability. Another risk is that, if you start a blog and then abandon it, unless you actively remove it from your platform (and the platform allows you to do so), it will remain there potentially forever, an embarrassing reminder of a failed project or just a project you lost interest in. The issue is that "dead" pages do not look good, creating the opposite effect of a vibrant, up-to-date blog. Before starting a blog, consider if you have the time and energy to commit to maintaining it.

There are many platforms for blogging, vlogging, photoblogging, and a host of other media. Micro-blogging transitions into social media: Indeed, posting on Facebook or Twitter/X can be considered a form of micro-blogging. For longer forms, Wordpress and Blogger are quite popular. Substack is more recent and based on a newsletter model. Sal, who runs his own mini newsletter on Substack, finds the platform surprisingly easy to use. Do some research before choosing a platform (see Bair, 2023) to find the best option for you.

Action item!

If you want your blog to be easily discoverable by people, keywords are your best friend. But there is an art to it when it comes to online content. Here are three resources you can use to research keywords for your blog or other types of online posts.

- Ahrefs (https://ahrefs.com/): free tool if you have a website; includes useful free tools such as a keyword generator.
- Google Keyword Planner (https://chrome.google.com/webstore/detail/keyword-planner/ohffmmbmebhcljgcdijjlepjaoladfag): a free Google Chrome extension tool for keyword research and analysis.
- Ubersuggest (https://neilpatel.com/ubersuggest/): a free Google Chrome extension tool that provides keyword ideas and content suggestions.

23.1.2 Podcasts

Podcasts are sound files that may be downloaded or streamed (giving the option to be "live"). With currently around three million separate podcasts, this popular genre includes many formats, including interviews, news commentary, discussions of a given topic, self-help, and even fiction. Some podcasts are enhanced by a form of video (like slides), while others are full-video podcasts. A podcaster may operate alone or with co-hosts. You will most likely want to do a podcast on your topic of expertise, or you can try for a "salon" vibe (in the sense of the French salons from the seventeenth century), a gathering of diverse but interesting personalities and ideas. The length may vary from a few minutes to over two hours. There are no rules, really.

Technically, a podcast does not require a lot of equipment, at least in its simplest format. However, you (or a producer) will need to do some editing. Most smartphones have excellent microphones and cameras nowadays, but if you are going to be serious about it, you will want to get some more sophisticated audio recording equipment, a mixer, and editing software. There are videos and websites with detailed instructions and reviews of equipment. There are also books on the subject (such as Meinzer, 2019 or Morris & Tomasi, 2020), as well as various companies that handle the practical aspects of streaming, such as Spotify, Apple, and Google.

Podcasts, much like blogs, require regular or frequent issues, so consider the level of commitment it will require before starting. Also, most podcasts are scripted or work from an outline. Don't think that you can just sit down and ramble for an hour and have a podcast. The same goes for interviews: a good interview requires deep knowledge of the subject matter by both interviewer and interviewee and carefully prepared questions.

In most "short-form" pieces, like podcasts, blogs, and newsletters, the benefits of exposure, networking, and breadth of reach in the field accrue incrementally, much like your audience. You need to be prepared for the fact that initially you will have only a few "followers," but you can grow your audience with time, consistency, and a solid product. For example, the blog "The Thesis Whisperer," which Inger Mewburn (Australian National University) has been writing for over ten years, has over 90,000 readers. For academics, those are dream numbers.

Action item!

There are many useful resources about scholarly podcasting to help you get started and address all these issues in depth. Check out some of the resources below.

- Book-length: *A Guide to Academic Podcasting*, by Copeland and McGregor https://scholars.wlu.ca/books/2/
- Article-length: *Storytelling in Acoustic Spaces: Podcasting as Embodied and Engaged Scholarship*, by Harter www.tandfonline.com/doi/full/10.1080/10410236.2018.1517549
- Web-based guide: *Podcasting and Audio Storytelling* (University of Michigan Library Research Guide) https://guides.lib.umich.edu/c.php?g=839924&p=6000285

Below are some examples of academic podcasts from different disciplines. Pick one to listen to as you consider these aspects:

- Is the style and tone of the podcast (narrative, dialogue, humor) appealing to you? Could this be adapted for your own podcast?
- How and for what purposes are sound effects and music used by the host?
- Is there participation from the audience or invited guests?
- What is your overall impression as the listener? What caused that impression?

Academic podcasts:

- Lexicon Valley http://slate.com/podcasts/lexicon-valley
- Backlisted www.backlisted.fm/
- Ologies www.alieward.com/ologies
- Design Matters www.designmattersmedia.com/
- Two Psychologists Four Beers www.fourbeers.com/

23.1.3 Social Media

We could easily fill this chapter with caveats about social media. As a blanket statement, be careful about what you post. That funny picture or that snarky remark may be very clever today, but it could come back to haunt you later. The key advice here is to carefully curate your online image. A public-facing social media account, which you will share with your employer and academic colleagues and researchers, is not the right place to discuss your partying style or your political leanings (although, see below). Think of posting on Facebook, Twitter/X, and so on as an email to your boss and to your boss's boss. Are you comfortable sharing that image or that thought with them (and with anyone else on earth, for the foreseeable future)? If so, post away. However, curation is not just avoiding embarrassing images or offensive language: curating means presenting an image of yourself that is conducive to your professional goals. Images of yourself

23.1 Types of Nontraditional Academic Writing

presenting at conferences, hanging out with your students at the conference (provided you are not dancing on the table), or visiting notable locations (Sal posted an image of himself exiting the Bodleian library that he's really proud of) are ideal. You may consider having two separate accounts, a professional one and then a private account for your friends and family where you can post anything you want – the key word here is "private."

Action item!

Let's say you would like to share a few thoughts from one of your recent publications on social media to help boost its impact and reach more people. One of the most commonly used techniques to do so is storytelling: you develop a narrative, based on your paper, and publish it as a series of subsequent posts accompanied by images (from your paper, but these could also be memes or gifs to serve as hooks for your audience). Each post needs to engage the audience but also keep them thinking about your posts and expecting the next one.

Here are a few examples:

- https://x.com/jamesptrujillo/status/1752196873975202103?s=20
- https://twitter.com/lucabischetti/status/1321035065124597760
- https://twitter.com/visual_linguist/status/1389567040273408006

Now it's your turn. Choose a paper, and follow these steps (you can expand each of these into more posts if you'd like or need to):

- Post 1: What is the key question your paper answers? Make sure to frame it in terms of its general impact (beyond academia) and avoid too much jargon. Use an image that will get people's attention (a meme of someone – or even better, a cat – thinking hard).
- Post 2: What have you done to answer that question? Avoiding jargon, explain in simple terms who or what you looked at and how. You could use an image from the method section of your paper, for example, if it helps to clarify your message.
- Post 3: What is a surprising or relevant finding? What does this finding mean for the general public and society at large? Can you connect it to a bigger issue or theme?
- Following posts: You can dig deeper into a specific aspect of your work, ask people questions by tagging them, or reply to any reaction you receive. It's important to engage with your audience.

Bonus tip: Make sure to tag relevant people and institutions in your posts and images, using appropriate hashtags #. Do a quick search before posting to find out who and what to tag for maximum engagement and exposure.

23.1.4 Video Pieces

A recent trend is the production of "support" videos for academic pieces, both articles (video abstracts) and books (book trailers). These can be produced professionally by companies hired by the publisher or self-produced by the author. They may vary significantly in production values, ranging from special effects to a simple talking head. What these forms have in common is that they are meant to stimulate interest in the article or book, which is itself not significantly different from other books or articles. In that sense, they are marketing tools. Other forms of videos, often distributed on platforms like YouTube or other social media, are broader, ranging from lecture captures, in which a speaker records and releases their own lectures, to "how to" videos, which may be as short as a few minutes and explain a technical point (e.g., how to do a Chi Square test in statistics). These are a subtler form of self-promotion. By releasing objectively helpful material, you establish a presence, while also helping out learners, which is a win-win situation. None of these forms is any different from writing a good abstract or delivering a good lecture, although the parameters, such as the audience, may be different in some cases. Just like a good abstract should include the main points of the text, a video trailer should cover the main points of the text.

Action item!

A good way to understand the differences between writing a typical academic text (be it an abstract, article, book, etc.) and a nontraditional academic video piece is looking at two versions of the same text side by side. Select and watch a video abstract from the journal *Foreign Language Annals* and then read the corresponding written abstract: https://onlinelibrary.wiley.com/page/journal/19449720/homepage/watch_video_abstracts.htm.

Consider the following aspects:

- Is the same information included in both texts (think content but also additional materials, like images and sound)?
- Is the same language used in both texts (think jargon and terminology)?
- How long is the video, and how long does it take to read the written abstract?
- What is the tone of the video, and how does it compare to the written abstract?

23.1.5 Interviews

Let's start by saying that interviews are a very good thing, and you should treat them as a valuable opportunity. Any attention to your research is good (unless you screwed up, and then you should not talk to the press before running it by your administration), regardless of whether it is traditional media or not. If this is all new to you, check with your institution (department, college, media office, or faculty affairs office) to see if there is someone who helps faculty prepare for media relations. Generally, a journalist or a producer will contact you asking if you are willing to do the interview. Respond right away, as press deadlines can be only hours away. Often, you can get featured because the other equally qualified scholars were slower to respond. In the contact email or call, they may or may not provide some information about their venue (newspaper, magazine, blog, podcast, etc.), the reason for the interview, and the length of the interview. This can range from a few minutes to hours. Answer positively but ask questions, if this information was not provided. What is the feature about? Why are they interested in it? If the reporter seems not to be aware of the general disciplinary background, you may want to suggest some background reading. Conversely, they may have researched the topic in depth. If possible, ask to see the questions ahead of time. Prepare your answers and practice them, especially if the interview is being recorded for a broadcast. Unless it's a video interview, it's OK to have notes and a list of points you want to make. You should not read a statement, however.

If the piece is about your research specifically, then enjoy talking about your work, but be generous with giving credit where credit is due. If the piece is not specifically about your work, it is OK to mention it, but remember that you're not the focus of the piece. The key here is to be helpful to the interviewer. The more you help the journalist, the more likely they are to be extra nice to you. Providing sources, especially your publications, is a good way to help, but you can also suggest other people to talk to, provide examples, and offer connections.

Keep in mind that anything you say to the interviewer is fair game (can be quoted on the record), so if you want to say something without it being attributed to you, you should specify that something is off the record or "background only." If what you want to say is something that could get you in trouble, it's probably best just to keep it to yourself. Generally, journalists will share the story upon publication. Read it or listen immediately and (politely) correct any errors that might have crept in. Most venues will gladly fix mistakes. Sometimes, but not always, journalists will let you read a draft of the story prior to publication to spot errors.

23.2 Advantages of Nontraditional Academic Writing

There is an intrinsic value in doing all these nontraditional academic activities. It's fun to publish a newsletter or a podcast: you are able to share your ideas, you receive feedback, and people send you examples or ideas to consider. It has been said that writing is a lonely activity, but this isn't true when you write in the social media space. It should be said that not all feedback is positive, especially in some "toxic" spaces like Twitter/X. You may want to carefully restrict who sees your writing, so that only academics can view it, for example. A mailing list, where you can determine who gets what, is another good solution. Conversely, if you want maximum exposure, posting to Facebook, LinkedIn, Substack, Twitter/X, and so on is the way to go.

Coming now to the extrinsic value, all of your activity on nontraditional media involves reading, thinking, talking, and writing, all of which is preparatory work for your traditional writing. Listening to yourself talk about a subject (or discussing the subject with students) may lead to new ideas, or you may like a turn of phrase and write it down. In the case of interview podcasts or podcasts that react to the news, new ideas may be sparked by the interaction between the participants or in thinking about a recent event. Once you've already done this work to think about the topic, it should be easier for you to do the work of putting together a chapter or article on the subject.

Regardless of the specific format, all these nontraditional academic writing venues can be excellent outlets for your passion about a subject. They may even become a passion that you can monetize, as some writers report significant earnings from platforms such as Substack. If your ramblings garner tens of thousands of readers/viewers/listeners, you may be in a prime position to monetize your work. It is best to talk to your institution before doing so. And best of luck from us.

Questions for Reflection

1. Is the idea of starting a blog, podcast, or newsletter appealing to you? If so, what differentiates your idea from what's already out there? What is the novel or interesting proposition that you will put forth?
2. What aspects of talking about your research for a general audience make you feel nervous? Which ones do you already feel confident about?

Questions for Discussion

1. What media do your colleagues and friends follow? What attracts them specifically to that media? What do they find useful about it?

2. Having a media presence is increasingly common among academics. Talk to some of your colleagues who already have a media presence, and ask them how they got started and how they keep going. What strategies do they use? How did they choose a specific platform, and what are the pros and cons of that platform?

Questions for Your Mentor

1. In this chapter, it is likely that you may know more about some of these matters than your mentor. However, they may have a particularly keen perception of the risks and problems you may encounter. Run any ideas by them before starting and solicit their feedback, while keeping in mind that you are your own researcher now.
2. If you are starting a podcast or blog, you may want to have your mentor as a guest for an interview or a guest post. With your mentor, brainstorm a topic they would be excited about discussing on your podcast.

Part IV

The Community

24 Having an Online Presence

This chapter explores the different ways in which scholars can join the academic conversation, that is, be more visible in academia and their own field and take on a more active role within the scholarly community. Here, we explain the value and characteristics of initiatives and platforms such as ORCID or Google Scholar and explore why and how it is important to create and curate a personal professional website. We may have said it in many different ways already, but it bears repeating: it is not enough *to do the work*, you also need to make sure that people know about it. We have already discussed some of the ways in which you can become part of the conversation, whether in scholarly communities (see Chapter 18 about articles or Chapter 19 on edited volumes) or beyond (see Chapter 23 on nontraditional academic writing, such as blogs or podcasts). Here, we talk about having and curating a professional online presence.

24.1 ORCID, Scopus ID, and Researcher ID

You probably have encountered the term "ORCID" at least a few times in your career, although if you haven't started publishing your research, you may not have created an account yet. We recommend you do and explain why below. ORCID refers to Open Researcher and Contributor ID, and it is essentially a unique number (a persistent digital identifier) that is assigned to you that allows you to be identifiable in a nonambiguous way throughout your career, even if you change your name or institution. Think of it as an ISBN or DOI for people, rather than for books or articles. Similar identifiers include Scopus ID and Researcher ID, which are not as widely used as ORCID. We will discuss these later.

After registering for a free account at http://www.orcid.org, you can set up your preferences for your personal or public record, which include adding a biography, employment, education, professional activities, publications, keywords, other websites related to your scholarly activity, and other research IDs. Besides curating your own page, you can also use the ORCID webpage to find other people based on a keyword search; if you want to be found, make sure to set your visibility to "public."

One of the main reasons people cite for using ORCID is to avoid confusion when two or more scholars have similar names, but there are other benefits. Keeping your ORCID updated can save you time when applying for grants (some grant platforms allow you to link your ORCID profile to transfer information automatically) and allows you to keep track of your publications and projects (but keep in mind that ORCID does not track citations). Many journals, presses, institutions, and funding agencies allow you to include your ORCID as a way of making sure your work is correctly attributed to you (some even require you to have one), and the information you provide is also used by other websites to index, confirm, or correct the titles of your publications.

Action item!

You probably saw it coming. We recommend you create an ORCID profile and pay special attention to updating the list of publications, keywords, and affiliation (employment). Use the search function to find the profile of other scholars in your field and have a look at their profiles in case you can learn something from the way in which they have curated them.

The process to obtain a Scopus ID or Researcher ID is similar, although these platforms offer some additional tools that may be useful to document the impact of your research (for promotion and tenure purposes, for example). Scopus ID, or Scopus Author Identifier, is maintained by the database Scopus and can be linked to your ORCID. You don't need to apply for one, as it will be automatically assigned to you once you publish in a journal that is indexed by Scopus, but you do have the option of editing your profile after it has been created. Besides making sure your work is attributed to you, within Scopus you can view impact metrics of your work, such as your h-index, citation counts, and trends over time, metric of collaboration, documents in top citation percentiles or in top journals, and more. These metrics will be useful when you have to document the impact of your research.

Researcher ID is a feature of Web of Science, Web of Knowledge, so it is useful to ensure your Web of Knowledge profile is accurate and reflects your actual work. It is possible to log in to a Researcher ID using your ORCID, which we recommend, so that the two platforms are linked. Researcher ID is also connected to Publons, so another option would be for you to create a Publons account, after which you will be automatically assigned a Researcher ID number. Some interesting features of Researcher ID include keeping track of your work as a reviewer (this happens through Publons, and you get to keep this information private so as to maintain anonymity as a reviewer) and tracking publications, citations, and access to your work via Web of Science.

24.2 Google Scholar

Probably the most-used platform by students and researchers alike, Google Scholar allows you not only to find resources (published works or scholars working in a given area) but also to curate your own scholar profile. The only caveat is that you need a Google account to set up your scholar profile (this is free to use, like ORCID, but Google is for-profit). Once you've created your Google Scholar profile, you can easily update your personal information (including email, affiliation, areas of interest, keywords, and picture) and revise your list of publications by importing them automatically, adding them manually, or editing (merging duplicates, changing titles, etc.). Areas of interest are a particularly useful feature, as you can select multiple keywords to represent your fields of interest. Make sure the words are not only spelled correctly but currently used by fellow researchers. We recommend you do an initial search for people who work in your field to see which keywords they use to represent their areas of interest and select only those that are widely used, as this will allow your profile to be searchable by using the same criteria. Keep in mind that these are language-specific and do not translate automatically, so if you are an applied linguist who works in and about English and Spanish, you may have to choose between *lingüística aplicada* and *applied linguistics*, or use both.

Unlike other services that we have discussed before, which tend to be linked to a specific database, Google Scholar does a pretty good job at finding your publications regardless of the language in which they were published or the venue where they appeared. Useful features you get access to include a list of coauthors (with a link to their profile) and impact metrics, such as citation counts and h-index. Additionally, you can explore who else is working in a given area by searching using the label function, as explained in the Action item below.

Action item!

Who is part of your professional network? Find out who shares similar scholarly interests with you by using the profile search on Google Scholar. Follow these steps (profiles will appear in order from most cited to least):

1. Click on one of the keywords listed on your Google Scholar profile to access a list of profiles with that same keyword.
2. Change the keyword you are searching for, following these suggestions:
    a. Use a low dash if your keyword includes two or more words (label: applied_linguistics)
    b. Use + to limit the search to the combination of two different keywords; the following will give you a list of profiles with both "applied linguistics" and "Spanish" as keywords: (label:applied_linguistics + label:spanish)

> c. Use a country internet extension to limit the search to a specific geographic area; the following will give you a list of profiles with "applied linguistics" as a keyword and a UK domain: (label:applied_ linguistics + ac.uk)
>
> Now that you have found your academic tribe, you can follow them to receive email updates about their publications.

24.3 Curating a Professional Website

Last but not least, besides being discoverable across scholarly platforms, we recommend you invest some time in building and then updating your own professional website. This will increase your visibility and make you and your work easier to find by potential employers, students, and colleagues, but, unlike the other options we discussed in this chapter, will give you much more flexibility and possibilities for personalization. The downside is you will have to make many decisions. Here, we discuss some important features to consider and give you recommendations and examples to get started.

You first need to decide what service you will use to build and host your website. Your decision will depend on your budget, the support offered by your university, and your tech skills. Free hosting and website building is entirely possible using platforms such as Wordpress, Weebly, Google Sites, or Squarespace. You will be limited to prebuilt editing options, at times within a given template, which is great if you are new to this or want to get it done quickly. If you choose a free hosting service, your website URL will also be marked as free by using the platform domain; for example, if you use Weebly, your URL will end in "weebly.com." However, if you have a budget, you may consider purchasing your own domain name or upgrading to a more professional service. A third option would be to work with the IT department at your institution to create your personal webpage under their domain. This option will most likely be free, but if you were to change institutions, you would lose access.

Once you have decided which platform to use, you should pick a domain name for your website (we recommend using your full name, as you want your website to show up first when people search your name online) and think about the main pages of your website. At the very least, you should include:

- A home page in which you introduce yourself. Remember to use a professional picture, a short bio for people to get to know you, and your

24.3 Curating a Professional Website

contact information to be reachable. If you feel comfortable doing so, you can also add an introductory video.
- A research page where you can list all your publications by type (articles, chapters, books, etc.) and include DOI links and reviews. Be careful with adding a copy of your published work for people to download, as you may be infringing copyright laws. We recommend checking with the publisher before doing so (see Chapter 29).
- A teaching page where you can list the courses you teach and any relevant details you may want to share with the public (syllabi, class projects, stellar comments from students).

Additional pages could cover your talks at conferences and other institutions, software (if you work with programming languages), creative works (artistic performances), current and past students, research projects (funded by grants), and even personal interests and hobbies. Besides pages, you can also add links to your other profiles and institutional websites, such as Google Scholar or your department's profile page, social network feeds (that link to your Twitter/X account), a comment section, or a search function. The amount of detail and pages you include is entirely up to you. The more you decide to share, the more time you will need to dedicate to keeping your page updated, so it is important that you have a clear sense of what you want your page to accomplish before getting started.

Besides content, here are a couple of technology-related suggestions that we'd like you to consider:

- Choose a theme for your website that is mobile-responsive, that is, that will adapt automatically if accessed on a mobile phone or tablet (you typically have a preview function to check how your site will look when accessed using different devices).
- Pick fonts and colors that are easy to read and accessible. This may mean choosing a font that enhances readability (sans serif, with spaced out letters, or even designed specifically for people with dyslexia, such as https://opendyslexic.org/) and a color palette that is color-blind friendly.

Before you publish your website, we highly recommend you ask family and friends to have a look at it. Since they are most likely nonacademics, they can help you streamline your website and make sure it is easy to navigate and does not include too much jargon. After you publish your website, you should link it across your accounts and platforms: add the URL to your email signature, crosslink it on your social networks and institutional pages, and even post about it so that people know about it.

The point we have developed in this and the previous chapter is that, to some extent, you need to act as your own publicist. You don't want to be the best kept secret of your field. You want the right people to read and be aware of your work, and this increasingly means having an online presence. It's not enough to go to conferences and to publish in academic journals anymore. People need to be able to find you and your scholarship. Mind you, we are not advocating starting a TikTok account and creating a dance to go with your latest paper on the influence of postmodernism on American comics (although if you did, please send us a link). In fact, we recommend curating the image you project very carefully. However, the reality is that the discussion groups on Facebook, Discord servers, Substacks, mailing lists, and WhatsApp chats are where the social interactions among your colleagues take place. If you want to network (and you do!), this is where you need to be. They call them social media for a reason.

Questions for Reflection

1. Create an online presence map: List all social media platforms on which you have an account that is primarily or largely used for academic purposes. Include webpages, blogs, and services such as ORCID. Think about what your goals are and which platforms would be the most useful to achieve those goals.
2. Think about the ways in which you can make people aware of your book besides the traditional ones, such as having an Amazon Author page or having your book featured on an academic podcast. What are the pros and cons?

Questions for Discussion

1. Ask your peers about their online presence. What do they see as the benefits and/or drawbacks to individual platforms? Check out any platforms you might have missed.
2. Ask your peers where they go to keep up with the professional "chatter."

Questions for Your Mentor

1. If all of this is overwhelming to you, ask your mentor (assuming they have a strong online presence) which platform is "it" in your field and why, so you can start from there.
2. If your mentor does not have an online presence, gently explain to them why they need it. Be prepared to listen to a speech on how when they were young they did not need any of this nonsense. Agree with them and create a Wikipedia page for them without telling them.

25 Self-Marketing

If you've made it to this chapter of the book, you have probably already published your work or are planning to do so in the near future. Here, we take you through some actions that you should consider to market yourself and build momentum after publication so that your work is read by a large group of scholars instead of family and friends, who pretend to read it and then hang the first page of your article on the fridge. In this chapter, we explain various strategies and formats to disseminate academic work, including conference presentations, book launches, and journal reviews. Sharing is caring, and you should care about your work after all the time you've dedicated to it, so let's make sure it reaches a wider audience.

Conferences are the most common way for scholars to share and disseminate their work. If you already have your PhD, chances are you have gone to a few conferences already, at least as an attendee, so you are familiar with local, national, and international conferences in your chosen field(s). You most likely attended some conferences during graduate school and maybe even presented at a few. This chapter will use conference presentations as a starting point, but we'll discuss other venues for sharing your academic work, including panels, round tables, symposia, book launches and talks, and getting your book reviewed. Participating in a variety of opportunities to share your research will raise your academic profile, make you and your work more visible, and help you build a stronger and wider professional network (see Chapter 26).

25.1 Academic Conferences

Presenting your research at a conference is the most common way to make your work visible and accessible to the academic community. So, how do you prepare a successful conference presentation? Surely not by copying and pasting text from your latest publication into a PowerPoint slide. That would be a really bad call, because people would most likely not be able to follow and would disengage. Common criticism of bad presentations includes giving too much information, using a lot of jargon, and giving information that is not relevant (Meyers & Nix, 2011).

> **Action item!**
>
> What makes someone a good presenter? You can approach this question in two ways: First, you can ask fellow academics to give you a few adjectives that they think describe a good presenter or a good presentation. Second, you can think about a good presentation you recently saw and jot down adjectives to describe it. Once you have your list, identify three adjectives (the most common ones, the most important to you), and write one concrete action you can take to incorporate those characteristics into your presentations. Here are a few examples, but you can add your own:
>
> - *Respectful of audience and other presenters*: You can do this by respecting the allotted time for your presentation and the Q&A. Another way to be respectful is by not dismissing a question you don't know the answer to. Even if you are nervous or the question is uncomfortable, it's still better to give the question careful consideration. If you are able, think ahead of time about tough questions that you might be asked and brainstorm some possible answers.
> - *Articulate*: Speak at an adequate volume (not too high, not too low) so that everyone can hear you clearly (use a microphone if there is one, so you can speak at your normal volume, control your voice better, and guarantee that even the furthest audience member will hear you). Vary your pace and tone to emphasize key points and make your talk more dynamic and less monotone.
> - _____
> - _____
> - _____

Here we are going to focus on a couple of recommendations to build and deliver a good conference presentation that you can apply to any topic and any field. First, visuals matter (see Chapter 10 on data visualizations). As Gunther Kress anticipated in the 1990s (Kress, 1998), we are now past the time in which the written page dominates the world of communication, and people expect others to use visual elements in an appropriate and effective way. In your presentations, keep the amount of written text you share with the audience in check (i.e., short, to the point, and easy to read from a distance – you don't know how big the room will be or how small the screen), and try to rely on images or design elements (colors, symbols, animations – in moderation) to support what you will say.

Second, tell a story. This is what experienced presenters do (have a look at the Action item in Chapter 23). Telling a story will make your work more memorable, accessible, and engaging. An important step to do so, from Cohen and Dreyer-Lude (2020), is to start by crafting a short, jargon-free core message (one or two "golden phrases," Cohen & Dreyder-Lude, 2020, p. 13) that encapsulates the essence of your work and the one thing that you want your audience to take away from your talk. Think of these golden phrases as the key ingredients of your elevator pitch (see Chapter 26).

Additionally, if you are presenting in a language and/or culture that is not your first or dominant one, you should familiarize yourself with their conventions, as there may be important differences in terms of what is expected of you and what you are or are not allowed to do. For example, not all cultures start presentations with a joke.

25.2 Panels, Round Tables, and Symposia

Proposing a panel, round table, or symposium is, in many ways, similar to editing a volume (see Chapter 21), although it's relatively easier because the number of people involved is much smaller. All of these activities involve a group of experts on a given topic discussing in front of an audience. Typically, a panel happens during a conference and is allotted a long time slot (from one to two hours) to accommodate multiple speakers. Each speaker gives their presentation using visuals, as if it were a regular conference paper, and the time for Q&A typically occurs at the end of the panel as a way to engage with all the different perspectives that were presented. To organize a panel, you will have to propose one and get it accepted, which means you will be responsible for selecting the topic and title, writing a general description (similar to an abstract, see Chapter 7), and then hope it gets accepted by the organizing committee. Depending on the conference, you may have to wait for the acceptance before you can invite people to participate via a call for papers or direct invitation (see a sample email in Appendix E), or you may have to contact people ahead of time to be able to secure their interest and participation if the panel gets accepted. In this last case, you may also have to include the names, titles, and abstracts of all participating speakers in your submission.

A round table is similar to a panel, with a few exceptions: Usually, participants are invited, there is no call for papers, and the discussion tends to be more spontaneous and dialogical (there may be no slides or visual support), with the organizer acting as the MC and asking questions to get the conversation going. A round table can be organized as part of a conference by people who belong to the association organizing the conference or are part of the organizing committee at the host institution, or it can be a stand-alone event. In both cases, your job as the organizer is to invite people who are experts, ask them engaging questions during the round table, and, if the audience is not participating a lot, make sure there are no awkward moments of silence.

Last, if your department receives a generous donation or you are feeling ambitious enough to write a grant for funding, you may consider hosting a symposium, which is similar to a panel but typically happens as a stand-alone event. The experience of organizing a symposium is similar to that of organizing a conference, but on a smaller scale. Remember that you will need to take care of all the promotion and organization, on top of inviting participants and being the MC for the event.

Here is what you should consider when organizing a symposium, a panel, or a round table:

- Where will the event be held? Will you have support for the practical aspects (refreshments, coffee, etc.)? An attractive location will make it more likely that those you invite will accept, but it will also be more expensive.
- Who will you invite? Big names generate a lot of buzz, but often new and exciting ideas are produced by junior scholars.
- Will you publish the proceedings? This is like editing a collection of articles (see Chapter 21).
- When will the event take place? You should avoid overlapping with other important events in your field. It is crucial that you announce the event at least a year in advance, to give people time to plan.

Each of these events (roundtables, panels, symposia) are a lot of work, but they allow you to make personal contact with experts in your field who may or may not know you and your work; engage with their work; gain visibility for yourself, your department, and your institution; and lay the groundwork for potential future collaborations. While it is true that you are not necessarily presenting your own research at these events, you will talk about it through the questions you ask and the topic and focus of the event. Each of these events allows you to join the conversation, that is, to have a seat at the table (in the literal and figurative sense) with the top experts in your field, discussing your research topic and making lasting professional connections. And it doesn't stop there. It's not uncommon to collaborate with the colleagues you invited to your event on a collective paper, edited volume, or other research projects in the future.

25.3 Book Launches and Talks

Book launches are a special kind of academic event that can boost your visibility but, if like Elisa you feel extremely uncomfortable being the center of attention, they can also be quite stressful. Essentially, this is a celebration of you and your work, so you (and your book) will be the main event. However, unless you are already a famous academic, a book launch event does not fall

25.3 Book Launches and Talks

from the sky into your lap. It may seem contradictory or even egotistic, but typically you have to organize it yourself. This is definitely worth doing, even if it feels a little strange to promote your work in this way. Especially if there is any chance for you to get support from your department or another institution (like an academic association), we suggest you go ahead and organize your own book launch. You should also be aware that some universities or organizations will not organize launches, for a variety of reasons. If that's your sad lot, read on for some other options.

A book launch can have different formats. In general, however, it tends to involve up to three invited speakers who are experts in your area, have read the book, and have agreed to give a (positive, we hope) commentary about it. In other cases, there are no external speakers and it's more of a book launch party. You will be there, copies of the book will be available, and you will be expected to sign copies. If the event will have other speakers, you, as the author and expert on the subject, are the best person to select and invite them. They will likely be scholars with whom you have crossed paths multiple times at conferences or maybe co-authored an article. If in doubt about who to invite as a speaker, ask senior colleagues in your department.

When you invite your guest speakers (also called readers in some areas), you should make sure they have a copy of your book beforehand and understand the expectations of the event: How long should their intervention be? Who will be in the audience (faculty, students, the general public)? Are there any specific aspects of your work they should highlight in their commentary or in the questions (this is your chance to help them and also make sure they do not overlook some elements of your work that are particularly relevant for your audience)? Who will the other guest speakers be? How much time will be allocated to each commentary and to the questions? Will they be allowed to use some slides or visuals? As you organize the academic component of the book launch, consider that it is common for these events to be followed by a reception during which people can relax, mingle, and take pictures with and talk to the author, so be ready to be social and enjoy your celebration. Also, dress up. Pictures will be taken.

Alternatively, for other types of book launches, you will be the one expected to talk about your book, explaining its premise to the audience and reading fragments from it. A book talk can take anywhere from thirty minutes to an hour, and there is generally time for questions afterwards (and a small reception with cookies and wine, if university policies and budgets allow for it). The semester (or academic year) in which your book is published is a great time to give a few book talks at other universities. It's completely acceptable for you to reach out to colleagues at other institutions and ask for an invitation to give a book talk at their universities (see Appendix D for a sample email for reaching out to colleagues). You should reach out to colleagues early to be sure that it's possible to get your talk scheduled. Although it can feel intimidating, giving book talks is a great way to spread the word about your research and solidify your professional networks. This can lead to better sales, more reviews, and future opportunities for collaboration and speaking events. If you are part of any professional organizations (a society dedicated to film study, for example), asking to give a book talk over Zoom is a fantastic opportunity to promote your research to a wide audience that you otherwise wouldn't have access to.

Action item!

In addition to promoting your book via launches and talks, book awards can be an important way to bring attention to your research. Depending on your publisher, they may nominate your book for prizes, or it may be up to you to do so.

1. Make a list of prizes your book might be eligible for. To get started, check out the professional organizations you're involved in.
   a. Do any of them offer yearly book prizes (e.g., the MLA awards several book prizes yearly)?
   b. Do you and your book qualify for any special demographics (there are prizes for first books, first-generation scholars, books on a specific topic, etc.)?
2. Talk to colleagues in your field. What book awards do they know about?
3. Talk to your publisher. Whose responsibility is it to nominate your book for awards? Keep in mind that to be considered for many awards, the nominator has to send in several copies of the book. If your publisher tells you that you need to nominate yourself, at least try to negotiate that they will send the copies of your book, free of charge.

25.4 Getting Your Book Reviewed

Just like book launches, book reviews don't fall from the sky either, particularly if this is your first book in a niche area that few scholars work in. There is a chance your book will be noticed by a couple of review editors (see Chapter 31 to know who they are and what they do) at journals affiliated with the same press that published your book or journals in the very same niche area as your book. If that is the case, congrats! The editor may reach out to you to let you know that they would like to review your book and ask you how to get a copy and/or to recommend a potential reviewer. Don't be surprised if this happens. You are the one who wrote the book, and you know who is interested in and understands your

25.4 Getting Your Book Reviewed

work enough to be able to review it. Have a look at Appendix F to see a sample email to potential reviewers of your book.

If this doesn't happen, don't despair. This is normal. Our recommendation is that you reach out to potential reviewers to see if they are interested and available to review your book and, at the same time, inquire about the possibility of publishing a review of your book with review editors of respected journals (see sample email in the Appendix G). When selecting which review editors to contact, consider these points, and if in doubt, ask your mentors:

- Select journals that publish book reviews, as not all do (it will say so on their webpage or, if not, check the latest issues they published to see if any reviews were included). Some may treat reviews the same as articles, in which case the review will undergo the same peer-review process; others may only do an in-house review (by the editors); and others may only publish reviews by invitation, in which case you can only bring your book to their attention, but they will decide if it is going to make the cut.
- Select journals in different geographical spaces or even languages, if your work fits and you know people who could write a book review in that language. This will ensure maximum visibility and a broader readership.
- Select journals in different disciplinary spaces that intersect with your work. Once again, this will make your work more visible across disciplines and allow it to reach a wider audience. If you do this, you should also contact potential reviewers who can speak to these different audiences and engage with different disciplinary traditions; otherwise your review may not be well received, meaningful, or even accessible to your intended audience.

Action item!

Keeping in mind the factors that we just mentioned, which journals could potentially publish a review of your book? Explore their webpages to learn more about these journals and then select your top three. List them below, followed by why each one would be a good choice.

1. _____
2. _____
3. _____

As academics, we don't often think about publicizing or marketing our work and building our "brand"; in fact, we may frown about such "commercial" practices. However, what is a reputation if not a personal brand? What are citations if not public acknowledgments that other scholars have benefitted from our work or at least found it worthy of discussion? How much easier would it have been for them to find our work if they had been aware of it without having to search for it? Academic research can and should benefit the world. How can those outside of academe find out about our research if we keep it to our little clique of colleagues? It's high time we stepped out of the ivory tower and brought our research to those who can benefit from it.

Questions for Reflection

1. What aspect of public speaking (conference presentations) would you like to improve? If you have a video of yourself, watch it; if not, consider recording your next presentation or a practice presentation. Although it's painful, watch the video and take notes about aspects you can change or improve.
2. What strategies do you typically use to prepare a conference presentation? Chances are that the strategies you mobilize do not tackle the aspect you want to improve, so being aware of these issues is the first step to getting better.

Questions for Discussion

1. What experiences have people had with panels, round tables, or symposia? Were they the organizers or participants? What went well, and what do they wish they could change?
2. Talk to colleagues who have published books. Were they reviewed? Were all reviews positive? How did they deal with negative comments?

Questions for Your Mentor

1. Is a book launch an event your department can sponsor and support? What logistic decisions does it entail at your institution?
2. Which journals would be appropriate venues to publish a review of your book? Does your mentor have any contacts that could be useful to get things started?

26 Professional Networking

The academic world is first and foremost a social community; it is essential to establish and cultivate relationships like in any other social area, but these relationships also bear a professional weight. Academia is not a community you can easily remove yourself from if things don't work out, unless you are willing to overhaul your entire life and find a different job. Moreover, academic network involvement leads to direct employment opportunities, career advancement, publication opportunities, and even research outside academia (Heffernan, 2020). Scholarly recognition leads to increased citations of your published work (Faria & Goel, 2010). With that in mind, we will focus in this chapter on how to represent yourself in the best way possible, put your name out there as a respectable scholar, and maneuver the pitfalls that come with professional relationships as they pertain to academia.

26.1 Navigating the Department

Your department is your local network, and managing it well can result in career advancement benefits (Heffernan, 2020; Van Helden et al., 2023). This may be stating the obvious, but our experiences indicate that some people need to hear this explicitly: You need to get on well with the people in your department (even if you have to bite your tongue once or twice – a day). That doesn't mean you need to regularly socialize with them or see them outside of work, but you need to maintain professional courtesy with everyone, even if the person is a known pain in everybody's necks. Over time, you can more clearly see who you can be more friendly with and who you should steer clear from. A peer mentor can also do wonders for you. To find a mentor, you can use your best initial judgment to approach someone in the department, or ask your department head if you can be assigned one (see Chapter 27). Either way, be extra careful at the beginning. People are people; the same rules of engagement apply as in any new environment.

While navigating your local network, it is important to adhere to institutional hierarchy. There may be things that you are not aware of that your direct supervisor can inform you about before you go up the chain of command. In a US higher education setting, for instance, it is not a good look if you have asked the Provost for additional funding and the Provost calls the Dean to ask them why they haven't told their department heads that all additional funding has been suspended this year. They probably have, but you didn't give the department head a chance to tell you that because you skipped over them. Now you have annoyed three (very important) people in one go. Or let's say you go directly to your department head without looping in your program coordinator. Chances are, the department head will have to bring them into the conversation as there is a reason people are in these positions. Now you have irritated your program coordinator. The truth of the matter is, people tend to find out if you go over their heads, and who needs that kind of tension in their life? To prevent disaster scenarios like this, follow the chain of command: If you have something to ask of the Provost, you need to go through the Dean; to contact the Dean, you need to go through your department head.

Your professional network in the department also includes student and professional staff. Executive assistants or secretaries, for instance, hold the power to make your life easier. Many executive assistants are gatekeepers for chairs, deans, and other administrators, so little gifts of chocolate and sincere recognition of their work goes a long way. Treat secretaries like the queens and kings they are, and you shall reap the benefits (see what we did there?).

As a scholar, you also need a global network, not of people who you work with at the same institution but of people who study and are passionate about the same subjects as you. While you will expand this network naturally along the course of your career (the people you graduated with, the people they introduce you to, the people you publish with, etc.), there is a more clear and explicit path to networking, which is what we now turn to.

26.2 Organizations You Can Join

All academic disciplines have organizations that represent and try to improve them. Examples include the American Psychological Association (APA), the National Council of Teachers of English (NCTE), and the International Pragmatics Association (IPrA). Organizations like these help determine the standards in the field, consolidate extant research to determine areas of work that need attention, provide online resources for their members, send out periodic newsletters to keep members informed, and even publish periodicals or guidebooks.

Action item!

Search for professional organizations that you could potentially join. You can consider the following points:

- Is it a professional organization tied to a field or discipline, or is membership based on other factors (country, gender, role, etc.)?

- When and where is the organization's conference typically held? Would you be able to attend?
- What benefits does the organization offer to its members (access to publications, grants, discounted conference attendance, etc.)?
- Who is on the board (people you know, others with shared interests, well-known scholars, etc.)?

In terms of networking, three of their services are especially worth mentioning. First, professional organizations have online user platforms that function like social media but are accessible only to members. You can find and contact members, join online discussions, ask questions of your own, and so on. If you want to be even more discipline-specific, you can join interest sections that narrow down the scope of interaction even further so you can be in touch with the people who share your research interests. Some interest sections organize events, webinars, virtual coffee hours, or similar opportunities where you can engage with other members. A second networking opportunity becomes an option after you have been a member with the organization of your choice for a while. Aside from very few paid staff members at the headquarters, these organizations are run by academics who are performing service to the field. These leadership opportunities are announced to the membership every time there is a vacancy, and if you have the time and energy, you can apply or volunteer (which you should consider, as leadership in academic organizations comes with the territory after all). These leadership roles are priceless networking opportunities; it's easy to make friends while you work together toward a common goal and get to know each other naturally in a professional setting. The third noteworthy opportunity from membership in a professional organization is conferences, but they deserve their own section, so that's what we turn to next.

26.3 Conferences

Academic conferences are the bread and butter of professional networking for scholars. This is where (usually) ongoing research is presented to other scholars to get initial feedback before publication. Any significant errors in your argumentation or design can be caught in a good academic conference presentation, and the Q&A sessions at the end can give you further ideas or direct you to form your written discussion in the most cohesive manner. As a participant, you can keep up to date with your field and gauge the current trends in research, with the added bonus of lending a helping hand to fellow researchers with well-thought-out questions or feedback.

The best way to network during conferences, therefore, is to do a solid job both as a presenter and as a participant. It won't go unnoticed. When you can engage people intellectually at an academic conference, it becomes a lot easier to approach them later (or vice versa) to start a casual conversation, to exchange ideas and, more importantly, contact information. If anyone you are thrilled to have talked to gives you their contact information at a conference, do follow up after the conference with a line or two to remind them of yourself and your conversation. Academic conferences are usually a blur by the end; we learn so much, see so much, and do so much that things and people slip the mind. A courteous email will rekindle the relationship that was started, and you never know where things may go after that. Hilal recently caught two world-class scholars' attention during the Q&A session of their panel at an international conference, they got to talking after the panel, and she ended up making a good connection.

There are also opportunities to meet people who make you feel starstruck. Don't be afraid to approach them and introduce yourself. Sal, for instance, would walk up to someone and just tell them, "Hi, I'm so and so and I'm a big fan of your work!" Everyone loves to hear that their work has made an impact on someone. The interaction may never progress beyond this conversation, but it also has the potential to lead to an academic friendship or research collaboration.

Action item!

Let's break the ice and finally summon the courage to talk to one of your personal heroes (professionally speaking, of course). If you want to expand your network, you need to talk to people, and conferences are a great place to do that. The best part is, you already know who is going and where they will be, so you can prepare. Follow these steps:

- Once you know who you would like to talk to (after looking at the conference program beforehand), have a look at their profile on Google Scholar or a similar platform. Are you familiar with their publications? We assume you are at least a little bit familiar, otherwise you would not be interested in talking to them.
- Pick a couple of recent publications and refresh your memory by reading them. Make a note of the title, publication venue, any interesting argument, novel findings, or anything else that sparks your interest.
- Think about your shared interests, and be ready to mention them. Are you working on a similar topic? Are you using their work, or did their findings inspire your research?

- Write up your introductory line. It will be short and to the point, something like this: "Good morning/afternoon, Dr. Personal Hero, my name is [your name], at [your institution]. I really liked your paper about [topic of the article], [reference to interesting argument/findings in that paper]."
- Practice your line to make sure you are not saying their name or the title of their article wrong, for example (you'd be surprised).
- At the conference, if you see them and they seem approachable (not surrounded by millions of people, not right after their talk, not running toward the exit), give it a try.

Conferences are a good opportunity to meet with editors and publisher representatives as well. Most of the time these people are located across the country or even the globe, so being at the same venue as them can be priceless. Say you have a book idea, for instance, but you are not sure whether there is a market for it; you can put feelers out with publishers and see what comes back. At a more developed stage, you can even pitch them your book idea (see Chapter 31).

26.4 The Elevator Pitch

Starting with graduate school, you should work on your elevator pitch, a bite-sized summary of your research that you can recite in under a minute to people who may or may not be in your field. As the name implies, you should be able to finish it in the time it would take to ride a few floors in an elevator, should you get the chance to introduce your work to a fellow scholar. It's not a good look to hesitate and grapple when asked what your work is on, so have it ready. Write it on a piece of paper and memorize it if you must; you will see that it comes in handy. In time, you will know how to customize your elevator pitch depending on who you are giving it to, but a go-to blanket version is a good starting point.

A successful academic career clearly depends on solid, relevant work that takes the scholarly conversation further, even if by a fraction of a step. A close second is networking. We are not islands in this profession; the basis of our work is literally building upon knowledge gained through other scholars' work. Do not be dismissive or alienating of anyone, regardless of their current status, as you never know when and in what capacity they might play a role in your life again. Plus, knowing the right people (or rather, the right people knowing you) can lead to exciting opportunities.

Action item!

Prepare an elevator pitch for your dissertation or new project and time yourself delivering it. Remember, you are going a few floors and not all the way to the penthouse! Keep it short and to the point.

Now, practice under stress or in a more realistic situation. Pick the situation that works for you:

- Practice telling it after one beer or glass of wine.
- Practice telling it to your spouse, partner, or cat while they wear a funny hat or fake mustache.
- Practice telling it while wearing shoes or clothes that feel uncomfortable.
- Practice telling it after a long, hard day at work.

Questions for Reflection

1. At the last conference you attended, did anyone seem excited about your research or give you their contact information? Have you followed up or done anything with it? After reading this chapter, make a mental plan for what you will do when a similar situation arises in the future.
2. Think of all the networks you are a part of. Do they meet your needs? Do you make the most of them? Should you be looking to add new ones?

Questions for Discussion

1. Has anyone in your group introduced themselves to a "big shot" in the field? How did it go? What pointers can they share for what worked well and/or what was not effective?
2. Does anyone in your group feel especially shy when it comes to approaching people in academic settings? How can the group help them overcome this obstacle before their next conference?

Questions for Your Mentor

1. Ask your mentor to tell you the most interesting networking story they have. How did the connection come about? Did it lead to any tangible cooperation or opportunities?
2. Tell your mentor (or a senior scholar in your field, if your mentor is in a different field) about the professional organizations you are a part of. Are you missing any important ones? Does your mentor have any recommendations for you?

27 Mentorship

In *The Hunger Games*, one crucial aspect that improves tributes' chances of survival is a solid relationship with a competent coach. Likewise, having a good mentor who can advise you on your research goals and help you grow as an academic writer can really help you to succeed. While the stakes may not be as high in academia as they are in the arena, a good relationship with a mentor can help you thrive (even though your mentor probably can't teach you how to use throwing stars as a weapon or funnel water out of a tree for hydration). In this chapter, we discuss different types of mentorship, how to find a mentor, expectations and guidelines for the mentorship relationship, and, finally, we ask you to consider whether you might want to become a mentor.

27.1 Formal and Informal

Mentorship can happen in a variety of ways, either formally or informally. Dissertation advisors often serve as early mentors, although their level of input and involvement can vary greatly. Other types of formal mentorship may be offered by your place of employment or professional organizations you are part of. When a new hire joins an academic department or workplace, many department heads or supervisors will assign them a formal mentor. The structure of this relationship will depend on the established program and the two people involved. You may have structured monthly meetings with your mentor, or they may simply tell you to reach out if you have any questions. Your formal mentor could come from within your program or department, or you might be paired with someone outside of your immediate area. Each option has pluses and minuses. A mentor from your program will be able to tell you all the details of how your department works, information that someone from across campus won't know. However, a mentor more removed from your immediate program can give you a broader view and different perspective of your university or organization, will have different connections and information to share with you, and may possibly be someone with whom you can vent frustrations that you might not want circulated in your department. Another way to find formal mentorship is through professional organizations tied to your discipline. This can be a great way to expand your network beyond your campus and learn more about a specific aspect of your field, especially if you are the only scholar at your workplace who studies a particular area.

Informal mentorship can be harder to find, but it has the potential to be extremely rewarding, as mentor and mentee establish this relationship organically without it being forced upon them by supervisors. These are the types of relationships that may never be formalized as mentorship. They can happen when you find yourself working closely with someone whose expertise you admire, or they can be a blend of friendship and mentorship. It's always nice to have a mix of formal and informal mentorship, if possible. Do keep in mind that research shows it can be harder for scholars of color, women, and other minority groups to find mentorship relationships, in comparison with their white, cishet male counterparts, as people tend to gravitate toward others like them when looking for mentees. Faculty of color and women faculty often have "higher attrition rates and lower tenure line advancement rates" (Hsieh & Tran Nguyen, 2020, p. 169) than their white, male counterparts, and they may struggle to find mentors who share similar experiences to theirs due to the lack of diversity within academia. Even well-meaning mentors from majority groups may not understand (or they may attempt to minimize) the particular institutional challenges or individual discrimination their mentees face (Hsieh & Tran Nguyen, 2020). We know this is discouraging research, but we hope it won't keep you from seeking out a mentor (and even if you have different intersectionalities, the relationship can still be successful). If you are struggling to find a mentor, please know that the flaw is with the system, not with you.

You may need more time or the assistance of your professional network to find a good mentor, but we firmly believe it's worth doing, as many studies have demonstrated the wide range of benefits that mentorship provides for both mentors and mentees. Mentees commonly increase their scholarly research and publications, experience improved job satisfaction (Jackevicius et al., 2014), and develop and become more confident in their research skills (Káplár-Kodácsy & Dorner, 2022). Mentors often report a sense of accomplishment from working with mentees, experience renewed interest in their own research, and increase their networking (Káplár-Kodácsy & Dorner, 2022). Establishing a mentorship relationship can help you to feel more confident in your research abilities while also allowing you to integrate yourself more meaningfully into your workplace.

27.2   Choosing a Mentor

Sometimes mentorship relationships happen organically or are arranged by administration, but if mentorship opportunities are not readily offered to you, you can intentionally seek one out. Let's discuss some strategies for identifying

27.2 Choosing a Mentor

a potential mentor. As we mentioned, one of your first mentors should have been your dissertation advisor. You probably chose your advisor from a limited pool of options in your department, based mostly on how closely their specialization lined up with your research interests, and maybe a little on personality. After graduate school, everyone will have a different relationship with their advisor, but for many individuals, graduate school advisors no longer have the same amount of time to dedicate to former students, as they must continue working with current students. This is the time to find a new mentor, someone who is more advanced in your field and their career, who can offer you advice and support. This can be someone at your institution, from a professional organization, or maybe even someone you've clicked with at a conference. When you're thinking about asking someone to be your mentor, consider the following questions first. You may also want to meet a potential mentor for coffee and ask them some of these questions, too.

- What skills or knowledge do I hope to gain from this relationship?
- What are the specific areas I hope to improve through this relationship (writing abilities, content knowledge related to my research, networking and professional development advice, etc.)?
- Is there enough overlap between our research to make this relationship productive?
- Is this person's personality/work style/approach to research compatible with my own?
- Do I enjoy this person's communication style?
- Are we on the same page about how frequently we will meet and how much of a commitment this will be for both of us?
- What are their goals for this mentorship relationship (what do they hope to teach me, and what do they want to get out of this relationship)?

It's OK to chat with a few potential mentors before making a commitment. If all goes well, this is a relationship that may be part of your academic life for years to come, so you both want to be sure that it's the right fit for you both.

Action item!

Identify potential mentors. Make a list of what you need, that is, the areas in which you would like to be mentored. Now, browse your institution's webpage (beyond your own department) and see if you can identify leaders in those areas. Is there someone with an impressive list of publications? If you're looking to improve in the classroom, maybe find someone who has received a teaching award.

27.3 Guidelines and Expectations

The human element of mentorship relationships is what can make this part of academic life so rewarding, even though it also adds an element of unpredictability. For this reason, it's always a good idea to enter into a mentorship relationship by establishing clear expectations for both mentor and mentee. While every mentorship relationship will be as unique as the two people involved in it, here are a few things you can generally expect from a mentorship relationship.

Assuming that you have chosen a mentor to guide you in your research trajectory, you can expect your mentor to give you honest, but not cruel, feedback. While it is their job to point out ways in which you can grow as a researcher and writer, which can be uncomfortable, you should not feel belittled or berated by your mentor. You can expect your mentor to give you advice on possible venues for publication of your research, as well as introducing you to others in the field, organizations, and conferences that will be beneficial for you. A good mentor will also look out for opportunities to collaborate on research with their mentees (studies, conference presentations, etc.) and to build them up (promote their work, cite them, connect them with others doing similar work). Good mentorship relationships are ones in which mentor and mentee meet regularly. The frequency (weekly, monthly, etc.) can depend on your schedules, but in order to establish trust and maintain good communication, this is key.

In order for your mentor to do all this for you, they will need time to read, think about, and comment on your work. You should keep in mind that your mentor may have similar relationships with other mentees. Even though your research is at the forefront of your mind, your mentor has a full plate and will not be able to provide immediate feedback, as they also have their own research agenda. When you submit drafts for your mentor to read, you should try to turn in the best and most polished work possible. Don't expect your mentor to be a copy editor, and if they give you advice once (such as, don't end paragraphs with direct quotes), be sure to apply that advice wherever it's relevant instead of making your mentor repeat themself. To uphold your end of the mentorship relationship, you should communicate clearly about your needs and questions. You should do your best to not miss scheduled meetings or deadlines that your mentor has set for you, as you want to respect their time. The two of you should establish some boundaries early on in your relationship about appropriate communication, such as the best way to reach one another (email, text, Facebook, etc.) and whether there are times of the day or week in which your mentor does not want to be contacted. Establishing healthy boundaries early on should help to minimize conflict.

You might be wondering how long a mentorship relationship is meant to last. Like almost everything else in this chapter, the answer is that it will depend on the relationship. You might go into a mentorship relationship having set a clear finish date from the beginning (one year, semester, etc.), but often, no official timeline for mentorship relationships is discussed. Some mentorship relationships will gradually fizzle out, either due to incompatibility of personalities or schedules or perhaps because the mentee no longer needs as much guidance. If you're lucky, your mentor might support you throughout their entire career. Mentorship relationships do not necessarily need to last forever. If your mentor is effective, you will ideally reach a point where you feel confident enough to tackle your research and career goals without relying so heavily on your mentor. It's lovely to have a mentor who is available to support you and answer questions when needed, but you should also learn to trust in your own expertise.

27.4 Becoming a Mentor

Once you become more confident in your own abilities and knowledge, you should consider becoming a mentor. Mentoring can be a great way to give back, and you don't have to wait until you think you know everything before you start doing it. For example, after about seven years into her current position, Heather realized that she had to stop referring to herself as "new faculty," as she in fact knew quite a bit about her university and department and had been successfully producing and publishing research for a while. The point is, you may have accumulated much more knowledge than you have realized, and chances are, there is a newer colleague who could benefit from your guidance. If you are directing theses and dissertations, you will naturally find yourself mentoring those students, as you guide them in the process of sharing their research and publishing. Once you are comfortable doing that, you may consider starting a writing group for students. If you have acquired some special skill set, for example by serving on your institution's ethical board or IRB panel, you may want to advise junior faculty or graduate students on how to successfully navigate human subjects' protection.

Finally, we should warn you of a potential pitfall in mentoring that can also happen in other areas of academia or, really, in any situation where two people are working closely together. As these relationships progress, mentors and mentees have been known to develop non-academic feelings toward the person they are working with. If you recognize that you are starting to feel unprofessional feelings for your mentor or mentee, distance yourself from the relationship or interrupt it. If you feel that your mentor or mentee is in danger of crossing boundaries into unprofessional territory, you have every right to walk away from the relationship and/or seek out appropriate resources and support from others on campus. We believe the majority of mentor/mentee relationships are professional and productive, but we would feel remiss if we didn't mention this.

We've talked about basic roles and responsibilities for mentors and mentees, but the central idea of this chapter bears repeating: So much of being a good mentor is being available to support your mentee. For individuals who are new to an institution or a position, having someone to serve as a sounding board for their ideas, concerns, and research questions can make all the difference in helping them feel integrated and valued within their role. Regardless of whether you're a mentor or mentee, these relationships can be extremely important in fostering a sense of academic community and helping newer researchers achieve their goals.

Questions for Reflection

1. Are you on the lookout for a new mentor? Take a moment to write down your top three priorities for a new mentorship relationship. What characteristics or qualities are non-negotiables for you in a mentorship relationship?
2. While mentors can be wonderful resources, it is also important to be confident in your own abilities. Write a list of writing- or research-related topics to consult your mentor about. Write a second list of topics that you feel confident handling on your own. Revisit this list every six months or so, and you may be surprised to see how your confidence in your own abilities is growing.

Questions for Discussion

1. Ask colleagues or members of your writing group to share about their experiences with past and present mentors. What were some of the most effective lessons learned from them? What advice or mentorship styles did not work for mentees and why?
2. How have members of the group found mentors in the past? Share tips on places to look for mentors, how to identify potential mentors, and questions to ask possible mentors.

Questions for Your Mentor

1. Ask your mentor to share something positive they have gotten out of a mentorship relationship (with you or another mentee). In your mentor's opinion, what are the benefits of being a mentor?
2. Ask your mentor to (anonymously) tell you about a moment of interpersonal conflict within one of their previous mentorship relationships. How did they handle that conflict? In general, what are the techniques or strategies they use to maintain open communication with their mentees?

28 Writing with Others

We have all heard of (or experienced) horror stories where two or more people decide to write a paper together, and then they never hear from that one group member again. Trying to write with someone who is not on the same wavelength as you can be a test of your patience and faith in humanity, but with the right colleagues, collaborative writing can be a joyful experience. It can even increase both the quality and the impact of your work (Franceschet & Constantini, 2010; Thelwall et al., 2023). Some people prefer to work on projects together while others have no choice due to circumstances, but all in all, collaborative writing is a part of academia for many scholars. There is variation across fields and countries, but the majority of all researchers in the most Scopus-indexed countries engage in academic collaboration (Thelwall & Maflahi, 2020). In this chapter, we share our insights about writing with others, along with some tools and strategies that you might find helpful.

28.1 Collaborative Writing Tools

In terms of collaborative writing, the latest technological advancements have been a gift to scholars. The tools we now have at our fingertips allow us to work with anyone across the globe, synchronously or asynchronously. No one needs to hear about video conferencing software like Zoom and Teams, of course, since we all got up close and personal with it during the pandemic. Still, it gets an honorary mention for making our lives (and academic collaborations with geographically distant colleagues) easier.

Shared cloud storage and online word processing with live changes (Google Workspace, MS Office, etc.) have also been a blessing. With this technology, it is possible to have one master draft of a document with all version and comment histories saved; you don't have to write something in an offline file, send it to multiple people via email, get their respective changes or comments, consolidate them back into one file (and lose your zest for life in the process), make the changes (hoping that you don't have any questions about any of it), and send it back to the collaborators, only to repeat the process all over again.

All of this is now possible in one shared folder or document, with comments and changes updated in real time and accessible to everyone.

For any academic collaboration, reference management software such as Zotero, Mendeley, or Endnote is helpful, especially one with a shared bibliography function so that everyone can save their references in one place. Keeping an accurate and up-to-date bibliography in the document itself is already a near-impossible task even for solo writing; things get forgotten, cut, changed, or moved. With more people, there are simply more errors. One person can be responsible for the references, sure, but then how is this person supposed to recover a full reference from a parenthetical citation if it wasn't even theirs? Having everyone commit to adding any reference they use to the shared reference management system folder ensures that anyone can pull up a full bibliography for the manuscript at any time. It will still need to be checked (because, humans), but it's sure to be a time saver anyway.

To write this book, for instance, we are using Google Workspace, Zoom, and Zotero. We have a shared Google Drive folder that includes all our Google Docs and Sheets. We read and comment on each other's writing through the cloud, and though we do meet weekly because we are in the same writing group and every now and then need to discuss topics related to the book, we can minimize the amount of meetings we need. We save our references in Zotero, so when we are done with the first draft of this manuscript, we'll pull the full bibliography and paste it at the end of the Google Doc. At the time of writing, some of us have never physically met each other, and some of us haven't seen each other in years, but we have been able to complete an entire book project seamlessly through online collaborative writing tools. We might therefore be biased, but we highly recommend them.

28.2 Strategies for Collaborative Academic Writing

If this is the first time you are collaborating with someone (or multiple someones) and you don't have an accurate feel of their work style, the first thing you might want to do is go over your expectations for each other. Starting a collaborative project where one person tries to check in daily or weekly and the other gets annoyed (because, what are deadlines for?) would not be conducive to a happy writing journey. Neither is wondering who will get first authorship the whole time. The good news is that as long as each party is willing to pull their weight and be fair, things will work out. We will assume you have a courteous, functional relationship with your collaborators and delve right into some strategies that we have seen to be effective.

Action item!

Authorship conversations with your collaborators do not have to feel awkward. Here we offer you a list of things to consider when talking to your collaborators about authorship:

- Ideally, these conversations happen early on in the project and are revisited periodically, so that expectations are clear and set from the beginning and as the project evolves. If that didn't happen, you can work backwards based on the actual work done (this can be tricky, though, and we do not recommend it).
- You should start by openly discussing what counts toward authorship (in some disciplines, creating a figure of graph may count, while in others, it would not) and what activities or tasks constitute a *substantial contribution* that grants authorship.
- You should discuss the specific practical responsibilities associated with each task, including deadlines, revisions, and possible changes (in publication venue, etc.), as well as ethical research standards.
- You could also consider other practical aspects, such as if this publication is part of a bigger project (will first authorship and corresponding responsibilities rotate or stay the same?), if a team member is going up for promotion (they could be interested in doing more work and appearing as first author), if someone is unavailable at a given time (can you work around it or will that impact authorship?), etc.

Additional resources about authorship:

- ORI Authorship Guidelines https://ori.hhs.gov/content/Chapter-9-Authorship-and-Publication-Authorship
- Contributor Role Taxonomy https://credit.niso.org/
- COPE Authorship Guidelines https://publicationethics.org/authorship

You and your collaborators may assign portions of the research to be written up individually and later combined, but we suggest you consider simultaneous writing, which happens when collaborators work on a document together at the same time. One way to do this is to actually write the sentences together, speaking your thoughts out loud, bouncing ideas off of each other, and making word choices together. This might sound headache-inducing, but it can make the whole process easier by taking away your self doubt, in the sense that you don't have to wonder whether something comes across the way you mean it, because there's already one other person that understood what you were trying to say. Hilal uses this method a lot with her collaborators, and she finds writing entire proposals, presentations, and other academic work to be a breeze when done collaboratively. You know how you sometimes get stuck while trying to craft a sentence or paragraph? You have a vague idea of the direction you want to go, but you can't quite put it into words or make it make sense? In synchronous simultaneous writing, that time suck is reduced greatly, because you are doing one thing with two brains.

Another type of simultaneous writing is when the collaborators work on the same document at the same time, but in different sections, only to pull each other in when there is a need, or at periodic intervals. Recently, Hilal and a coauthor had to revise a book chapter manuscript, and they had different tasks to work on in the same document. They met on Zoom, pulled the document up, asked each other any initial questions they had about their respective tasks in the document, and got to work, together yet separately. Every now and then when they weren't sure about something, they asked for help from each other. This way, the entire process was completed in a matter of hours.

Then there is asynchronous collaborative writing, where everyone writes their own parts (paragraphs, sections, chapters, etc.) alone but the parts eventually come together to make a collaborative whole. Collaborators may take a different approach to how they sign off on what others have written. They may read and make comments in the document, or they may get together and discuss each other's parts. In the process of writing this book, we are doing both. Once someone finishes a chapter, everyone reads it and makes comments for feedback, suggestions, and ideas for elaboration. Then, at the end of each section, we get together virtually to go over the comments in each chapter. We try to resolve each comment as we go, but sometimes we have to assign tasks to one or more of us to be completed later. For instance, if the wording is off somewhere, we can easily fix that problem live, resolve the comment, and move on. But if the comment someone made involves bringing in our own examples on a certain matter, that would be too much to try to accomplish right then and there. Plus, it's not something that requires four brains.

28.3 Collaborating with Students

Collaborating with students can be a very rewarding experience. Sal has done it frequently and swears by it. The key is to be realistic about what the student can do. Their skill set and expertise will naturally vary, so it's crucial to gear your expectations to the specific student. Generally speaking, you will have initiated the collaboration, so you need to think about what the student can bring to the table that's most helpful. For example, if they actually ran an experiment, they are the most qualified person to write up the methodology section. If they wrote a thesis or dissertation on a topic, they may be best qualified to write the literature review. Sometimes data coding can be most revealing as discussing complex or unexpected data points can lead to insight. If the student did the coding but also participated in the discussion, then they may deserve coauthorship, even though they may not have actually written any of the final text. That will depend on how you feel about the significance of their contribution to the ideas presented in the paper. Of course, everything is relative to the student: Sal has had the pleasant experience of reading a chunk of text written by a student coauthor and just dropping it into the document in progress virtually without changes. Likewise, he's had to almost completely rewrite text that was awkward or just didn't follow academic conventions.

The most important thing to remember is that writing with a student is part of mentoring, not a way to get free or low-cost help. Writing with a student is more work than writing by yourself. You will need to read anything they write extremely carefully and vet it against possible involuntary plagiarism. Many an academic has gotten into trouble for blindly trusting what their research assistant produced. However, writing with a student is a valuable teaching tool, if you use the opportunity to show the student how to be an effective academic writer, by modeling proper research practices, approaching the writing systematically, and sharing other expertise with them. For the student, the experience of working with a seasoned author can be foundational. Writing a paper is like riding a bicycle: once you know how to do it, you don't forget it easily. The best things about writing with students are the fresh insights they bring, or the expertise in areas unknown to you, in addition to their enthusiasm for the process.

As long as you find collaborators with similar work ethics and expectations to yours, and you can agree on the terms of your collaboration, the strategies you can employ to write collaboratively, and the potential for positive results, are endless.

Questions for Reflection

1. Have you ever collaborated with anyone on academic writing? How did you feel about the experience? Whether it was pleasant or unpleasant, what made it so? Consider whether you could have made the experience better through clearer communication.
2. Do you have any project ideas that you have been sitting on because you can't do them alone? Would it be possible to bring in a collaborator or two to take care of the parts you don't feel confident about?

Questions for Discussion

1. How do the people in your group feel about strategies shared in this chapter? Which one would everyone prefer? Why?
2. Share any other online tools that might be useful for collaborative academic writing with your group.

Questions for Your Mentor

1. If you are in certain parts of the publish or perish world, you may need to produce a certain number of solo publications first, or collaborative projects may not count at all. Sometimes, collaborating with certain people may even be detrimental to your career. Ask your mentor how this works in your institution/field.
2. Has your mentor collaborated on research with students in the past? If so, ask them to share about the experience. What were the benefits of this experience for them? What were some of the unexpected challenges or difficulties of working with a student in this way? In what contexts or for what types of scholarship would your mentor recommend that you collaborate with students?

29 Open Access Science

The Open Access (OA) movement is one of the most exciting and interesting developments in the science and research world. While this is not the place to discuss the epistemological significance of this move, we will review a little about open access in general so you can understand how and why OA can help you.

29.1 What Is Open Access?

Simply put, an open access journal is one that does not charge its readers to access, read, and download its articles. How do open access journals manage to pay for the costs of producing and distributing a journal, if they don't charge for their product? Here we need to look briefly back at two factors: digital publishing and online distribution. In the 1990s, all the big academic publishers that collectively account for 50 percent of all publishing (Elsevier, Springer, Wiley-Blackwell, Taylor & Francis, and Sage) adopted digital online publishing and distribution of journals and books. Hard-copy books obviously still exist, but increasingly journals are primarily distributed and accessed online. This slashes or entirely eliminates the cost of producing and distributing books: shipping hard copies of journals is expensive, not to mention the price of paper. Digital publication and distribution is essentially free.

However, there is still the cost of producing the material (editing, selecting the articles, etc.). How do they cover those costs if they do not charge the readers? They charge the authors. Obviously, paying "page costs" has always existed, especially in the sciences, where typesetting of complex mathematical formulae or reproduction of images, and very restricted audience, made a business model of breaking even based on subscription fees very hard to work. However, in the humanities and social sciences this was much rarer.

The allure of open access publication overcame this potential obstacle: it has been established (McKiernan et al., 2016; Tennant et al., 2016) that open access articles get downloaded more and get quoted more than paywalled articles (you have to pay to read them). In short, if you want better citation counts, open access is the way to go. However, this dynamic gave rise to predatory publishing: when revenue depends on the number of authors willing to pay to get published, quality is bound to drop – and this is exactly what happened.

> **Action item!**
> A growing number of institutions worldwide are adopting open access policies. To avoid missing out on open access benefits that you may have, thanks to your institution, we strongly recommend that you contact your librarians well ahead of publication to inquire about the following:
> - Is there financial support for open access publications (small grants to partially or totally cover the cost of OA fees)?
> - Is the institution you belong to part of an OA program (you may have the opportunity to publish OA without paying any fees if you are the first author of the paper and your institution is part of one of these programs)?
> - Are there policies in place regarding OA and copyright?

29.2 Gold, Diamond, and Preprint Open Access

The success of OA has been enormous. To get a sense of its impact, we suggest that you explore some of these resources: Directory of Open Access Journals (www.doaj.org), which includes 12,000 journals without APC; Open access Journals Search Engine (www.oajse.com/); or a general list of OA journals available on Wikipedia (https://en.wikipedia.org/wiki/List_of_open-access_journals). Fifty percent of academic articles were available through open access in 2019, up from 30 percent in 2010 (Heidbach et al., 2022). It is important to differentiate various types of OA. First, the so-called "gold" open access is the model we described above: the author pays "article processing charges" (APC). There is a "diamond" or "platinum" tier, in which neither the reader nor the author pays any charges. Platinum journals are supported by volunteer work and academic institutions. Hybrid OA are journals that publish some papers in OA, but other papers are behind a paywall. Essentially, the publisher gets two revenue streams. There is also a "bronze" open access, which just means that while the paper can be read for free, there is no clear license attached to it. Gold and diamond OA papers will state how the article can be reproduced (commercially or not) and used (perhaps for instruction purposes only). Black open access is the distribution of copyrighted materials illegally either through a website (Sci-Hub) or by word of mouth (by posting a request on social media using the #ICanHazPDF).

Another practice, which is becoming more frequent, is to upload your paper in a preprint repository. For the sciences, arXiv.org is the largest and best known, but there are others in many fields, including Medieval studies, education, sociology, and media. People may decide to publish a preprint for a variety of reasons that typically include establishing priority (your preprint has a timestamp so you can demonstrate that you were the first to come up with that idea even though the official publication process may take much longer). This can be useful when you have to meet promotion or grant deadlines, to increase visibility of your work (preprints are open access and were shown to receive high numbers of citations, Piwowar et al., 2018), or to receive feedback as you finish up the manuscript for publication.

The appeal is obvious. There is no wait time to upload your paper on a preprint site, so you can get your research out there, get feedback, and stake a claim. However, you should be extremely careful if you are interested in prepublication OA: some journals consider them to be publications, period, so they will not accept a submission that has been "published" elsewhere. You should do your homework before you submit anything. Wikipedia has a very useful page that lists the policy of various journals vis-à-vis accepting preprint submissions (https://en.wikipedia.org/wiki/List_of_academic_publishers_by_preprint_policy). Most journals will have a posted policy on the subject. Failing that, you can always try contacting the editorial team to ask, but there is no guarantee they will respond.

Wikipedia also has a page listing preprint repositories (https://en.wikipedia.org/wiki/List_of_preprint_repositories) that can be searched by discipline and provides information about any restrictions (e.g., by language, by affiliation of the author, etc.).

29.3   Green OA

Green OA is a bit different, in that it consists of self-archiving your published papers in publicly accessible repositories, meaning it is entirely author-driven. For a long time there was a sort of "gray" open access, meaning that authors would post nonformatted copies of their papers or even postedited copies in clear violation of copyright agreements. The reasoning was that publishers were unlikely to sue their own authors. With the mainstreaming of OA, publishers took a more permissive stance and now generally agree that self-archiving of post-print (the published paper) is allowed.

There are a few factors to be considered: First, you have to make sure that no one is profiting from the archiving. In other words, you should not sell or donate your paper to a service that charges for access. The best way to do so is to personally upload your paper on your website (assuming you do not charge access) or to a repository in your institution.

Next, you need to check and respect any embargo period, a time in which OA is not permitted. Once the embargo is over, Green OA is allowed. Most publishers have an embargo period of a year, but this can vary, so it is important that you check carefully with the publisher's website or, if necessary, by contacting them and asking in writing about their Green OA policy. Keep the answer for your archive.

The reason for ensuring that your entire production is in green OA is simple: As we saw, OA papers get downloaded more often and thus have a better chance of getting quoted. If you cannot afford or refuse to pay the Gold OA fees, Green OA levels the playing field with scholars with deeper pockets. The embargo period is not significant in terms of citations. Most papers get cited long after they are published, at least in the humanities and social sciences (see Galiani and Gálvez, 2017).

29.4 Standards of Quality

As we saw in Chapter 15, OA caused the unintended consequence of spawning predatory publishing. The problem is that in the traditional model of publishing in which the reader pays to access the article or book, the incentives for the publishers align quality with financial rewards (your journal attracts more readers, and hence generates more revenues, if the articles are good, significant, and useful). In the gold OA model, unfortunately, the financial incentives are aligned toward quantity of publication. In other words, the more articles a journal publishes, the more revenue it generates. This means that even with the best of intentions, a gold OA journal or publisher is forever tempted to increase the number of papers or books they publish, since the more they publish, the more money they generate. In principle, there is no problem if, for example, a journal publishes twenty high-quality papers instead of ten. However, when the journal wants to publish 100 papers, it may find that it needs to lower its standards to find that many papers. Indeed, many studies have shown that OA journals sometimes publish nonsense papers. This is not to say that all OA journals are predatory. Obviously, there is a difference between a journal or publisher that sets out to scam its audience by pretending to be a scholarly publisher or journal but is in fact only interested in collecting the APCs, and an OA journal or publisher who starts out as a bona-fide publisher but sees its standards eroding under commercial pressure. A good way to conceptualize this is to see both predatory and OA journals and publishers as part of a continuum, ranging from outright deception to full commitment to quality.

From everything we've said so far, you want to be in the high-quality camp, while also wishing to achieve maximum distribution of your work. The straightforward solution is diamond OA and/or green OA. There seems to be little or no reason to spend money on gold OA. You may object that it doesn't matter where you publish, as long as your work is out there. However, remember the saying, "you are the company you keep." Even if your scholarship is flawless, if it appears in a low-quality venue, it will be regarded as less valuable.

29.5 Preregistration and In-Principle Acceptance

An even newer practice linked to the open science movement, preregistration allows you to describe in detail the plans you have for a study (including a literature review, methods, expected results, and their impact) and register your plans. By doing so, you are clearly stating whether your research is exploratory or confirmatory and avoiding confounding the two (an issue that is as problematic as is fairly common across disciplines). This practice is increasingly common in a variety of disciplines, and Nosek et al. (2018) break down some of the challenges researchers may face, as well as solutions and numerous instruments (templates, courses, guidelines, etc.) to increase and facilitate preregistration. In some cases, preregistration means that your report is published and available to others. However, you can also preregister your study with an embargo, meaning that it won't be available to the public until published.

In line with this trend, some journals have started accepting preregistered studies in principle. In-Principle Acceptance is based on successful peer review of the preregistered study (also called registered reports), which essentially means that reviewers are giving you feedback on your plan to conduct a study, including the methods you plan to use. After the study is conducted and the full manuscript is written up, it undergoes a second review to check that the plan was executed appropriately and the results are fully reported. This does not mean that there can't be variations to the initial plan, but rather that these need to be justified and explained convincingly. Additionally, one of the benefits of this practice is that it is not, in principle, biased against reporting negative results.

Action item!

Is preregistration and in-principle acceptance common or available in your field? You can find out by searching the journal or publisher's webpage, typically under author services or guidelines. Here are some examples:

- Wiley: https://authorservices.wiley.com/author-resources/Journal-Authors/submission-peer-review/registered-reports-policy.html
- Taylor & Francis (Routledge): https://authorservices.taylorandfrancis.com/choose-open/
- Nature: https://www.nature.com/nmeth/submission-guidelines/aip-and-formatting

Additionally, you can explore preregistered reports in the OSF repository (https://osf.io/).

29.6 Transparency

Another aspect of open science is the transparency of the whole research process, starting with data collection and continuing all the way through publication. This approach has made more progress in the sciences, but is beginning to be felt in the social sciences and humanities as well. The whole idea boils down to making the research process more or fully transparent, thus helping to root out sources of bias, scientific misconduct, or just poor practices. Consider the p-hacking phenomenon. You may not be familiar with it, so let's use an example to explain. You collect data on first-year writers by gathering samples of their writing. The idea is that students who spend more time reading may do better at writing. With the help of the instructors, some of the classes were assigned extra-credit reading, while others were not. Once you start analyzing your data, you realize that one of the classes where the extra credit was given did particularly badly, for a variety of reasons. You decide to drop that class from your sample. You just committed p-hacking. It is likely that you will find a correlation between the students who read more and the quality of their writing. So, the important question is whether the correlation is above chance level (that is what "p" stands for; generally a p-value of 0.05 is considered above chance level, since it means that there is only a 5 percent chance that the results you found are due to chance). By dropping the class that did poorly, you altered the p-value. There are other ways of tampering with the statistical validity of your results, for example by running statistics on all the variables you collected but only reporting some of them. An even more insidious strategy is to change your hypothesis midway through the study. For example, if the class that did particularly poorly happened to be taught in the evening, you add a variable "time of day" to your analysis and revise your hypothesis accordingly. Journals rarely publish studies that find nonsignificant results or, worse, no correlation, so if you want to be able to publish your work, you have to come up with some statistically significant results. The temptation to "tweak" your data is always there. This is true for qualitative researchers, too: if you interviewed twenty teachers, you cannot pick and choose whose comments you include in your study, transcribe, run a thematic analysis on, and so on.

Open science aims at making it harder to do this kind of manipulation by registering hypotheses in public repositories, making raw data available to other scholars, making presubmission articles available, and even publishing formulas for the statistical analysis (which makes them replicable) or entire datasets. In fact, if your research is funded, the funding agency may have an open data policy that requires you to publish your data so that these are freely available for anyone to access and reuse. While you may still be on the fence about sharing your data, keep in mind that this may lead to more citations of your work (Colavizza et al., 2020).

> **Action item!**
> Use https://v2.sherpa.ac.uk/juliet/ to find out which funding agencies have an open data policy.

There is no question that the open science movement is laudable, but you need to be very careful about depositing any parts of your research in public repositories. You should check with your advisor or with experienced researchers about the possible drawbacks. For example, not all journals allow preprints. Another risk is being scooped by another scholar who replicates your study and gets it into print before yours appears. Consider that some journals will keep a manuscript literally for years before accepting or rejecting. This has happened to one of us, admittedly under unusual circumstances, but still, we speak here from experience. A way to prevent being scooped is to file your hypothesis as close as the moment you start collecting your data as possible; you can also aim to publish your results immediately after the analysis is complete.

> **Questions for Reflection**
>
> 1. Do you have any materials (articles, data, etc.) that you could make open access (especially green OA)?
> 2. Open reviews are another piece of the open science movement. Would you consider doing one? Why or why not?
>
> **Questions for Discussion**
>
> 1. With your peers, discuss the idea of publishing your research open access. What are the benefits and drawbacks that people have heard of and thought about? Is the movement (increasingly) common in your field?
> 2. In a similar vein, ask people if they have or have not decided to share their instruments, data, code, and so on as open access resources. What were their motives?
>
> **Questions for Your Mentor**
>
> 1. Ask your mentor how OA articles are evaluated in your department. Do they carry the same weight as an article published in a more traditional journal?
> 2. Share what you know about OA with your mentor. Are there any practices that they see as particularly valuable or risky?

30 Serving as a Reviewer

Serving as a reviewer is not only important but also vital to the advancement of science. The National Science Foundation reported 2.9 million articles in peer-reviewed journals and conference proceedings in 2020 (White, 2021). There's an average yearly growth of 3.99 percent (White, 2019), so the number will only grow. Three million articles worldwide means at least six million reviews each year, and this is a conservative estimate of only two reviewers per publication. Depending on the field and journal, it's possible to have three or more reviewers, and having only one round of reviews is not the norm. Our estimate also does not include reviews of conference proposals, grant applications, book proposals, or full book manuscripts. So, assuming that you are willing to contribute to your field with service, in this chapter we will cover some reviewing basics, focusing on journal articles.

30.1 Getting Started

If you are at the beginning of your academic career having never reviewed anything, serving as a reviewer can sound very flattering. That is because it is. You need to be an expert in your field and recognized as such for editors to trust your judgment on whether or not something gets published or axed. You play a role in someone's academic journey, which is no small feat. Once you have publications out, and assuming the editor deems them good enough, you will be added to journals' reviewer lists. The journals in which you publish are usually the first to ask you to review for them. What if you want to start reviewing before the review requests start rolling in of their own accord, though?

The first thing you can do is express your interest to your mentor. Without your own publication record to speak for itself, your mentor is the best person to know whether you have reached the academic maturity to start judging others' work. Your mentor can take an empirical approach to it and ask you to review one of the papers they have been sent for review, with the approval of the editor of the journal, who generally speaking will only be happy to have found a reviewer. An established academic always has an uncompleted review lying around, and they would be happy to give you a shot. Then they can look at your review and decide whether you are ready. If you have done a good job, they can sign off on it, and, voila, you're in the club! This kind of scaffolded approach is the best; you don't know what you don't know until you know, so let a seasoned scholar help you at the beginning.

Of course, not everyone has a reliable mentor, and not every mentor has the time or desire to go that much above and beyond for their mentee. If you are alone in this, you can write to editors or fill out reviewer interest forms online and wait for your shot. If you do get a review request this way, please understand that you need to do an absolutely bang-up job with it and impress the editor, or you might never be invited back, and word can spread. As we have emphasized many times before, academia is small, so we can't afford to burn any bridges, and doing subpar work in this fast-paced world where time is precious can definitely burn bridges. See the next section for how (not) to review academic work.

30.2 Do's and Don'ts

The academic review process is the foundation of quality scientific work. It ensures that standards are met and relevant work is explicitly and sufficiently tied to each other, giving credit to prior work where it is due. It is important to bear this higher purpose in mind while reviewing others' work; it is, after all, an act of service to our discipline. A bit more selfishly, your name is tied to it. Even for double-blinded reviews, there are still people in the process who see your name. People who have been in the field long enough can sometimes tell who their reviewers are, even if the process is double-blinded. You want to remember that your name is attached to any review you submit and present yourself accordingly. With all this in mind, do:

- Only accept manuscripts that you can actually do a good job of reviewing. If you don't know enough about the subject, you can miss important scholarly connections even if you may still help with other aspects of the paper.
- Be honest. Don't be afraid to point out any errors, flaws, missing points. It is crucial for you to call it like you see it. There is a misconception that any negative review makes you the dreaded Reviewer #2; it doesn't. Sometimes manuscripts are just bad, and it's the reviewer's job to point it out.
- Tell the author(s) what needs to be done to improve the draft specifically. "Important theoretical work is missing" isn't very helpful; whose work are they missing? Just tell them.
- Point out the strengths as much as weaknesses. Not only does that help the author(s) when they read the evaluation of their work, but it also helps you realize the pros and cons of the paper instead of seeing only the cons because that's what you've been focusing on.

- Pay attention to deadlines. Be realistic about whether you can do a review by the proposed deadline. Let the editorial team know if a review you agreed to do in a specific time frame is no longer feasible.
- Anonymize any document you're submitting with your comments (e.g., by using the redact function on Adobe) if you want to stay truly anonymous. Be careful that many software programs (MSWord) will save the names of those who have edited the paper in the settings or document information. The only 100 percent safe way of anonymizing a file is to cut and paste it into a plain text file. That removes all meta-information (but of course not what's in the text).

And don't:

- Be a Reviewer #2. Remember that another human being will read your comments. A little kindness goes a long way. That doesn't mean to sugarcoat or overlook the flaws in the manuscript; just state them professionally instead of insultingly.
- Mistake a bad manuscript for a bad scholar. Being aware of that distinction will help you write your comments more respectfully.
- Try to get the author(s) to write a whole new paper based on your vision. Is what *they* wrote salvageable? If not, you can list your reasons and recommend a rejection.
- Recommend that the author(s) cite your own work unless it's absolutely relevant and they did actually miss it. There's a special place in hell for reviewers who try to up their citation counts through this process.
- Speaking of special places in hell, don't recommend that a native speaker read the manuscript before resubmission. Not only is it elitist, it also disregards the fact that there are many native speakers who can't put together an error-free sentence. What you mean is professional proofreading, so say that instead.
- Do not include an explicit recommendation for or against publication in your review. You can make that recommendation in a separate place to the editor, but the decision to accept or reject does not lie with you. It is the editor's privilege, and if they disagree with you, they will need to edit your review, which may be annoying.

30.3 How to Deal with the Perception That You Are Doing Free Labor

A lot of academics are wary of the review process in academia, considering how publishers make millions of dollars off of academic publications while the reviewers who are integral to the process get zero percent of the big bucks. Just think about how journals charge the author (or their affiliated institution) thousands of dollars to make a publication open access. Think about how they charge readers per article if they don't have a subscription to the journal. All that money adds up, and none of it goes to the reviewers that ensured the scientific integrity of the work, or to the actual authors who, you know, actually wrote the thing people are trying to read.

How do we deal with this knowledge, then? First off, you can be the change that you want to see and do something about it. You can refuse to do reviews for journals that charge Article Processing Charges. You can petition the professional organizations in your field to do something. A less dramatic approach many academics choose to adopt is to recognize that while some entities make a financial profit off of publishing, reviewers and authors also make a profit, albeit not a financial one. Service is a component of many academic jobs, so your institution most likely will count reviewing toward fulfilment of your yearly service goals that are part of your job. There is also the issue of reciprocation. Academics who rage about not getting paid for their review work don't seem to realize that their work has also benefited from this seemingly free labor. In that sense, the review process can be seen as a give and take; you don't do free labor for the publishers, but pay what another scholar has done for you forward by reviewing another scholar's work yourself.

30.4 How Much to Review

If we approach reviewing journal articles as a matter of reciprocity, then the math on how much to review becomes clear. For every new submission you send to a journal, review an equivalent number of papers to the number of reviewers who evaluated your submission. For instance, if you have made three submissions this year, and two of them received three reviewers and one of them was assigned two, that's a total of eight reviewers that took the time to read and assess your work. You can pay it forward by reviewing eight papers yourself, and call it even.

This is, of course, not the only criterion you should take into consideration while deciding whether you should accept a review request. If you have the time, you can do more. If a new request has come after you have met your self-imposed quota or when you simply don't have the time, but it is right up your alley and you are one of the best people out there who can do that manuscript justice, then you might reconsider. Just make sure you don't find yourself being unable to attend to your other responsibilities or wanting to make quick (read: subpar) work of a review because you have said yes to too much.

People also often wonder how much time they should spend on a given manuscript. The bad news is, there is not a set amount of time we can give you. The good news is, there is an easy principle to follow: give it as much time as it takes to do the work justice. You need to commit to fully reading and understanding the paper in order to give it the comments it deserves, and that will vary from paper to paper. For some, it may be so close to your own work that you don't need to look anything up and can write your comments from memory. For some, you will know of a theory or publication (or five) that they need, but you will need to look these up. The nature of the flaws that need attention will also play a role; mechanical errors are a lot easier to indicate than those pertaining to argumentation or presentation. There are some things you can do to make your job easier regardless, though. For instance, if you work on the manuscript digitally, you can take notes as you go using the comment feature of the program you opened the file in (usually Adobe or Word) so you don't have to type up your comments later. This way, you can also easily adjust your comments if you find yourself in the shoes of Sheldon Cooper, a fictional theoretical physicist in *The Big Bang Theory* (2007), who, as he reads an article, says, "Why?! Why?!" in deep frustration, only to say, a couple of pages later, "Oh, that's why." You can also opt to summarize your comments in the textbox provided on the review platform, but you should still refer to page and line numbers to direct the readers to your points of reference, and that takes additional time. The upside is that you don't have to worry about your wording in the comments you make as you go, and you can focus your energy on being constructive in the summary version. If you go with the first option, though, you should still write a summative statement or two in the textbox and direct readers to the file attachment for details.

Action item!

When you are doing a review, it's useful to have a set of categories to consider. Of course, if the journal directs you to their categories, you should use them, but if they give you latitude, these may help.

- What is the main point of the paper?
- Is that claim sufficiently supported by evidence?
- Is the paper well organized, clear, and accessible?
- Does the paper show awareness of prior relevant research, and is this research incorporated in the discussion?
- How novel is the claim and/or methodology?
- If statistical tools are used, are the statistics reported fully (not just a p value)? If you are not sufficiently trained to assess them, clearly state so. Editors and authors alike will appreciate your candor.
- Make a list of typos, ungrammatical sentences, and other improprieties. Again, editors and authors alike will appreciate your help in improving the paper.

30.5 When and How to Say "No" to Review Requests

So far, we have assumed that you want to and should do the reviewing. However, there are circumstances in which you should refuse. The most obvious one is if you cannot be impartial. If your ex who broke your heart in graduate school is the first author, or conversely if they are your BFF, you should recuse yourself. Another valid reason is if you are too busy. If you are finishing a book project or are about to turn in a major grant, you don't have time to be dealing with other people's research (and you may do a poor job if you try). Inform the editor and give them a time frame of when you'd be able to deliver the review. Sometimes an editor will choose to have a reliable review a month later than they'd want rather than no review at all. It also goes without saying that you should refuse to work for predatory journals. Whether you should work for free for journals that charge authors steep article processing charges to publish is an ethical question that you will need to tackle for yourself. Moreover, you may refuse to re-review an article if the author does not seem to be genuinely interested in correcting the errors you pointed out or in making the improvements you suggested. Politely but firmly point out to the editor that the author seems to be non-cooperative and move on. Nobody has time for that, and it's the editor's job, not yours, to see that the article is publishable. Finally, if you refuse to review an article, you should always suggest another person who you think would be appropriate and might have the time and inclination to do the review. It is pointless to suggest a major name in the field, as the editor is most likely familiar with them anyway, but an advanced graduate student or a junior faculty member may have not made it onto their mental map.

30.6 Reviewing Books and Grant Applications

Reviewing books is not very different from reviewing an article, except that the scope of the work is much broader, so the publisher will want to know more about how the book fits within the field, how innovative it is, and what its competition looks like. When reviewing books, you may be asked to do so based on a proposal (see also Chapter 20 for more on book proposals) or the whole manuscript. Sometimes it will be a combination of the two, as when reviewing a book that is already published because the authors are planning a new edition. In any of these scenarios, you will be given specific instructions by the publisher in the form of a set of questions to address. Here, we include some of these questions and some words of advice.

- What is the commercial potential for the book? Often this question is simply worded as "Would you adopt this book for one of your classes and why?" Be

honest, but remember that the field is very small and it's usually easy to find out who wrote what.
- Does the book offer a comprehensive and up-to-date coverage of the field? Consider if all the key topics are covered or anything important is missing. If so, explain why that topic should be included or given more coverage. In this case, remember that "filling a gap" is not a good enough reason for the authors to add a new chapter. Rather, consider who will use the book and for what purposes.
- Is the organization and format of the book logical? This requires you to look at the table of contents and the sequencing of chapters. If there is an introduction in which the authors explain how the book is organized and why, read that as well. You may also think about a potential college course based on the book and see what the syllabus would look like.
- How useful is the approach, writing style, and use of figures, tables, and so on? Once again, we recommend you answer this question by considering the intended audience of the book, as a textbook for graduate students at the beginning of their career will be different from a research monograph for experienced researchers.

Last, reviewing grants is different from reviewing articles or books. We recommend you familiarize yourself with how to write a grant application before reading any further (see Chapter 22). If you have been selected to review a grant application, it means that the funding agency has identified you as an expert on that topic (yay, you!) or the applicants have suggested your name as a potential reviewer because they know you are familiar with their topic. Either way, it is a big responsibility, as your evaluation will determine if the project gets funded or not. Unlike articles or books, each funding agency has its own set of criteria for reviewers; these are not necessarily shared, as each agency has its own mission, goals, and leadership officials to whom it must justify how the money is spent. You will probably be given an evaluation matrix or rubric with all the criteria to consider already weighted (with a set of points assigned based on their importance for the agency), organized in sections, and linked to a specific part of the grant application. Typically, you will be asked to consider how the application fits within the scope of the specific grant and the funding agency, its scientific quality, feasibility, and impact. You will also receive specific instructions about how to assess each component and what your final evaluation score will mean (e.g., a negative score on the fit of the proposal may disqualify it from further consideration, but the same score in the impact category may not). The best way to prepare yourself to be a good reviewer is to familiarize yourself with the agency mission, the specific grant type you will be reviewing, and the criteria guidelines that you will receive.

Overall, serving as a reviewer makes you a valuable part of the global scholarly community, which speaks to your merit as an expert in your field. Though you can take some purposeful steps to be inducted into the process sooner, it occurs naturally as a result of publishing your own work. Your constructive criticism of your fellow academics' work helps ensure that scientific work is held to the highest standards. Just remember to be professional about it, if not to save the author's face, then to protect yourself.

Questions for Reflection

1. Have you been Reviewer #2 in the past? If handy, pull up one of your past reviewers and take a look. Is there anything you could have worded differently?
2. How much time do you spend on reviewing manuscripts, both individually and in total for a given time period (semester, academic year, etc.)? What are some techniques or strategies you adopt to make the process quicker and more effective for you?

Questions for Discussion

1. Some scholars argue that an insulting or rude tone in academic reviews is a result of the time crunch reviewers are in and should not be taken personally. They maintain that polite criticism takes longer to craft and is therefore not worth it. Do you agree or disagree? Can you think of any strategies to help you be a polite yet efficient reviewer?
2. How have people in your group dealt with particularly challenging manuscripts without resorting to rude or elitist comments?

Questions for Your Mentor

1. If you haven't yet reviewed a journal article but would like to, speak to your mentor. Do they have something they can give you to try? The next time they get a request, would they consider telling the editor to send it to you instead?
2. Does your mentor have any stories about reviews and reviewers that they'd like to share with you that would supplement our points in this chapter?

31 People in the Publishing World

Throughout this book, one of our main objectives has been to demystify the academic writing process, helping you to gain a sense of confidence that might even bring you moments of joy as you become a more effective and proficient writer. By now, you should have a writing routine that works for you, as well as a bunch of information about how to structure your writing time and achieve your writing goals. Once you're happy with your article or book draft, the next step is to publish it, which will require interaction with a variety of editors and agents. In this final chapter, we explain the roles and responsibilities of a variety of individuals within the publishing world and offer you some guidance for how and when to have conversations with the editors and agents who can help you get your writing out into the world.

31.1 Journal Editors

At some point, you are going to send your work to a journal for potential publication. If the idea of submitting your article for publication makes you nervous, you may want to submit to the *Journal of Universal Rejection* first (universalrejection.org). You'll definitely be rejected, but this can be a good way to work through any anxieties linked to the submission process. The editorial structure of every journal will vary slightly, but most large journals have an editor-in-chief, associate editor(s), review editor, and an editorial board. The editor-in-chief is the person with the most authority at the journal who oversees the scope and direction of the journal. When submissions arrive, editors-in-chief either reject them or assign them to associate editors, who will send them out to reviewers. They have oversight over journal issue content, making the final decision if reviewers are divided over the merit of a submission. In smaller journals, the editor-in-chief directly handles the assignments of reviewers. In *really* large journals, the journal management software directs submissions to appropriate editors, and the editor-in-chief is not directly involved. Later in this chapter, we'll discuss how and when to reach out to different editors. It's pretty easy to remember when to reach out to the editor-in-chief of a journal, though, because the answer is almost never.

31.1 Journal Editors

Editors-in-chief have multiple responsibilities related to the journal, in addition to their obligations as professors, and they may not take kindly to your message popping up in their inbox, asking a question that an associate editor could have fielded.

Associate editors are more closely involved in the process of vetting and polishing submissions, as they oversee the details and production of journal issues. To a lesser extent than the editor-in-chief, they can propose topics for issues and help shape the trajectory of the journal. While a journal will have one editor-in-chief, it may have many associate editors, which makes sense, given their heavy workload. Depending on the size of the journal, associate editors may have the job of assessing whether a submission's topic falls within the scope of the journal and, if so, finding an appropriate reviewer for that submission. Depending on the structure of the journal, they may directly accept or reject articles, or they might make recommendations to the editor-in-chief. Associate editors serve as go-betweens for reviewers and aspiring authors. Associate editors will closely review revisions made to submissions to be sure the content is up to the journal's standards. Most likely, you will be communicating with an associate editor from the submission stage through the revision process. Journals also have a bevy of subeditors or copy editors who revise your work for typos and other small errors once it has been accepted for publication, but your interactions with these editors will probably be minimal. Many journals from large commercial publishers outsource proofing and some aspects of editing.

Review editors coordinate the work surrounding book reviews. Many journals publish a set number of reviews of books related to the field in each issue. Every journal has different guidelines for book reviews, so be sure to read their online instructions before investing ten hours into a review of the latest book on competitive hotdog eating for a journal whose scope only includes croissant-based scholarship. Most journals will not accept unsolicited reviews, but review editors will have a list of books for which they need to find reviewers. Depending on the journal's policies, either you can write directly to the review editor and ask if they will assign you a book to review or the review editor will reach out to individuals. It is usually the case that when someone has been asked to write a review, they will receive a free copy of the book from the journal, whether that be a physical copy or an electronic version. While book reviews are short and do not hold the same weight as journal articles, they can be important pieces of scholarship (see Chapter 17) that allow you to further integrate yourself into the academic community.

Finally, most journals have an editorial board. Quite honestly, boards can feel mysterious. What do they do? When do they meet? How many members should a board have? There are no uniform guidelines for editorial boards, but the basic function of the board is to guarantee the academic quality of the journal. Board members are often big names in the field who have been invited to join the board because their names bring prestige to the journal. Many board members are not required to actively contribute to the journal. Board members could potentially be asked to serve as reviewers, to offer suggestions about topics for issues, or to give feedback on whether submissions should be published. As someone submitting an article to a journal, there should be no need for you to directly contact editorial board members. If you are ever asked to serve on an editorial board for a journal, though, say yes, and then let us know what the board actually does.

31.2   Acquisitions Editors

When you are planning on publishing a book, you will need to speak with an acquisitions editor. These editors serve as the first point of contact in many publishing houses. They are extremely knowledgeable about current trends and conversations in the field, as well as the unique scope of their own publishing house's books and series, as they are the individuals who make decisions about which book proposals will be forwarded on within the publishing house and which will be rejected. While you can always email an acquisitions editor with no prior contact (we'll get to this soon), if you're attending your national conference (or sometimes a bigger regional conference), you can chat more informally with acquisitions editors in the book room. This is a space where acquisitions editors, books reps, and various other publishing house employees hover by a table displaying their publishing house's latest books. If you're researching publishers for your book, taking a stroll around the book room is a great opportunity to see the kinds of topics and conversations that specific publishers have been interested in lately. While you should of course be professional, it's completely fine to introduce yourself to acquisitions editors and give them an elevator pitch for your book project. Listen very carefully to what they say to you; you often can gather immediate feedback on your ideas that can be invaluable. Later, when you email them the formal proposal, you can remind them that you spoke about the project at your national conference. Another possible way in which you might have a conversation with an acquisitions editor at a conference is through invitation. Acquisitions editors look through conference programs to find titles of presentations that are of interest to them. They then reach out via email to those scholars and ask for individual meetings. Even if you're not currently planning to turn your conference paper into a book, it's always a good idea to accept these invitations. At the very least, they allow you to make a personal connection with an acquisitions editor, which may make them more inclined to read your book proposal once you're ready to submit it (whether it's about the topic you presented on at the conference or not). Remember that editors are people too, and while it is important to network, you can do so while also having genuine conversations about a topic of shared interest. One way to get on the radar of acquisition editors is to review books for them. You have to wait for them to ask you, but in our experience, once your name starts popping up, invitations to review will not be very far behind. If you do a good job and they find you helpful, they will ask you again.

31.3 Series Editors

If an acquisitions editor decides that your book proposal is promising, you may be offered a contract or passed on to an area or series editor. Some monographs will be published as stand-alone books, in which case you will work with a content editor. Generally speaking, if your book fits into a general area of specialization (say, teacher preparation or medieval history), you will work with the area editor responsible for that subject. If your book fits within one of the publishing house's standing series, you will work with a series editor. These are the editors who will send your manuscript out for review and closely monitor the content of your book to be sure it matches the expectations of the publishing house and/or series. These editors should be invested in promoting your book, discussing book tours with you (you can always hope), and submitting your book for prizes, which is a great way to promote your work, the series, and the publishing house. Content or series editors also often attend national conferences, visiting panels to see who is working on research that they might want to publish. A good series editor may also help you network, introducing you to other scholars who have published with them. Establishing a relationship with a content or series editor is extremely valuable. If your series editor invites you out for dinner or drinks, they may ask you about your ideas for a second book. This is not just idle conversation, and you should have a thoughtful answer prepared. Many editors enjoy working with repeat authors, especially if they prove reliable, easy to work with, and produce good scholarship.

31.4 Agents

Finally, if you become a huge deal in your field, you may acquire an agent. An academic agent has similar roles and responsibilities to a literary agent for a novelist. They find publishers for your work, negotiate your contracts with those publishers, and promote you and your writing. Agents will take a percentage of your profits, as they work for you individually rather than being paid by a publisher. While this won't be a relationship that most academics will find necessary, if you do become rich and famous enough for an agent, remember us little people who gave you advice so long ago. Don't worry, we'll send you our banking information.

31.5 How to Reach Out

When you are ready to submit a potential article to a journal, you will be addressing an editor in some way. Before starting your submission, read through the journal's submission guidelines carefully. You don't want to make a bad impression by sending the wrong documentation or submitting your article via the incorrect platform. Many journals now use online systems that don't require you to email an editor directly. Even so, online systems usually still have a space for the equivalent of a cover letter, where you briefly address the editor and make a small case for your submission. Whether through an online system or as an email directly to the editor, you should find the editor's name so that you can personalize the message. You also want to briefly highlight what makes your submission unique and exciting scholarship that is relevant to this particular journal. See the sample in Figure 31.1 from an email that Heather sent out with an article submission. Keep in mind that, in contrast to journal articles, book proposals are generally emailed directly to acquisitions editors, rather than submitted via an online system. You can read two sample emails in Appendix B.

After you have submitted your work and received confirmation of submission, you may find yourself in the position of needing to reach out to an editor asking for an update. This is not ideal, but sometimes journal editors' decisions can be greatly delayed (due to a variety of reasons, such as difficulties in finding reviewers); in the most nightmarish of situations, your submission can also be lost. On their websites, most journals will indicate the normal amount of time between submission and decision, which can officially range up to six months. Different academics will tell you different things, but our rule of thumb is that if the journal or press hasn't gotten back to you by a month *after their official range*, it's OK to contact them. This email, sent to the associate editor with whom you were in contact at the time of your initial submission, should be short, courteous, and avoid placing any blame. Even though these decisions can be extremely high stakes, especially for scholars on the tenure track, your email will be most effective if all emotion is set aside. Have a look at a sample email in Appendix C. In general, when you correspond with editors, stay professional and keep your message to the point. Editors often have a tremendous amount of work to do; by being concise and courteous, you will hopefully make a good impression.

While interacting with people in the publishing world can feel intimidating at first, you will become more skilled at it with time and practice. No matter what stage of your career you're currently at, you are a legitimate member of the academic community who can both benefit from the experience of others and also contribute to your field. Even though this is the end of the book (be sure to check out the appendices, too), please come back to individual chapters as you need. Also, don't be afraid to trust in yourself,

Letter	Annotation
Dear Dr. [editor's last name], Please find attached my submission and title page for [journal].	Use the last name of the editor-in-chief and clearly state your purpose in reaching out.
My article, [title] is an examination of the intricate connections between gender, religion, and race within colonial Equatorial Guinean society, produced through an analysis of cover illustrations from La Guinea Española, a magazine published in Equatorial Guinea between 1903 and 1969 by the Spanish religious order of the Sons of the Immaculate Heart of Mary.	Clearly state the title of your submission and the parameters of the research.
My article uncovers a representation of Catholicism that evolved from feminized to masculine to best serve shifting colonial interests and needs. During the early years of colonization, La Guinea Española's version of Catholicism is feminized, projecting a peaceful and benevolent attitude toward the indigenous population, only to become hypermasculine in the 1960s as Spain's colonial power weakened, in an attempt to portray a message of Spanish domination and power.	Use strong verbs to demonstrate the core of your argument, as well as how your submission adds something unique to the conversation.
With reference to Laura Wexler's Tender Violence: Domestic Visions in an Age of U.S. Imperialism, I analyze what these photographs reveal and conceal about the race, gender, and religion of both the colonizers and the colonized—including the violence masked by altruism and the masculine Spanish crisis of empire hidden under the mask of bravado.	Acknowledge the theoretical framework that you are referencing.
I look forward to your response and would be happy to take any suggestions you may have for improving the article. Thank you for your time and consideration	Show that you are grateful and willing to be flexible when it comes to potential revisions. It is common courtesy to thank the editor for their time in looking at your submission.

Figure 31.1 Sample submission email to a journal with annotations

your writing group, and your mentor, as our communities make us stronger. You have all the knowledge and tools you need to approach academic writing from a competent and joyous perspective.

Questions for Reflection

1. Look at the email you sent to the editor with the last article that you submitted for publication. After reading this chapter, what did you do well in that email, and what are some areas that you could improve for the future?
2. We know that approaching a publisher's booth at a conference can be intimidating. Even though you may feel nervous about it, you are on a valuable information-gathering mission. Think about the benefits of such a conversation. How might this conversation help you? What can you do to better prepare yourself for the conversation?

Questions for Discussion

1. Look at the sample emails to editors with your writing group. Does anyone in the group have additional boilerplate phrases that they could share with the group that might come in helpful when contacting editors?
2. What kind of people in the publishing world have your colleagues been in touch with? How did they establish these connections? What kind of conversations are they having?

Questions for Your Mentor

1. Ask your mentor to roleplay a conversation with an acquisitions editor with you. Can you brainstorm some potential questions for the acquisitions editor together and work on your elevator pitch for your book?
2. Does your mentor have any stories about a time in which they needed to reach out to an editor with a request (timeline update, etc.)? How did they approach that tricky conversation, and what advice do they have for you?

Appendices: The Occluded Genres

Appendix A Say-no Punch Card

Appendix A

Appendix B Sample Submission Emails for a Book Proposal

To Use These Templates, Remove the Square Brackets and Add in Your Information

Sample 1

Dear [editor],

I hope you are well and your semester started off smoothly.

I am writing because I am working on a book manuscript based on my dissertation, provisionally titled [title]. [name of scholar] suggested the book series that you edit with [publisher], [title of book series], where they are also a board member, as a possible publication avenue. I also thought my work would be a good fit for your series after we talked at [conference], and I have attached the proposal for you to review. Please let me know if you also need one or more sample chapters.

Thank you for your time. I am looking forward to hearing from you.

[your signature]

In this context, the author knows the editor of the book series, although not well. The two met a couple of years before at a conference and exchanged a few emails in which they discussed several topics that are also treated in the book (which is why the author brought it up in the email). The author was confident that the editor would know who she was and remember her, and so decided not to remind the editor who she was. In a different situation, if you are not sure whether the editor remembers you or not, or you have never been in contact with them, it would be good to add a couple of lines in which you tell them who you are (university, department, your position and title, your main areas of research).

Sample 2

Dear [editor],

It was a pleasure to meet you at [conference] in [month/year] and discuss my book project with you. I am writing to you with a proposal for my book project, [title of the book], for publication with [press/publisher]. I am familiar with [press/publisher]'s strong support of [field] overall, particularly the [book series

Appendix B

title]. My book would complement [name of author with book published in the same series]'s recently published [title of book], expanding [author]'s astute conversation of [specific topic] through a shift in focus to [your own topic].

[title of your book] seeks to change the conversation about [topic] through an examination of [topic]. My book is unique in that it analyzes [topic].

This book will be a resource for scholars and professors of [field/s] who wish to expand their curriculum related to [topic/s in your book].

My manuscript is approximately [number] words, with [number] chapters. The manuscript is currently [percentage] complete, to be fully completed by [date]. Parts of Chapter [number] and Chapter [number], in their previous forms, have been published in [journal/year] and [journal/year]. Please, note that this is not a simultaneous submission. Attached to this email, please find my book proposal, CV, and a sample of Chapter 1.

I would be happy to discuss the project in greater detail or answer any questions you might have. Thank you very much for your consideration.

[your signature]

In this sample email, the author is establishing that they are familiar with this specific press (whether that includes a particular series or not) and wants to indicate that they are well versed in the field. By citing an author from this press, the author is again signaling that their work belongs in this series by suggesting similarities with other books, yet hinting that the series has space for something novel, which their book brings to the table. Be careful here, as you want to situate your book within the series without seeming to insult the series or press for what it is lacking.

Appendix C Follow-up Email after Submitting a Book Proposal or Journal Article

To Use These Templates, Remove the Square Brackets and Add in Your Information

Sample 1

Dear [editor],

I hope this email finds you well. I was wondering if you had any chance to have a look at the book proposal I sent you a few weeks ago for the series [title of the book series] (attached).

I am looking forward to your feedback.

All the best,

[your signature]

Sample 2

Dear [associate editor],

I am writing to inquire about the status of my submission to [journal], "[title of your submission]," for which I received confirmation of submission on [date].

I understand that the review process is important and therefore can be lengthy.

However, I wanted to ask if you had a sense of when I might be receiving an update, as I am in the process of putting together my materials for my yearly review and still have time to make revisions to my CV before the end of the month. Any new information would be helpful and appreciated.

Best regards,

[your signature]

Here the idea is to use the approaching deadline as a justification to gently prod the editor. Obviously, you should replace the text with your own personal circumstances. Don't make up dramatic twists of fate; it's enough to say that your annual evaluation is due.

Appendix D Email to Inquire about a Possible Book Talk

To Use This Template, Remove the Square Brackets and Add in Your Information
Dear [name],

I hope that you're doing well and that the semester is off to a fantastic start for you. I'm writing because my book [title] is coming out with [publisher] in [month and year], and I would love to do a couple of book talks related to this project. I could easily come to [institution] in [month or semester] if your department would be interested in me giving a book talk. This email is a little early in the year, but I know how quickly our calendars fill up. If this sounds like something that you all would be interested in, please let me know, and we can discuss some possible dates. I'm including a brief description of the book below as well.

   [book description]
   Thanks for considering this idea,

   [your signature]

Note how you are not asking for any compensation, not even mileage or an honorarium. In other words, you are offering them a freebie, in exchange for the visibility. Generally, this sort of thing is followed by the host taking you out to lunch or dinner, but you should not count on it.

Appendix E Sample Panel Invitation Email

To Use This Template, Remove the Square Brackets and Add in Your Information

Dear Dr. [last name],

[organizers' names] are thrilled to announce the upcoming online panel [title] organized by the [organization] and scheduled to take place on [date]. Please keep in mind that because we are trying to accommodate an international audience, the panel will likely take place in the morning (if you are based in a US time zone) or afternoon (if you are based in a European time zone).

The [organization] aims at fostering discussions, research collaborations, and methodological innovation around [topic]. Because this is an inherently interdisciplinary area that has experienced a lot of growth in recent years, scholars have at their disposal a wide array of methodological options. To help members explore new research approaches, methods, and instruments, we are organizing an online panel focused on research methods. The panel will last one and a half hours and tentatively include three panelists. Our plan is to have each panelist give a short presentation (twenty minutes) and then have thirty minutes for discussion.

We would like to invite you to participate as a panelist with a presentation about [topic]. If you were to accept our invitation, we would love for your talk to discuss your recent work in this area, and more specifically, the theoretical framework(s) used and the methodological innovations and issues raised by such approach(es). Additionally, we are asking all panelists to prepare and share with us ahead of time some questions that they think could help us shape the discussion (questions you would like to ask or answer).

We would be grateful if you could confirm your interest within a week. After that, we will ask that you submit an abstract (max. 500 words not including references, tables, or figures) to [email] by [date].

We are looking forward to your reply, and do not hesitate to contact us if you have any questions.

All the best,

[signature]

Appendix F Sample Email to Potential Reviewers of Your Book

To Use This Template, Remove the Square Brackets and Add in Your Information

Dear [name],

I hope that you're doing well. I'm writing because my book [title] just came out with [publisher], and I was wondering if you would be interested in writing a book review of my manuscript for the journal [name of journal]. Here you can find out a bit more about the book: [link to publisher's page]. If you are interested, then I will reach out to [review editor of journal] to confirm and put you in touch with them. I will also need your address to arrange for a copy of the book to be sent to you.

Thanks for considering this,

[your signature]

Appendix G Sample Email to a Review Editor

To Use This Template, Remove the Square Brackets and Add in Your Information

Dear [name],

I hope this email finds you well.

I am reaching out to inquire whether [name of the journal] would be interested in receiving a review of the book [title of the book you would like to review], published by [author] in [year of publication].

[I already have a copy of the book, so it will not be necessary for you to send me one.]

OR

[If you are interested, please arrange for a copy of the book to be sent to the following address: your address]

Thank you very much for your consideration,

[your name and affiliation]

Appendix H Sample Cover Letter for Article Submission

To Use This Template, Remove the Square Brackets and Add in Your Information

Dear [editor],

We are writing to submit our manuscript, [title], for consideration to [journal]. This article is the first to [describe the novelty of your article, using verbs like compare, assess, describe, outline, map out, contrast, explore, etc.].

[The following paragraph is important if the article is related to others you published before on the same topics, or as part of a larger project.]

The present study builds upon the findings of a previous one, published in [journal], in which [explain general goal of the first study as well as its limitations, presented only aggregated data, did not consider the variable age of participants, etc.]. The present study addresses this limitation through [explain methods that allow you to address limitations and build on first study]. This approach to studying [topic] by analyzing [topic, variables] represents a novel methodological contribution that could be replicated for investigating [topic] in other fields besides [main field of your study].

[The following paragraph justifies the need for your study and frames it within the current literature on your topic.]

The literature review demonstrates the need for such a study in the broad field of [field], as not many studies have been conducted on [your topic]. The study of [topic, variable] has increased substantially in the last decades, and the article provides a model that can be replicated for other [fields, variables]. The article is important because [outline contribution of your study to the specific field].

[The following paragraph explains and justifies the methods of your study, focusing on replicability.]

The study follows the highest standards of inquiry, having applied [your research design, methods]. It is based on a unique set of data collected through [summarize instruments, participants]. The study could be easily replicated by using the information provided in the article and measuring the same aspects of [topic]. In the design of the study, attention was paid to [underscore important features such as special or under-researched populations, variables].

[The following paragraph explains the results, their relevance, and practical implications.]

The results contribute to the understanding of [topic] and inform future initiatives to [topic]. The study also contributes to [practical topic] by: [list key practical applications or implications resulting from your findings].

The authors confirm that this manuscript has not been previously published and is not currently under consideration by any other journal. Additionally, the authors have approved the contents of this paper and have agreed to abide by the [journal]'s submission policies.

[signature]

Appendix I Sample Initial Emails to Authors for an Edited Volume

To Use These Templates, Remove the Square Brackets and Add in Your Information

Sample 1

Dear [author's name],

[colleague's name] and I would like to extend an invitation to you to contribute a chapter to the anthology we are co-editing, titled [title], which is under contract with [publisher] (full manuscript due by the end of [year]). The anthology will have three sections that will analyze [theme 1], [theme 2], and [theme 3]. We would like you to write a chapter analyzing the [topic of invited chapter].

The chapter would need to have an extension of [number of] words (including footnotes and bibliography) and be written in English. We would need the chapter no later than [date], so that we could edit the chapter and give you time for revisions. I am attaching the style guide, as well as the original CFP.

If you have any questions about this project or invitation, please let us know. We'd be happy to discuss this with you further. We hope you will be willing and able to contribute to this anthology.

Best,

Sample 2

Dear [author's name],

I am writing to officially invite you to contribute a chapter to the [title of the volume], which will be part of [series]. Publication is expected in [year]. The title of your chapter is [title]

As you may be aware, there are currently no competing publications that will provide an in-depth introduction targeted at advanced undergraduates, graduate students, and faculty in [topic of the volume] and to the growing community of [discipline/field] scholars worldwide. The idea is to provide a complete overview of the field in a definitive and yet accessible volume.

Because this will be the first such publication, this is a very significant event, and I am honored to have been solicited to edit the [volume]. I am recruiting the top scholars in each field, and a few select emerging scholars, to provide a thoughtful, original, and in-depth overview of their field of expertise.

In a separate appendix, I will provide you with the current list of chapters. As you will see, some of the authors have already agreed to write their chapters. As more people sign up, I will circulate the updated list, to encourage exchanges between the authors. If you would prefer not to be included in the exchange, I will obviously accommodate your request.

If you agree to contribute a chapter, you will be contacted by [publisher] and you will have to sign an individual contributor agreement, which will specify your obligations (writing the chapter, making the changes required by the editor, and correcting a set of proofs) and compensation (a free copy of the [volume], upon publication).

More information on the structure of the [volume] and the deadlines are provided below. Needless to say, if you have any questions, please feel free to contact me at the address below.

Structure of the book and of your chapter
The [title of volume] will consist of about [number of] chapters, of [number of] words. Each chapter word count will include the references and endnotes (if any).

Each chapter will include the following sections: Historical perspective; Core issues and topics; Methodology and sample analysis; New debates; References. These are explained in more detail below.

- Historical perspective: Chronologically organized development of the materials, which articles/books were the precursors of the field, how did they influence those that came after? The historical perspective section is meant to contextualize the research for students new to the field.
- Core issues and topics: The "meat" of the chapter. What are the major findings/results of the field? What is the contribution that this particular area [name of core area of the volume] has brought to the general field of [general field/discipline]? Authors are encouraged to focus on the central, most significant issues in the field, thus ensuring that the core areas of research are covered.
- Methodology and sample analysis: The authors will be invited to describe their methodology (data collections, analysis, etc.) and to analyze a sample text or fragment thereof. This section may be omitted in chapters in which it is not relevant.
- New debates: What areas or issues are controversial or debated currently? What areas have not been the object of systematic research or are in need of more research? Is the field moving in a given direction? Are several new

approaches/directions competing for the attention of scholars? This section should look forward to the future of the discipline, by highlighting current debates/controversies in the field.
- References: The authors should list enough sources to provide a representative panorama of their subfield. This bibliography is NOT meant to be exhaustive.

Deadlines: I will need to receive the first draft of the manuscripts by [date], so that they can be peer-reviewed and revised by [date], so you have roughly a year to write your chapter, overall. I may ask you to review another chapter and/or I may ask you to coordinate the contents of your chapter with another author, when there is overlap. Some overlap is to be expected, but we don't want to be repetitious.

Please feel free to contact me if you have any other questions.

References

Ahmed, S. J., & Güss, C. D. (2022). An analysis of writer's block: Causes and solutions. *Creativity Research Journal, 34*(3), 339–354. https://doi.org/10.1080/10400419.2022.2031436.

American Psychological Association. (2020). *Publication manual of the American Psychological Association: The official guide to APA Style* (7th ed.). American Psychological Association.

Annesley, T. M. (2010). Bars and pies make better desserts than figures. *Clinical Chemistry, 56*(9), 1394–1400. https://doi.org/10.1373/clinchem.2010.152298.

Anwar, M. A. (2004). From doctoral dissertation to publication: A study of 1995 American graduates in library and information sciences. *Journal of Librarianship and Information Science, 3*(4), 151–157. https://doi.org/10.1177/0961000604050565.

Azar, O. H. (2004). Rejections and the importance of first response times. *International Journal of Social Economics, 31*(3), 259–274. https://doi.org/10.1108/03068290410518247.

Badenhorst, C. (2013). Writing relationships: Collaboration in a faculty writing group. *All Ireland Society for Higher Education – Journal, 5*(1), 1001–1026.

Bair, A. L. (2023). *Blogging all-in-one for dummies* (3rd ed.). Wiley.

Bernstein, E. E., LeBlanc, N. J., & McNally, R. J. (2022). Response and ongoing skills use following a single-session virtual cognitive behavioral workshop for graduate students. *Journal of American College Health, 72*(9), 1–10. https://doi.org/10.1080/07448481.2022.2098036.

Bloom, L. (1985). Anxious writers in context: Graduate school and beyond. In M. Rose (Ed.), *When a writer can't write* (pp. 119–133). Guilford Press.

Boring, E. G. (1951). The book review. *The American Journal of Psychology, 64*(2), 281–283.

Borkin, M. A. (2013). What makes a visualization memorable? *IEEE Transactions on Visualization and Computer Graphics, 19*(12), 2306–2315. https://doi.org/10.1109/TVCG.2013.234.

Bourke, P., & Butler, L. (1996). Publication types, citation rates and evaluation. *Scientometrics, 37*, 473–494. https://doi.org/10.1007/BF02019259.

Bravata, D. M., Watts, S. A., Keefer et al. (2020). Prevalence, predictors, and treatment of impostor syndrome: A systematic review. *Journal of General Internal Medicine, 35*, 1252–1275. https://doi.org/10.1007/s11606-019-05364-1.

Burd, A. (2009). Book reviewers and book reviews: Potential conflict of interest. *Journal of Plastic, Reconstructive & Aesthetic Surgery, 62*(4), 446. https://doi.org/10.1016/j.bjps.2009.02.045.

Butler, J. (1990). *Gender trouble*. Routledge.

References

Chandra, S., Huebert, C. A., Crowley, E., & Das, A. M. (2019). Impostor syndrome: Could it be holding you or your mentees back? *CHEST, 156*(1), 26–32. https://doi.org/10.1016/j.chest.2019.02.325.

Chomsky, N. (1959). A review of BF Skinner's Verbal Behavior. *Language, 35*, 26–58.

Clance, P. R. (1985). *The impostor phenomenon: When success makes you feel like a fake*. Peachtree.

Clance, P. R., & Imes, S. A. (1978). The imposter phenomenon in high achieving women: Dynamics and therapeutic intervention. *Psychotherapy: Theory, Research & Practice, 15*(3), 241–247. https://doi.org/10.1037/h0086006.

Clance, P. R., & O'Toole, M. A. (1988). The imposter phenomenon: An internal barrier to empowerment and achievement. In E. D. Rothblum & E. Cole (Eds.), *Treating women's fear of failure* (2nd ed., pp. 51–64). Haworth Press.

Cleveland, W. S., & McGill, R. (1984). Graphical perception: Theory, experimentation, and application to the development of graphical methods. *Journal of the American Statistical Association, 79*(387), 531–554. https://doi.org/10.2307/2288400.

Cohen, I., & Dreyer-Lude, M. (2020). *Finding your research voice: Story telling and theatre skills for bringing your presentation to life*. Springer Nature.

Colavizza, G., Hrynaszkiewicz, I., Staden, I., Whitaker, K., & McGillivray, B. (2020). The citation advantage of linking publications to research data. *PLoS ONE, 15*(4), 0230416. https://doi.org/10.1371/journal.pone.0230416.

Columbus, C. (2002). *Harry Potter and the chamber of secrets [adventure, family, fantasy]*. Warner Bros.

Connor, U., & Mauranen, A. (1999). Linguistic analysis of grant proposals: European Union research grants. *English for Specific Purposes, 18*(1), 47–62.

Connor, U., & Upton, T. A. (2008). The genre of grant proposals: A corpus linguistic analysis. In Connor, U., & Upton, T. A. (Eds.) *Discourse in the professions: Perspectives from corpus linguistics* (pp. 235–255). John Benjamins Publishing Company.

Crawford, W. S., Shanine, K. K., Whitman, M. V., & Kacmar, K. M. (2016). Examining the impostor phenomenon and work-family conflict. *Journal of Managerial Psychology, 31*(2), 375–390. https://doi.org/10.1108/JMP-12-2013-0409.

Crown, S., Lee, A., & Ramsay, R. (2000). And now the book reviews... *The British Journal of Psychiatry, 177*(5), 388–388.

Csikszentmihalyi, M. (1990). *Flow: The psychology of optimal experience*. Harper & Row.

Daly, A. J. (1985). Writing apprehension. In M. Rose (Ed.), *When a writer can't write* (pp. 43–82). The Guilford Press.

Dinham, S., & Scott, C. (2001). The experience of disseminating the results of doctoral research. *Journal of Further and Higher Education, 25*(1), 45–55. https://doi.org/10.1080/03098770020030498.

Duffy, M. (2016). *Fun ways of deciding authorship order*. Dynamic Ecology. https://dynamicecology.wordpress.com/2016/09/21/fun-ways-of-deciding-authorship-order/.

Dwivedi, Y. K., Hughes, L., Cheung, C. M. K. et al. (2022). Editorial: How to develop a quality research article and avoid a journal desk rejection. *International Journal of Information Management, 62*, 102426. https://doi.org/10.1016/j.ijinfomgt.2021.102426.

Dwyer, A., Lewis, B., McDonald, F., & Burns, M. (2012). It's always a pleasure: Exploring productivity and pleasure in a writing group for early career academics.

Studies in Continuing Education, 34(2), 129–144. https://doi.org/10.1080/0158037X .2011.580734.

Elsevier. (2015). *5 ways you can ensure your manuscript avoids the desk reject pile.* www.elsevier.com/authors-update/story/publishing-tips/5-ways-you-can-ensure-you r-manuscript-avoids-the-desk-reject-pile.

Elsevier. (2018). *Eight top tips to help you turn your PhD thesis into an article.* www .elsevier.com/connect/eight-top-tips-to-help-you-turn-your-phd-thesis-into-an- article

Evans, S. C., Amaro, C. M., Herbert, R., Blossom, J. B., & Roberts, M. C. (2018). "Are you gonna publish that?" Peer-reviewed publication outcomes of doctoral dissertations in psychology. *PloS One, 13*(2), 0192219. https://doi.org/10.1371/journal .pone.0192219.

Extracting a journal article from your thesis: Top tips from award-winning author. (n. d.). Taylor & Francis Author Services. https://authorservices.taylorandfrancis.com/ blog/get-published/extracting-a-journal-article-from-your-thesis/.

Fabre, A. (2015). Publication of pediatric medical dissertations in France. *Archives de pédiatrie: organe officiel de la Societé française de pédiatrie, 22*(8), 802–806. doi .org/10.1016/j.arcped.2015.03.013.

Faria, J. R., & Goel, R. K. (2010). Returns to networking in academia. *NETNOMICS: Economic Research and Electronic Networking, 11*(2), 103–117. https://doi.org/10 .1007/s11066-010-9048-z.

Feak, C. B., & Swales, J. (2009). *Telling a research story: Writing a literature review.* Michigan University Press.

Feng, H. (2002). *Genre analysis of research grant proposals* (MA Thesis, University of British Columbia).

Feng, S., Park, C. Y., Liu, Y., & Tsvetkov, Y. (2023). *From Pretraining Data to Language Models to Downstream Tasks: Tracking the Trails of Political Biases Leading to Unfair NLP Models.*

Fink, A. (2019). *Conducting research literature reviews: From the internet to paper.* SAGE.

Franceschet, M., & Costantini, A. (2010). The effect of scholar collaboration on impact and quality of academic papers. *Journal of Informetrics, 4*(4), 540–553. https://doi .org/10.1016/j.joi.2010.06.003.

Freeman, J., & Peisah, C. (2022). Imposter syndrome in doctors beyond training: A narrative review. *Australasian Psychiatry, 30*(1), 49–54. https://doi.org/10.1177/ 10398562211036121.

Galiani, S., & Gálvez, R. H. (2017). *The life cycle of scholarly articles across fields of research*, Issue w23447. National Bureau of Economic Research. https://papers.ssrn .com/sol3/papers.cfm?abstract_id=2964565.

Green, R. G., Hutchison, E. D., & Sar, B. K. (1992). Evaluating scholarly performance: The productivity of graduates of social work doctoral programs. *Social Service Review, 66*(3), 441–466. doi.org/10.1086/603932.

Halpern, F., & Phelan, J. (2020). Transforming a dissertation chapter into a published article. *Inside Higher Ed.* www.insidehighered.com/advice/2020/08/27/how- adapt-your-dissertation-so-it-works-published-article-opinion.

Hartley, J. (2006). Reading and writing book reviews across the disciplines. *Journal of the American Society for Information Science and Technology, 57*(9), 1194–1207.

References

Heffernan, T. (2020). Academic networks and career trajectory: "There's no career in academia without networks." *Higher Education Research & Development, 40*(5), 981–994. https://doi.org/10.1080/07294360.2020.1799948.

Heidbach, K., Knaus, J.,Laut, I., & Palzenberger, M. (2022). Long Term Global Trends in Open Access. *A Data Paper. Max Plank Digital Library.* https://pure.mpg.de/rest/items/item_3361428/component/file_3361648/content.

Helden, D. L., Dulk, L., Steijn, B., & Vernooij, M. W. (2023). Gender, networks and academic leadership: A systematic review. *Educational Management Administration & Leadership, 51*(5), 1049–1066. https://doi.org/10.1177/17411432211034172.

Hill, K. (1997). Book reviewing: Keeping the audience in mind. *Nurse Author & Editor, 7*(1), 4–7.

How to Write a Journal Article from a Thesis. (2019). Elsevier. https://scientific-publishing.webshop.elsevier.com/publication-process/how-to-write-a-journal-article-from-a-thesis/.

Hsieh, B., & Tran Nguyen, H. (2020). Identity-informed mentoring to support acculturation of female faculty of color in higher education: An Asian American female mentoring relationship case study. *Journal of Diversity in Higher Education, 13*(2), 169–180. https://doi.org/10.1037/dhe0000118.

Huisman, J., & Smits, J. (2017). Duration and quality of the peer review process: The author's perspective. *Scientometrics, 113*(1), 633–650. https://doi.org/10.1007/s11192-017-2310-5.

Jackevicius, C. (2014). Faculty development: A formal mentorship program for faculty development. *American Journal of Pharmaceutical Education, 78*(5), 1–7. https://doi.org/10.5688/ajpe785100.

Jarin, T., & Zahin, A. U. R. (2023). Inter-caste gender performativity in Indian Hindu Culture: A postcolonial gender study in Mulk Raj Anand's Untouchable and Arundhati Roy's The God of Small Things. *Zakariya Journal of Social Science, 2*(1), 11–22. https://doi.org/10.59075/zjss.v2i1.228.

Johnson, M. (1995). Writing a book review: Towards a more critical approach. *Nurse Education Today, 15*(3), 228–231. https://doi.org/10.1016/S0260-6917(95)80111-1.

Káplár-Kodácsy, K., & Dorner, H. (2022). Rebuilding faculty capacities in higher education: An alternative for relational mentoring. *Innovations in Education and Teaching International, 59*(3), 359–369.

Klingsieck, K. B. (2013). Procrastination. *European Psychologist, 18*(1), 24–34.

Kress, G. (1998). Writing and learning to write. In Olson, D. R. & Torrance, N. (Eds.), *The handbook of education and human development: New models of learning, teaching and schooling* (pp. 219–246). Wiley.

Kumar, S., & Jagacinski, C. M. (2006). Imposters have goals too: The imposter phenomenon and its relationship to achievement goal theory. *Personality and Individual Differences, 40*(1), 147–157.

Lally, P., Jaarsveld, C. H. M., Potts, H. W. W., & Wardle, J. (2009). How are habits formed: Modelling habit formation in the real world. *European Journal of Social Psychology, 40*(6), 998–1009. https://doi.org/10.1002/ejsp.674.

Lee, W. M. (2000). Publication trends of doctoral students in three fields from 1965–1995. *Journal of the American Society for Information Science, 51*(2), 139–144. https://doi.org/10.1002/(SICI)1097-4571(2000)51:2.

Maynard, B. R., Vaughn, M. G., Sarteschi, C. M., & Berglund, A. H. (2014). Social work dissertation research: Contributing to scholarly discourse or the file drawer? *British Journal of Social Work, 44*(4), 1045–1062. https://doi.org/10.1093/bjsw/bcs172.

McAndrew, D. A. (1986). Writing apprehension: A review of research. *Research and Teaching in Developmental Education, 2*(2), 43–52.

McKiernan, E. C., Bourne, P. E., Brown, C. T. et al. (2016). Point of view: How open science helps researchers succeed. *Elife, 5*, 16800. https://doi.org/10.7554/eLife.16800.

Meinzer, K. (2019). *So you want to start a podcast: Finding your voice, telling your story, and building a community that will listen.* HarperCollins.

Mesquita, L. (2018). *Eight top tips to help you turn your PhD thesis into an article.* Elsevier Connect. www.elsevier.com/connect/authors-update/eight-top-tips-to-help-you-turn-your-phd-thesis-into-an-article.

Meyers, P., & Nix, S. (2011). *As we speak: How to make your point and have it stick.* Simon and Schuster.

Motta-Roth, D. (2001). A construção social do gênero resenha acadêmica. *Trabalhos em Linguística Aplicada, 38*.

Moore, S. (2003). Writing retreats for academics: Exploring and increasing the motivation to write. *Journal of Further and Higher Education, 27*(3), 333–342. https://doi.org/10.1080/0309877032000098734.

Morris, T., & Tomasi, C. (2020). *Podcasting for dummies.* John Wiley & Sons.

Neff, K. (2003). Self-compassion: An alternative conceptualization of a healthy attitude toward oneself. *Self and Identity, 2*(2), 85–101.

Nicolaisen, J. (2002). The scholarliness of published peer reviews: A bibliometric study of book reviews in selected social science fields. *Research Evaluation, 11*(3), 129–140.

Nosek, B. A., Ebersole, C. R., DeHaven, A. C., & Mellor, D. T. (2018). The preregistration revolution. *Proceedings of the National Academy of Sciences, 115*(11), 2600–2606. https://doi.org/10.1073/pnas.1708274114.

Okabe, M., & Ito, K. (2008). *Color universal design (cud) – How to make figures and presentations that are friendly to colorblind people.*

Onwuegbuzie, A. J., & Collins, K. M. (2001). Writing apprehension and academic procrastination among graduate students. *Perceptual and Motor Skills, 92*(2), 560–562. https://doi.org/10.2466/pms.2001.92.2.560.

Orteza y Miranda, E. (1996). On book reviewing. *The Journal of Educational Thought (JET) / Revue de La Pensée Éducative, 30*(2), 191–202. http://www.jstor.org/stable/23768989http://jfly.iam.u-tokyo.ac.jp/color/.

Peate, I. (2008). The anatomy of a book review. *Journal of Paramedic Practice, 1*(2), 82–83.

Penney, S., Young, G., Badenhorst, C. et al. (2015). Faculty writing groups: A support for women balancing family and career on the academic tightrope. *Canadian Journal of Higher Education, 45*(4), 457–479.

Piwowar, H., Priem, J., Larivière, V. et al. (2018). *The state of OA: a large-scale analysis of the prevalence and impact of Open Access articles.* https://doi.org/10.7717/peerj.4375.

Porter, R. (2007). Why academics have a hard time writing good grant proposals. *Journal of Research Administration, 38*(2), 37–43.

Price, H., & McIntyre, D. (2023). *Communicating linguistics: Language, community and public engagement*. Routledge. www.routledge.com/Communicating-Linguistics-Language-Community-and-Public-Engagement/Price-McIntyre/p/book/9780367560119.

Rad, H. S., Samadi, S., Sirois, F. M., & Goodarzi, H. (2023). Mindfulness intervention for academic procrastination: A randomized control trial. *Learning and Individual Differences, 101*, 102244. https://doi.org/10.1016/j.lindif.2022.102244.

Recht, B., Roelofs, R., Schmidt, L., & Shankar, V. (2019). Do ImageNet classifiers generalize to ImageNet? *Proceedings of the 36th International Conference on Machine Learning*, 5389–5400. https://proceedings.mlr.press/v97/recht19a.html.

Riley, L. E., & Spreitzer, E. A. (1970). Book reviewing in the social sciences. *The American Sociologist*, 358–363.

Rittgerodt, R., & Wagenhofer, S. (2021). How to turn your dissertation into a book. *De Gruyter Conversations*. https://blog.degruyter.com/how-to-turn-your-dissertation-into-a-book/.

Rojon, C., & Saunders, M. N. K. (2015). Dealing with reviewers' comments in the publication process. *Coaching: An International Journal of Theory, Research and Practice, 8*(2), 169–180. https://doi.org/10.1080/17521882.2015.1047463.

Rose, M. (Ed.). (1985). *When a writer can't write*. Guilford Press.

Rowling, J. K. (2000). *Harry Potter and the chamber of secrets* (Reprint). Scholastic Paperbacks.

Sakulku, J., & Alexander, J. (2011). The imposter phenomenon. *International Journal of Behavioral Science, 6*(1), 75–97.

Sandoval, C. (2000). *Methodology of the oppressed*. University of Minnesota Press.

Santos, M., Willett, P., & Wood, F. E. (1998). Research degrees in librarianship and information science: A survey of master's and doctoral students from the Department of Information Studies, University of Sheffield. *Journal of Librarianship and Information Science, 30*(1), 49–56. https://doi.org/10.1177/096100069803000105.

Schwartz, B., Ward, A., Monterosso, J. et al. (2002). Maximizing versus satisficing: Happiness is a matter of choice. *Journal of Personality and Social Psychology, 83*(5), 1178. https://psycnet.apa.org/doi/10.1037/0022-3514.83.5.1178.

Shin, J., & Grant, A. M. (2021). When putting work off pays off: The curvilinear relationship between procrastination and creativity. *Academy of Management Journal, 64*(3), 772–798.

Silva, J. A., Al-Khatib, A., Katavić, V., & Bornemann-Cimenti, H. (2018). Establishing sensible and practical guidelines for desk rejections. *Science and Engineering Ethics, 24*(4), 1347–1365. https://doi.org/10.1007/s11948-017-9921-3.

Simon, H. A. (1956). Rational choice and the structure of the environment. *Psychological Review, 63*(2), 129–138.

Sirois, F. M. (2023). Procrastination and stress: A conceptual review of why context matters. *International Journal of Environmental Research and Public Health, 20* (5031), 1–15. https://doi.org/10.3390/ijerph20065031.

Squires, B. P. (1989). Biomedical review articles: What editors want from authors and peer reviewers. *CMAJ: Canadian Medical Association Journal = Journal de l'Association Medicale Canadienne, 141*(3), 195–197.

Squires, C. (2020). The review and the reviewer. In A. Baverstock, R. Bradford, and & M. Gonzalez (Eds.), *Contemporary publishing and the culture of books*. Routledge.

Steel, P. (2007). The nature of procrastination: A meta-analytic and theoretical review of quintessential self-regulatory failure. *Psychological Bulletin, 133*(1), 65–94. https://psycnet.apa.org/doi/10.1037/0033-2909.133.1.65.

Steel, P., & Klingsieck, K. B. (2016). Academic procrastination: Psychological antecedents revisited. *Australian Psychologist, 51*(1), 36–46. https://doi.org/10.1111/ap.12173

Swales, J. (1990). *Genre analysis: English in academic and research settings.* Cambridge University Press.

Tennant, J. P., Waldner, F., Jacques, D. C. et al. (2016). The academic, economic and societal impacts of Open Access: An evidence-based review. *F1000Research, 5*, 1–55. https://doi.org/10.12688%2Ff1000research.8460.3.

The Big Bang Theory. (2007). Chuck Lorre Productions, Warner Bros. Television.

Thelwall, M., Kousha, K., Abdoli, M. et al. (2023). Why are coauthored academic articles more cited: Higher quality or larger audience? *Journal of the Association for Information Science and Technology, 74*(7), 791–810. https://doi.org/10.1002/asi.24755.

Thelwall, M., & Maflahi, N. (2020). Academic collaboration rates and citation associations vary substantially between countries and fields. *Journal of the Association for Information Science and Technology, 71*(8), 968–978. https://doi.org/10.1002/asi.24315.

Thompson, T., Davis, H., & Davidson, J. (1998). Attributional and affective responses of impostors to academic success and failure outcomes. *Personality and Individual Differences, 25*(2), 381–396. https://doi.org/10.1016/S0191-8869(98)00065-8.

Walker, B., & Unruh, H. E. (2017). *Funding your research in the humanities and social sciences: A practical guide to grant and fellowship proposals* (1st ed.). Routledge. https://doi.org/10.4324/9781315159034.

Wessely, S. (2000). A review of reviewing. *The British Journal of Psychiatry, 177*(5), 388–389.

White, K. (2019). Comparisons of Overall Scientific Publication Output. *NSF – National Science Foundation.* www.nsf.gov/statistics/2019/nsf19317/overview.htm.

White, K. (2021). Publications Output: U.S. Trends and International Comparisons. *NSF – National Science Foundation.* https://ncses.nsf.gov/pubs/nsb20214/executive-summary.

Whitman, M. V., & Shanine, K. K. (2012). Revisiting the impostor phenomenon: How individuals cope with feelings of being in over their heads. In P. L. Perrewé, J. R. Halbesleben, & C. C. Rosen (Eds.), *The role of the economic crisis on occupational stress and well being* (pp. 177–212). Emerald Group.

Wordsrated. (2023). https://wordsrated.com/self-published-book-sales-statistics.

Yan, Z. (2020). *Publishing journal articles: A scientific guide for new authors worldwide.* Cambridge University Press.

Index

abstract, 98, 149, 160, 163, 192
accessibility, 123
acquisition editor, 249
agent, 249
AI, 92, 94
Amazon Author page, 204
American Psychological Association (APA), 214
American Society for Indexing, 97
anxiety, xiii
apprehension, 12
Article Processing Charges (APCs), 126
associate editor, 246
audience, 92, 115, 116, 118, 119, 120, 134, 141, 149, 152, 155, 156, 158, 159, 160, 162, 165, 167, 187, 189, 190, 191, 192, 194
author, 88, 91, 94, 97, 98, 99, 105, 120, 123, 137, 138, 139, 143, 149, 160, 166, 192, 227, 229
author guidelines, 149
authorship, 226, 227, 229

backward calendar, 23
bibliography, 100, 226
bibliometrics, 121
blog, 141, 188, 189, 193, 194, 195
Blogger, 188
book, 88, 90, 92, 93, 94, 95, 96, 97, 98, 99, 100, 101, 115, 116, 121, 124, 125, 126, 132, 133, 134, 135, 136, 137, 138, 139, 140, 141, 142, 143, 145, 151, 152, 153, 154, 156, 158, 159, 160, 161, 162, 163, 164, 165, 166, 167, 168, 187, 192, 204, 217, 226, 228
book chapter, 151, 152, 153, 154, 156, 164, 228
book launch, 205
book proposal, 134, 158, 159, 160, 163, 165, 167, 168
book review, 121, 136, 137, 138, 139, 140, 141, 143
book trailer, 187, 192
bottom-tier, 122
boxplot, 81
budget, 90, 91, 92, 93, 97, 162, 202

Cambridge University Press, 126
circular visualization, 85
citation, 90, 200, 201, 226
citation count, 200, 201
class paper, 116, 118, 120
collaborative writing, 225, 226, 228
color, 92, 112, 203
color palette, 203
Committee on Publication Ethics, 41
Committee on Publication Ethics (COPE), 41
conclusion, 132, 141, 155
conference, 115, 118, 119, 120, 125, 130, 146, 151, 153, 154, 156, 157, 164, 167, 191, 215, 216, 217, 218, 221, 222
conference paper, 118, 119
conference proceedings, 151, 154, 156, 157
conflict of interest, 45
controlled vocabulary, 60
copyright, 88, 89, 90, 91, 92, 93, 94, 203
Creative Commons, 89
curating, 199, 204

data visualization, 80
deadline, 104, 153
department, 128, 153, 187, 193, 202, 203, 213, 214, 219, 221, 223
depression, 10
Directory of Open Access Journals, 232
Discord, 204
dissertation, 115, 116, 128, 129, 130, 131, 132, 133, 134, 135, 158, 159, 160, 163, 166, 168, 218, 221, 228
dissertation advisor, 221
domain name, 202
donut chart, 82
dynamic visualization, 81

EBSCO, 73
edited volume, 143, 145, 151, 152, 153, 154, 156, 157, 199
editorial board, 148
elevator pitch, 217, 218

275

Endnote, 226
European Association of Science Editors, 41
European Association of Science Editors (EASE), 41
European Commission, 41

Facebook, 188, 190, 194, 204
fair use, 88, 89, 90, 91
findings, 89, 131, 139, 144, 145, 146, 147, 162, 187, 216
first-generation, 6
flow, 163

Gantt chart, 183
golden phrases, 207
Google Scholar, 199, 201, 203, 216
Google Workspace, 225, 226
grant, 200

handbook, 153, 155, 156
h-index, 121, 200, 201
histogram, 82
home page, 202
hook, 141
Human Research Ethics Committee, 40

images, 89, 90, 91, 92, 93, 94, 190, 191, 192
impact metrics, 200, 201
impostor cycle, 15
impostor syndrome (SI), 120, 128, 129
index, 95, 96, 97, 98, 99, 100, 101, 121, 138, 200
in-principle acceptance, 235
Institutional Review Board, 145
interview, 189, 193, 194, 195
introduction, 134, 138, 145, 155
inverted pyramid, 141
iThenticate, 43

jargon, 133, 142, 191, 192, 203
job market, 128
JSTOR, 73

keyword, 117, 133, 188, 199, 201, 202

list of predatory publishers, 126
literature review, 74

mandala visualization, 85
market, 89, 159, 164, 167, 217
market analysis, 164
Mendeley, 226
mentee, 220, 222, 223, 224

mentor, 99, 101, 103, 112, 120, 127, 135, 143, 148, 150, 153, 157, 168, 195, 204, 213, 218, 219, 220, 221, 222, 223, 224, 230
mentoring, 130, 223, 229
mentorship, 219, 220, 221, 222, 223, 224
meta-analysis, 131, 147
meta-synthesis, 147
methodology, 90, 130, 132, 145, 147, 155, 228
micro-blog, 188
mindfulness, 15
mixed methods, 145
momentum, 104
monograph, 143, 158, 160, 163
mosaic plot, 83

National Endowment for the Humanities, 125
National Science Foundation, 144
networking, 153, 157, 189, 214, 215, 217, 218, 220, 221
newsletter, 141, 188, 194

open access, 94, 123, 127, 149
Open Access Journals Search Engine, 232
Open Research, 89, 199
oral history, 40
ORCID, 199, 200, 201, 204
outline, 93, 133, 134, 135, 155, 162, 163, 189, 263

page costs, 231
panel, 216, 223
paper, 94, 102, 103, 104, 105, 106, 108, 111, 116, 117, 118, 119, 120, 121, 122, 123, 124, 125, 126, 127, 130, 131, 132, 133, 134, 135, 144, 147, 148, 149, 150, 166, 167, 191, 204, 217, 225, 229
paragraph, 106, 108, 110, 119, 160, 161, 228
paywall, 126
peer-review, 102, 116, 118, 129, 137, 151, 187
pie chart, 10
plagiarism, 229
podcast, 141, 142, 187, 189, 190, 193, 194, 195, 204
Pomodoro, 11
popularization, 141
predatory, 124, 125, 126, 127
predatory press, 125
predatory publisher, 124
predatory publishing, 124, 125
preprint, 146
preprint repositories, 233
preregistration, 235
procrastination, 12
project management, 176
PubMed, 73

reference management software, 226
report, 93, 125, 129, 144, 145, 187, 194, 220
research agenda, 152, 156, 222
research gap, 172
research question, 118, 130, 132, 133, 146, 155, 224
Researcher ID, 199, 200
review article, 145, 146, 147
review editor, 136, 137
review of the literature, 48
reviewer, 102, 103, 105, 106, 108, 109, 110, 112, 139, 159, 166, 200
Reviewer 2, 13
revision, 102, 103, 159
rhetorical moves, 138, 142
round table, 207

salami slicing, 130
scoping review, 147
Scopus, 121, 199, 200, 225
Scopus ID, 199, 200
secondary sources, 154
self-compassion, 15
self-plagiarism, 130
series editor, 159
slides, 118, 189
slope chart, 83
social media, 121, 187, 188, 190, 191, 192, 194, 204, 215
source, 110, 125
sources, 88, 110, 116, 125, 131, 154, 155, 193
static visualization, 81
stock images, 92
style guide, 100, 146, 154
submission, 104, 111, 117, 120, 124, 149, 166
submission guidelines, 250
Substack, 188, 194
suicidal thoughts, 10

systematic review, 147

Teams, 225
textbook, 92, 143, 158, 165, 167
The Thesis Whisperer, 189
thought control, 10
thought stopping, 16
throwing stars, 219
tiers, 122, 152
timeline, 135, 165, 223
title, 93, 144, 159, 162, 216, 217
topic sentence, 5
top-tier, 122, 133, 148, 149
tornado chart, 83
TurnItIn, 43
Twitter/X, 188, 190, 194, 203

URL, 202

video, 136, 188, 189, 192, 193, 203, 225
video abstract, 192

Web of Science, 121, 200
WhatsApp, 204
white paper, 121, 125, 129
word cloud, 73
word count, 117, 153, 155, 162, 163
Wordpress, 188, 202
writer's block, 12
writer's high, 5
writing group, 223, 224, 226

Youtube, 192

Zoom, 225, 226, 228
Zotero, 226

For EU product safety concerns, contact us at Calle de José Abascal, 56–1°,
28003 Madrid, Spain or eugpsr@cambridge.org.

www.ingramcontent.com/pod-product-compliance
Ingram Content Group UK Ltd.
Pitfield, Milton Keynes, MK11 3LW, UK
UKHW022232220226
468302UK00017B/252